PRAISE FOR *BECOMING A KING*

"I'm always reluctant to write blurbs for books, and I didn't want to write an endorsement for *Becoming a King*—but then I read it. It's not sanctimonious advice written by somebody who's never had his knuckles bloody or his hands dirty or his heart broken; it's the honest account of a man who's been where every man needs to go sooner or later. I don't like to sign my name to things that don't matter. This matters."

Randall Wallace, Oscar-nominated screenwriter, film producer, director, *Braveheart, We Were Soldiers, Heaven Is for Real*

"Morgan Snyder has taken the journey that he so compellingly invites other men to embark on in his beautifully written and wisdom-filled book. Courageously honest and true, *Becoming a King* is a worthy read that you will come back to time and time again and, as Morgan expresses so well, a noble calling to pursue. As a woman reading *Becoming a King*, I was inspired with how to better come alongside the men in my life, to lovingly encourage them in their lives' ultimate calling."

Stasi Eldredge, *New York Times* bestselling author of *Captivating*

"Morgan Snyder simply asks better questions. His pursuit of the root system of manhood, fatherhood, and royalty brings us within reach of deep truths that could help us outlast the modern brutal storm. This book is for the soul-hungry, sick-of-the-BS reader, which is why I love it. And Morgan picks a much better fight than you'd find in any ring in Vegas or any back-alley bar. His fight is for his own heart."

Jared Anderson, singer and songwriter of *The Great I Am*

"Morgan walks us into the basement of our souls, clicks on the light, and begins turning over skeletons and lies. What's at stake? You and me. But fear not. He's been here before. The scars are proof. This is neither theory nor theological wrangling. It's an excavation of the heart. A rescue mission to steal back the truth of us. This book may well shatter the paradigm you have of yourself—only to restore the one your Father has written on your heart. I love everything about this."

Charles Martin, *New York Times* bestselling author

"I love this book. It engages the deep matters of the heart. It is a book for men, but be warned. It is as much a book for women to understand what it truly means to grow as a man and to love a woman. Morgan awakens in me the hunger to keep moving forward with hope. His call to kingship will unnerve your complacency while calling forth the best of your heart to take on what is truly yours and to throw down what is not. This is a life-shaping journey into the heart of the Father."

Dan B. Allender, PhD, author of *Healing the Wounded Heart*; professor of counseling psychology, The Seattle School of Theology and Psychology; and counselor and founder, The Allender Center

"*Becoming a King* is a rare and essential invitation to living true and becoming a man God can entrust with more. Though Morgan is younger than me, words could never describe how I've been mentored by him for more than a decade. He's one I'd take a bullet for. What I've gained from this book is priceless and has already impacted me and generations to come. Every man, and every woman who loves him, needs this message."

Rick Hinnant, *American Ninja Warrior* competitor and cofounder/ co-owner of Grace & Lace (as seen on *Shark Tank*)

"For the rare few willing to enter into the quiet places of the soul, *Becoming a King* will prove to be one of the most radical, reorienting, and encouraging books you will ever read."

Zack Duhame, Screen Actors Guild Award winner and actor, *Lone Survivor*, *Dunkirk*, *Star Trek*, *Transformers*, and *The Matrix*

"I work with numerous men who are just now becoming kings and have been looking for a resource to use to come alongside them. I am profoundly grateful that Morgan Snyder, who truly knows this topic, has just handed me the tool I need!"

Carter Crenshaw, senior pastor, West End Community Church, Nashville

"If there is one book that you read this year on growing deeply as a man, this is it! I recommend not only Morgan's book but Morgan himself. You can no longer say, 'I don't know where to begin.' It begins with this book."

Bill Lokey, chief clinical director, Onsite Workshops (2010–2019)

"What boy doesn't love stories about kings and kingdoms and doesn't love crowns and swords and armor? What grown man doesn't still find himself drawn into their gallant stories? Maybe this says something profound about the way God made us as men as well as the desires he placed in our hearts. You are holding a map revealing the ancient path to the fulfillment of those desires. If you want to make that heroic journey, don't put it down. Read it."

Christopher West, ThD, president, Theology of the Body
Institute, and author of *Our Bodies Tell God's Story*

"*Becoming a King* is the map for living a wholehearted life. Morgan is a cartographer, lovingly drawing in the contour lines of a healthy man's soul grounded in a vibrant life with God. Become who you were intended to be and accept the adventurous and gracious wisdom reclaimed from God's intimate invitation to find and walk the ancient path of freedom."

Aaron McHugh, author of *Fire Your Boss*

"What Morgan has done to curate and distill the message of *Becoming a King* over the past few decades is honestly something I respect more than almost any other journey I've been honored to witness over my lifetime."

Chad Turner, chief financial officer, S&P 500 company

"I have waited a decade for Morgan Snyder's first book. This man is a true warrior of the Light, and these pages teem with the wisdom that can come only from fighting on the front line, conveyed with honesty, seasoned with humility, and refined by deep reflection. His work will inspire this generation and undergird the next."

Mike Carson, founding partner, Aberkyn, and
partner, McKinsey & Company

"No one has challenged me to become the man I was created to be, and shown me the path to getting there, more than Morgan has over the past several years. It's exciting that that path is now in print. I can't wait to get this book into the hands of all the men I know and the women who love them."

Greg Lindsey, lead pastor, Discovery Church Colorado, Colorado Springs

"I would not be the husband, father, business owner, and friend I am today without the message in this book."

Zach Thomas, franchise owner, Chick-fil-A, author of *Leader Farming*

BECOMING
A
KING

The Path to Restoring
the Heart of a Man

MORGAN SNYDER

W PUBLISHING GROUP

An Imprint of Thomas Nelson

Published in Nashville, Tennessee, by W Publishing, an imprint of Thomas Nelson.

Author is represented by The Christopher Ferebee Agency, www.christopherferebee.com.

Thomas Nelson titles may be purchased in bulk for educational, business, fund-raising, or sales promotional use. For information, please e-mail SpecialMarkets@ThomasNelson.com.

Unless otherwise noted, Scripture quotations are taken from the Holy Bible, New International Version®, NIV®. Copyright © 1973, 1978, 1984, 2011 by Biblica, Inc.® Used by permission of Zondervan. All rights reserved worldwide. www.Zondervan.com. The "NIV" and "New International Version" are trademarks registered in the United States Patent and Trademark Office by Biblica, Inc.®

Scripture quotations marked ESV are from the ESV® Bible (The Holy Bible, English Standard Version®), copyright © 2001 by Crossway, a publishing ministry of Good News Publishers. Used by permission. All rights reserved.

Scripture quotations marked MSG are from *The Message*. Copyright © by Eugene H. Peterson 1993, 1994, 1995, 1996, 2000, 2001, 2002. Used by permission of NavPress. All rights reserved. Represented by Tyndale House Publishers, Inc.

Scripture quotations marked NASB are from New American Standard Bible®. Copyright © 1960, 1962, 1963, 1968, 1971, 1972, 1973, 1975, 1977, 1995 by The Lockman Foundation. Used by permission. (www.Lockman.org)

Scripture quotations marked NLT are from the Holy Bible, New Living Translation. © 1996, 2004, 2007, 2013, 2015 by Tyndale House Foundation. Used by permission of Tyndale House Publishers, Inc., Carol Stream, Illinois 60188. All rights reserved.

Scripture quotations marked TLB are from The Living Bible. Copyright © 1971. Used by permission of Tyndale House Publishers, Inc., Carol Stream, Illinois 60188. All rights reserved.

ISBN 978–7852–3185–1 (eBook)

Library of Congress Control Number: 2020933167

ISBN 978-0-7852-3185-1 (HC)

Printed in the United States of America

20 21 22 23 24   LSC   10 9 8 7 6 5 4 3 2 1

To Cherie,

My bride, my chief editor, the champion of my heart and my truest companion. Your patience with me in my slow and bumpy process of becoming more of the man I was made to be has been a source of love and a window into God's heart beyond telling. You saw what I could not see. And you never gave up. Our deep yes to God twenty years ago was true to be sure. Yet to share two decades of responding to God's pursuit of our hearts and authoring of our story, together, has become the greatest treasure of my life. I love you with my whole heart.

Stand at the crossroads and look;
  ask for the ancient paths,
ask where the good way is, and walk in it,
  and you will find rest for your souls.

—Jeremiah 6:16

CONTENTS

Foreword by John Eldredge. XIII
Uncovering the Ancient Path to Becoming. XV

Chapter 1: Becoming Powerful 1
Chapter 2: Becoming a Son 11
Chapter 3: Becoming True 31
Chapter 4: Becoming the Man You Were Born to Be . . . 45
Chapter 5: Becoming a Generalist. 63
Chapter 6: Becoming a Warrior 85
Chapter 7: Becoming Good Soil 101
Chapter 8: Becoming Deep Roots. 125
Chapter 9: Becoming Like-Hearted 153
Chapter 10: Becoming a King 179

A Fellowship of Kings 195
Become Good Soil Prayer 197
Acknowledgments 205
Notes .209
About the Author 217

FOREWORD

Many years ago Morgan and I found ourselves deep in the Yukon wilderness, fulfilling a lifelong dream to bowhunt for moose. We had to overcome a wild set of challenges to even get there.

After driving down the Alaska Highway from Whitehorse, following the overflowing banks of the Yukon River, we flew by floatplane into remote wilderness with our guide, whom we nicknamed Muskrat (he wore a cap made of muskrat pelts he'd trapped himself). Then came a six-hour trek in an Argo (an eight-wheeled amphibious vehicle) deeper into moose country, chainsawing our way through tangled forest, paddling through swamps. Hours of grueling labor passed slowly. We were less than a mile from our camp when we hit a branch of the mighty Jennings River that we simply could not cross; the current was too strong.

It was getting late, we were exhausted, and we sat there assessing the gravity of the situation.

"One of you needs to put on some waders," Muskrat said, "and take that winch cable across. Wrap it around some willows. If we try this without it, we'll be swept to hell and gone." I wanted to discuss more reasonable options, but Snyder was already pulling on the waders. I walked to the river's edge and dipped a hand in the glacial waters; it was numb before I could pull it out. I wanted to say, "No—I'll do it," but I hesitated just long enough to make sure Morgan was already suited up.

That's the kind of guy he is: willing to go for it. Willing to take one for the team.

And because of that, we made it to our camp and spent one of the most magical weeks in the wilderness either of us will ever have.

I tell you this story for two reasons: because Morgan never will, and because you need to know what kind of man is offering you counsel in this book.

The plague on the church today is that too many leaders are teaching about too many things they have never really lived. It's all hip theory and sexy ideas that haven't been tested in real life, and it does a lot of harm. We need wisdom. We need guidance. We need to hear from men who have actually walked the "ancient paths." As you've noticed, there aren't too many around.

Now let me quickly add—Morgan lives in a typical suburban neighborhood with a wife and two kids and has a nine-to-five job and trash that needs to be taken to the curb every Tuesday morning. They own a minivan. It's important to reveal this stuff, too, because we need counsel and wisdom that can be lived out in ordinary life. As much as we'd all love to quit our jobs and go find adventure on the high seas, we've got our actual lives in front of us, and it's right here that we navigate the pressures, challenges, heartbreaks, and chaos of this world. It can be done. With joy, even.

The treasures in this book weave together into a map of the masculine journey, a guide into wholehearted maturity. It is a joy-filled process—liberating, strengthening—and the results are the kind of men God loves to bless; the kind of men he is earnestly looking for.

I've known Morgan for more than twenty years; we've seen a lot of wild stuff together: missions to places like Africa and Australia, hundreds of counseling sessions with men in some pretty dark places. I can assure you he has lived all of this deeply, with love and perseverance, before he took it in hand to write this book and offer what he's learned to you. In fact, it took him years to write it because he didn't want to rush.

That's the best endorsement I can give.

This journey will be well worth your time.

John Eldredge
Colorado, 2020

UNCOVERING THE ANCIENT
PATH TO BECOMING

Midway along the journey of our life
I woke to find myself in a dark wood,
for I had wandered off from the straight path.

How hard it is to tell what it was like,
this wood of wilderness, savage and stubborn
(the thought of it brings back all my old fears),
a bitter place! Death could scarce be bitterer.

But if I would show the good that came of it
I must talk about things other than the good.
—Dante, *Inferno*, Canto 1 (c. 1308)

More than a decade ago, I found these words painfully true. In a personal wilderness, I awoke—lost, alone, disoriented, and very afraid. In a bitter place.

I had a beautiful wife, two healthy and happy kids, meaningful work, and the beginning of a little nest egg for the future. What more could a man ask for?

But when I was finally honest with myself, the steady waves of discouragement and anxiety were undeniable. Looking at my life as an iceberg, the 10 percent above the waterline looked impressive. But the 90 percent below told another story: I was not well; I was submerged in pain and confusion.

While I had already committed the decade of my twenties to focusing on becoming a more mature and wholehearted man, as I rounded the bend into the thirties, my inner life was not what I'd envisioned. Perhaps better said, *I* had not become *who* I'd envisioned. At least at most junctures, I'd made what I thought were good, honorable decisions to get where I was. But where I was wasn't good, at least not on the inside.

And so, as every good story goes, I left the comfortable and set my soul on a quest. In time I became aware that God had already set my rescue in motion, as I began to discover answers to my questions in the least likely places.

Where Are You?

Looking back, I wonder now if God's pursuit of me was that different from his engagement with Adam. You may remember the story: Adam and Eve had just eaten from the Tree of Knowledge of Good and Evil, choosing to break trust with the One whose image they bore. Throwing off Love's authority and allowing the lines between good and evil to be blurred, they chose to call into question the goodness of God's heart.

Then the story takes a remarkable turn of kindness. Instead of withdrawal and attack, God offered relationship and pursuit. Love came *looking* for Adam and Eve, reaching out. Moving toward Adam in strength and engagement, the Hebrew Scriptures record, God offered this intimate and profound question: "Adam, where are you?"

This was not a question to collect data. God knew *where* Adam was. It was a question to pursue and connect soul to soul. And it might be one of the most important questions we ever ask ourselves. What's more, it might be the question God is curious about in this moment.

Where are you?

It was surely the question with which my heavenly Father pursued me in that bitter place a decade ago, and it's the question he continues to ask me today. To experience the depths of his intentions, we must pause to hear our own name beckoned by the heart of God.

Where are you?

The journey to becoming the kind of wholehearted man to whom God can gladly entrust the care of his kingdom will require courage, vulnerability, and beyond all, love. To open your masculine heart to receive a love that is being made available more deeply than you might even imagine. In order to do that, you must choose whether to risk being honestly vulnerable about where you are in your story. You are worth pausing—here in this moment—to consider how you are doing on the inside. Perhaps on a soul level there is disappointment or anger. Perhaps it is a deep sense of fatigue or of being overwhelmed. Perhaps a feeling of being behind. Whatever it is, let your soul speak for a moment. There are treasures waiting for you and deep hope infused in the pages ahead. The only way to receive all this is to start by being honest with yourself about the true condition of your heart, as a man.

Questions

I, too, chose to get really honest with myself. Over several weeks, my heart reached out in desperate pleas for God to make sense of my life. I poured out questions to him: *God, where are you in this? Where am I in this? How did I get here? Where do I go from here? Why is there such a disconnection between the goodness of my circumstances and the discontent within? What is this next decade supposed to be about? What are the pitfalls? What are the hopes? What's the one thing? Above all, how do I find the fullness of life I was made for and thirst after so desperately?*

Nothing. For weeks. Silence.

Then an impression from the Father started slowly coming to me: *Morgan, I am right here with you. I love your questions, and they will be your guides from here. To begin, I want to speak to your questions through the counsel of older, wise men. Go to the oldest men you know and respect, and ask them. Listen to me through their stories.*

God was inviting me to heal through relationships, through sitting at the feet of older, wiser men who had suffered and found life; my Father was directing me to the ancient path of *becoming* and to the rare men who had chosen to walk along it.

> Stand at the crossroads and look;
>   ask for the ancient paths,
>   ask where the good way is, and walk in it,
>   and you will find rest for your souls.
>
> —Jeremiah 6:16

And so it began.

The Ancient Path of Becoming

It began with a single letter. I found the oldest man I knew and respected, and I put pen to paper regarding the questions in my heart. In time I formed a list of all the older men who, in one way or another, had a place in my story. I sent letters to them, asking for their counsel. I asked those in faraway states or countries for a letter in return or a phone call. Responses from those in proximity came over time, in the form of conversations over a pint or with a cigar by a campfire. As the experiences grew, so did the list. I kept adding to the ranks more and more guides, men in front of me on the masculine journey. Over two years' time, the number grew to nearly seventy-five sages, with whom came a treasure chest of clues to an ancient path eager to be recovered. As I sat in their counsel with a stack of notes, I started to notice the themes of their responses, and with those in hand I began to add to their advice the counsel of the great heroes of our faith down through the ages. The Father's affection and assurance began to break through to my lost and weary soul.

Son, you're not behind. You are on time. And you're going to be okay.

The lives of these elders represented a variety of vocations, socioeconomic thresholds, faith practices, and journeys. Yet through the diverse experiences of these men, a common path emerged: each man had been entrusted with power and had to navigate a process of restoration to become the kind of man who could handle it. There were consistent themes, spoken in many different terms but all with the same heartbeat. Men reclaiming their identity, their strength, their integrity, and their purpose through *becoming a student, becoming a son, and consenting to the slow and steady process of inner transformation.* As the years transpired, a map took shape around signposts rendered from the joy and suffering I witnessed in the lives of these men. After a decade, through the urging of trusted friends and growing out of my work rescuing and restoring the hearts of men, I began to realize this map was not for me alone. It was meant to be shared.

This book is my effort to share that map, to help others recover the narrow path to becoming a king.

And it is intended to reach the man, to find the few.

To share that outright is the best way I can think of to honor you. Books offering quick, easy steps to change your life will sell, but they aren't sufficient to bring long-term transformation. This book is for the few who want life and are willing to be transformed in the pursuit. It is for men who are thirsty for adventure, meaning, recovery of soul. It is for men who desire to engage this pursuit through a fellowship with a small, heroic tribe along the way. Men who have suffered enough to be open to the possibility that recovering a life in and with God and his kingdom is the context in which the masculine soul will flourish. It is for men who are willing to trust that the process of inner transformation leads to the kind of legacy we dream to leave behind as we one day depart from this world.

As you will see, there is little new in these pages but much newly recovered. My intent is to serve as a curator and distiller of an ancient path to becoming a king. Fueled by a relentless pursuit of becoming a wholehearted man, I've invested the better part of the last two decades seeking the heart of God and the nature of reality as shared by these modern-day fathers I have sought out and come to trust. As mentors, John Eldredge, author of *Wild at Heart*, and Dallas Willard, author of *The Divine Conspiracy*, were central to recovering a map to the restoration of the heart of a man. While there were many other modern-day fathers with whom I've had the privilege of cultivating personal relationships, there have been others among this fellowship of giants who have recently crossed over from human history—men like A. W. Tozer, C. S. Lewis, and George MacDonald. Still others reach much further back into the story: the earliest disciples as well as more ancient forerunners of our faith such as Solomon, Isaiah, and Nehemiah—most of whom were, by all outward appearances, ordinary men whose noble hearts found life in and with an extraordinary God. Together, this collective has formed the basis for any wisdom saturating these pages.

This book is offered for those who choose to believe transformation of the masculine soul is possible and are willing to risk moving toward it. My intention is to build upon the faithful apprenticeship laid out before me and to share a map of the ancient path of becoming the kind of king to whom God greatly delights to entrust the care of his kingdom.

While it is my heartfelt intention for this book to deeply benefit women who desire to see the men in their lives restored, I wrote this book primarily for men. I hold fast to a facet of reality expressed in Genesis 1, that God authored gender and created humans as male and female in his own image. My experience is that recovering the fullness of what it means to bear the image of God *as a man* is central to the restoration of men and women.

After years of conversation with my wife and other women I deeply respect and admire, I'm convinced that men and women share many core desires and that these common desires are expressed in very personal ways, particular to the individual, to his or her calling, heart, preferences, and story. Being entrusted with a kingdom and lovingly reigning over it is one of our shared desires, as are the desires to explore, to discover, to create, and to be loved, to love, and to move ever closer to the Source of love. However, with humility, I'm choosing to honor the feminine soul and allow this book to focus on the masculine soul and the path to becoming a king.

This is a no-BS kind of message, and it requires soul-centered honesty, courage, and love. You'll find that to be my style. I will be myself with you, in the hope that you might find permission to become more of the unique man God created you to be.

Keep in mind, it is never too late. Be encouraged: this is a book for a man of any age who is willing to honestly consider what is lacking in his path to becoming wholehearted. Clearly, there are ages in most men's lives at which a level of deep inner transformation is more readily achievable. Yet rather than focus on age, this book explores the epicenter of the process that the masculine soul goes through to grow, heal, and mature into full manhood.

When I started my journey down this path years ago, little did I know the accuracy of Louis L'Amour's words: "There will be a time when you believe everything is finished. That will be the beginning."[1]

I invite you to a new beginning. To stand with me at the trailhead of a path into the wild. To risk taking one more step into the unknown. To trust that your suffering has not been wasted. To believe that you will find a good Father leading the way and celebrating your courage and vulnerability at every turn. May you find grounding in these truths as we plunge into the promise together.

You may be feeling weary, discouraged, defeated. You are not alone. There are other men who are holding on to hope that the abundant life is available. Men who know there is a life of deep meaning, adventure, beauty, courage, and intimate relationship, a life that is worth fighting for. There are men who want it and, perhaps like you, are growing in willingness to go for it. The offer is fullness of life for you and those you hold dear. It is available. It isn't cheap. It isn't easy. It isn't quick. But it's worth the cost.

Journey with me as we begin to make our way down the path laid out long before our days. It is a path that will remain long after we are gone. It is an ancient path we can recover even now. May we learn together how to become the kind of man—the kind of king—to whom God can entrust his kingdom.

To the few, the rare, and the brave:

Welcome.

1

BECOMING POWERFUL

The great problem of the earth and the great
aim of the masculine journey boil down to this:
when can you trust a man with power?
—John Eldredge

Do you remember your first taste of power?

I can still hear the blades engaging on our 1976 Cub Cadet riding mower. I was eight years old, and after I rode on his lap a few times, my dad put me behind the wheel. I distinctly remember taking the throttle for the first time as my dad stepped aside and turned me loose. I was given rule and dominion over the half-acre lawn that hugged a strip of western Pennsylvania woods. And I loved it. For the first time, I felt the masculine surge of fierce mastery over a domain. Even now, several decades later, the smell of freshly cut grass takes my soul back to that moment of being entrusted with power.

What have you done with the desire to be powerful?

Here is the unapologetic premise of this book: the desire to be powerful—to lead, care for, and bring goodness to a man's realm—is central to the soul. The story line of what we do with power is the path to recovering the depth and breadth of what God meant when he made you and me. While it expresses itself in infinite ways, this desire to be powerful is common to us all; it's in our design. Regardless of what we look like, where we come from, and what we do for work, all of us can identify with this desire uniquely expressed in our lives.

Think of what you long to have spoken about your life in your eulogy. What if, among stories of shared adventure and intimate relationships, the people closest to you were able to speak words like these:

> He lived and led with wisdom, vulnerability, and courage.
> He shaped the world for good and left a lasting legacy.
> He loved well and loved deeply from a sincere heart.
> And he finished strong.

The *Imago Dei*

The desire to be powerful transcends both social constructs and our boyhood dreams of becoming firefighters, policemen, NFL football players, Olympic athletes, fighter pilots, or soldiers. This longing transcends because it is the image of God in us.

We need to look no further than the opening chapter of Genesis for this reminder. God formed us from soil into his image, then breathed us to life in order that we might rule and reign under the authority of his goodness. To share valiantly and effectively in God's power was the first mission entrusted to humankind. With deep anticipation, God declared to Adam and Eve, "I want you to rule."

When we strip away the religious veil, this command is more rousing than we might first think; it is the invitation to become who we were *meant* to be. As bearers of God's image, we were meant to embody God's heart, character, and power, partnering with God to fulfill his purposes in our days. "Like a foreman runs a ranch or like a skipper runs his ship. Better still, like a king rules a kingdom, God appoints us as the governors of his domain."[1] A kingdom is, as Dallas Willard pointed out, simply the range of our effective will. It is where we have say, where our will is done. It is within the context of kingdom language and kingdom thinking that we must reconsider God's design for effective power-sharing with created yet creative human beings.

God's desire to share his power with us is displayed across the narrative of Scripture. From God's convocation of Adam and Eve to his ultimate reinstatement of the human race at the restoration of all things, described at the end of the book of Revelation, God is inviting humanity to collaborate in his dominion.

Even at a midpoint in the biblical story, David marveled that God endowed humans with the capacity to wield power within a universe charged with grandeur and magnificence.

> When I look at your heavens, the work of your fingers,
>> the moon and the stars, which you have set in place,
> what is man that you are mindful of him,
>> and the son of man that you care for him?
>
> Yet you have made him a little lower than the heavenly beings
>> and crowned him with glory and honor.
> You have given him dominion over the works of your hands;
>> you have put all things under his feet,
> all sheep and oxen,
>> and also the beasts of the field,
> the birds of the heavens, and the fish of the sea,
>> whatever passes along the paths of the seas.
>
> —Psalm 8:3–8 ESV

Yet what do we do with the dissonance between the wonder of the invitation and the poor way we've fulfilled it? A glance at current events and an honest look in the mirror both reveal that something has misfired. Yes, there are men among us who valiantly bear the image of God. And there are no doubt also moments where we find ourselves living strong and true. Yet by no means is pervasive and integrated masculine goodness the major theme of our day.

For me, as for many, Dallas Willard served as one of the central modern-day fathers of the faith. For several decades he mentored men and women in kingdom living as a teacher, philosopher, and author. Dallas captured the deep dilemma of masculine power with these words: "The primary work of God is finding men to whom he can entrust his power. And the story of most men is being entrusted with power and it bringing harm to themselves and those under their care."[2]

Willard suggested that throughout the narrative of Scripture and through the entire record of human history, again and again we observe this same pattern of men being entrusted with power intended for the good of others. And often that power is used for self-promotion or personal gain and in the end does not bring the greater good for which it was intended, neither to the man nor to the people and kingdom entrusted to his care.

Let that sink in. The power entrusted to most men often brings harm. Think of the stories that have come out in recent years.

Bill Cosby was a hero for a generation, an iconic family man. Yet at least fifty women have come forward accusing him of sexual assault. The harm he caused is incalculable; the fissure between his on-screen life and his private inner life has cost him—and many others—nearly everything.

Lance Armstrong. Seven-time Tour de France champion. Cancer survivor. Founder of the Livestrong Foundation, which has given hope to millions. Yet he chose to lie to the world—even to his own kids—about his reliance on performance-enhancing drugs to make every Tour championship title possible.[3] His extensive drug use is one of the greatest scandals in professional sports history. Having seven world titles revoked was only the beginning of the unraveling of his wide influence.

No coach racked up more wins in the history of college football than Penn State's Joe Paterno. More bowl victories than any coach in history. In his own words, "I don't fish. I don't golf. I don't cut the lawn. . . . Football is my life."[4] And it was true. Enough for him to overlook the conduct of his long-standing assistant football coach Jerry Sandusky, who was convicted of fifty-two counts of child molestation. At the height of his professional achievements, Joe was fired by the board of trustees and died within a month.

Disgraced Hollywood producer Harvey Weinstein was indicted on several predatory sexual assault charges and has been accused of sexual misconduct by more than forty women. What has come to light—from Hollywood to corporate America to politics—is systemic abuse of power through sexual harassment, misconduct, and abuse in every arena of our society. More than fifty other high-profile men were called out in 2018 alone.

Organized religion has not escaped these tragic stories. The Catholic Church faces perhaps its greatest crisis in modern times with pervasive and systemic sexual abuse surfacing around the globe. A grand jury issued an 884-page report identifying more than one thousand child victims of sexual abuse by three hundred priests in Pennsylvania dioceses alone. The now-disgraced founding pastor and forty-year leader of Willow Creek Community Church was ushered into "early retirement" by confirmed cases of power abuse and misconduct. The *Houston Chronicle* published an article detailing 220 Southern Baptist church leaders accused of sexual misconduct who have been convicted or have taken a plea deal in cases involving more than seven hundred victims.

Nearly any search of the news can yield a fresh batch of dethroned monarchs, religious or secular. Men entrusted with power but who, having unaddressed and unattended rifts in their masculine soul, have brought harm to women and men and children under their care.

Fallen kings and fallen kingdoms.[5]

Scripture is replete with similar stories. Remember the cowardice of Pontius Pilate when he refused to stand up to the crowd and save the life of Jesus? How about the impact of David's power upon the lives of Uriah and Bathsheba? The Old Testament Pharaoh killed thousands of Hebrew boys, and the New Testament King Herod repeated this horror in his jealousy and fear of a rival king. Though the characters change, the story line remains the same: broken, unfinished, uninitiated men breaking the lives of others with their power.

Think of the men who have held positions of authority over you in your own story. When did they use their power to meet their own unharnessed need for validation rather than offer their strength in the service of love? Coaches, teachers, pastors, bosses working out their core desire to feel powerful at the expense of those entrusted to their care. The list is long, and the damage is real. Kings of this world are notorious for using the talent of young men to serve their own needs to build their kingdom.

More sobering, when I survey my own domain and all that has been entrusted to my care, I see that my own mishandling of power has wounded those I love most. Though in ways I am growing and maturing in my capacity to love well, the harm I've caused others is undeniable and long-standing. I am not yet the man I was made to become. Both in acts of commission, where my power has hurt others, and in acts of omission, where I have failed to engage, to bring a genuine strength in love, I have brought harm. Even this morning I found myself needing to pause and invite my wife to sit face-to-face, heart-to-heart, so that I could take renewed responsibility for places where I have failed to bring into our story the strength and love she deserves.

And so we return to the question, when can you trust a man with power?

Initiation by Fire

"It felt as though I was on a huge roller coaster. It was all I could do to hold on." I was sitting in a truck, deep in the high country of Colorado, with one of the guides from whom I had sought out wisdom. He was reflecting on his years as a young husband, with young kids, in a young and growing career. He named the universal shift that happens for every maturing man, where we begin to move from being the center of our story to coming to the sobering realization that life is not primarily about us.

In the masculine journey, our early years of manhood often begin as a season of exploration and discovery. In youthful exuberance, we tend to view the world with ourselves at its epicenter. Passing through this in time, every man is faced with this profound, essential transition. While it may not be easy to name, the shift is felt deeply in the masculine soul.

I am not the center of the story.
A significant portion of my life is behind me.

And for better and worse, my decisions have deep consequences in the lives of others.

Sure, we are important and affect the lives of others at every stage of development. But at some point in young to mid-adulthood, we find our lives bound with others in inextricable ways. This shift is often initiated by marriage, having kids, and taking on a full-time job or other major responsibilities.

Signing up for a joint checking account with my wife, Cherie, and eventually purchasing a home in both of our names was sobering. The implications of "till death do us part" became concrete, hitting me with the pressure and fear that ultimately I did not have what was needed to come through.

When we stepped into marriage, both Cherie and I were intent on seeking God's heart, filled with a sense of promise and possibility. While many rocks lay strewn on the path in our first years, I remember the joy of lingering conversation and sharing what we were learning and what questions were emerging as we explored life, each other, God, and the world.

And then we became parents. We were delighted by God's good provision and felt the joy of being entrusted with these little ones. Yet as quickly as they came, so did all margin depart. I remember Joshua crying and being unable to comfort him, the sleepless nights, the disorientation of being the first among our peers to become parents, and feeling painfully out of place between couples with older kids and our peers who were single or newlyweds.

My dreams and desires became very simple: a few hours' sleep, a beer, a cup of coffee, or—someday—maybe even ten minutes of stillness. As margin evaporated, the negative impact of my style of relating with Cherie increased. I could see the check engine light on the dashboard of my soul illuminated, but our lives seemed to be functioning well enough, and as long as the car is still drivable, who has time or emotional space to check under the hood anyway? So we kept on driving our life and our marriage. (It's amazing how at times we can pay more attention to our vehicles than to the state of our souls.)

Do you remember this transition from a season of exploration and discovery into the season of being consequential to other people? While it caught me off guard, there were a handful of moments in which it was crystal clear that

I'd been catapulted out of one season of life and had landed with bumps and bruises in another. And I, too, found myself on a huge roller coaster. And it was all I could do to hold on.

I started to notice certain things for the first time. Professional athletes were actually younger than I was. One day my head was strangely sore after a short adventure with some buddies under the hot summer sun. I soon realized I had badly sunburned my scalp. I had no idea I'd lost enough hair to warrant replacing styling gel with sunscreen from the kids' swim bag.

With this shift into a new season of heightened responsibility, the pressure builds quickly and steadily, and most men reach for security with a determination to start building. The standard blueprint for this reactive building process often has three components:

1. **Making a name for ourselves.** Whatever we can do, big or small, we establish ways to secure our identity by what we do so it isn't rooted in who we are.
2. **Making a little money.** We lock onto our own version of the modern dream. We take the bait of thinking that building a bank account will validate us as a man or give us more of the lasting rest or satisfaction that our heart seeks.
3. **Getting something going.** Whatever it may be, we start building. We build resumes, social media networks, churches, businesses. We start hustling. Whatever it may be, much of it fueled by the desire to feel alive. To feel the thrill of accomplishment, success, and to have something of which we can be proud.

Consider these three central motives for building. Look back at your life over the years. Notice how these motives have been expressed and how much of your time and energy has been invested in succeeding in these pursuits. If we slow down and observe our lives, we often will find that many of our activities are a reaction to mounting pressure and responsibility. In and of themselves, none of these things are inherently bad. It is the motives with which we pursue them that must be unearthed. Notice how often, even if we are physically present with the people and things we attest to care most about, we find ourselves not soulfully present and engaged. Rather than bringing to our families playfulness and affection, we bring fatigue and frustration. Why is it we spend our best energy at work and show up at home with mere scraps? We determine to achieve something to call our own, to start that company, to conquer that initiative. Yet why is it we find ourselves scrambling to prove to a boss, to our spouse, or—even more—to our own souls that we have what it takes?

And the desire and vision we have for being powerful collides painfully with our inability to maintain integrity of soul under the weight of the demands. What if the desire deep within our souls, expressed in so many forms, to be powerful is whispering to us an ancient truth?

We are meant to be powerful.

And in order to become powerful, to become a wholehearted king, to become a man who can delight the heart of God through what he does with power bestowed, we must take a journey down a rarely traveled and adventurous path. We must risk believing that these desires placed within us were meant for good. They were set deep inside us by the Father heart of God. And in order to recover life, we must first venture far enough down this ancient path to recover the possibility and the promise of becoming a son.

2

BECOMING A SON

Since we are the sons of God, we must
become the sons of God.
—George MacDonald

It was a summer day in 2008 when I collapsed by the driver's side door of
my old Ford Explorer, my body crumpling to the surface of an asphalt
parking lot searing under the summer sun. I had just buckled our three-year-
old son into his car seat on the opposite side of the truck after returning a
tool to Home Depot for my dad. We were in Pittsburgh, Pennsylvania, with
my parents, having sought refuge in my childhood home from our quickly
deteriorating life. Several states away, Cherie was in a treatment center for
severe depression and anxiety, and my mother-in-law was caring for our one-
year-old daughter.

More than seven years earlier, our marriage began with such promise.
Cherie and I both engaged in profound conversions of faith during our college
years, which transformed our views of sexuality and marriage. We set off on
uncharted waters, choosing to invite God to be the centerpiece of our growing
relationship and our future marriage and sexual intimacy. The first years were
vibrant with hope. We were both fully immersed serving alongside John and

Stasi Eldredge to develop Wild at Heart*—a mission committed to rescuing and restoring the hearts of men and women around the globe. Yet after the birth of our second child, Cherie began to experience increasingly severe symptoms of anxiety and depression. Over the subsequent months, I did everything I knew to do—pray, seek a variety of professional help, call on every form of support from our faith community, change circumstances around her daily life to ease the demands. But nothing curtailed the riptide pulling her out to sea. Each day her symptoms heightened to the point that she was unable to perform even basic tasks like packing a suitcase. The severity of Cherie's condition did not fully hit me until the late hours of a summer evening, when a dear friend and counselor gently directed me, "You need to remove all the knives from your home."

Days later I was checking my bride into a sterile-looking treatment center. She'd expressed the desire to participate and had given her consent, but after she was admitted and I turned to leave, she balked. I will never forget how she desperately groped at my arms, begging me not to leave her. I looked her in the eye, whispered, "I love you," and walked out the double doors of the admittance hallway. When I got to my truck, I curled up in a ball and wept. I was a broken man. There I sat, three miles away from where our first kiss took place on our wedding day. What was happening to my life? All of it—my kids, my marriage, even my work in rescuing the hearts of men—felt like sand running through my fingers.

Cherie's mom graciously suggested I take a road trip to my parents' house with our three-year-old son, Joshua, to provide him some summer joy. I believe it was also her kind way of communicating that I, too, was a mess and that, frankly, I was a hindrance at this point in my wife's healing. You see, all the while, I'd been trying everything, desperately grasping to save my wife's life. I was burning through every option I could come up with—making calls and decisions, spending money and time—all in a frantic effort to save her. I was exhausted, and our boat was sinking more quickly than I could bail water.

On a nondescript summer day, my shattered soul finally came to a breaking point under the weight of my world, which I had been trying to hold up for days . . . for decades. It was the most terrifying and holy moment of my life.

---

* Ransomed Heart Ministries was renamed Wild at Heart.

Only later did I understand that collapse to be a severe mercy and the inception of the next chapter in God's long-range rescue of my heart. Two years had passed since I began collecting and integrating the counsel of mentors, but it was through this season of suffering that what I was hearing from them became what I experienced to be true. Though at the time I had intellectual assent that the Father of Jesus was my heavenly Father, what I lacked was the experiential knowledge of this relationship. And deeper than the present chaos of my life, this lack of experiential knowledge of God as my loving and present Father and of myself as his beloved and secure son was my central misery and the source of my greatest pain.

The recovery of our identity as God's beloved son and our experience of God's lavish love through sonship is foundational for our transformation into the kind of man who has the inner wholeness to wield power well. To understand any man's story, we must learn the narrative of the loss of the father and set our intention to see how the Father is searching for each man no matter how he lost his way, in order to restore what has been lost, stolen, and surrendered in the place of sonship. And we must consider what it would look like to participate in the restoration of the lost treasure of sonship.

The Heroic Fellowship

As John Eldredge and Brent Curtis articulated in *The Sacred Romance*, in John 1 we find a secret to the fabric of all creation. "In the beginning was the Word, and the Word was with God, and the Word was God" (John 1:1).[1] In the beginning, before all time, existed the eternal heroic fellowship of the Trinity. The person of the Father and the person of the Son and the person of the Spirit were joyously interacting and collaborating together—as Dallas Willard put it, "a community of unspeakably magnificent personal beings of boundless love, knowledge, and power."[2]

At the center of creation itself was loving relationship, particularly the relationship between a parent and a child, a Father and a Son. In the overflow of the generous love of the Trinity, human beings were created for adoption into the family of the Trinity as beloved sons and daughters. In his letter to the Ephesians, Paul put words to the wonder of God's pleasure in creating humans as the focus of his love.

> How blessed is God! And what a blessing he is! He's the Father of our Master, Jesus Christ, and takes us to the high places of blessing in him. Long before he laid down earth's foundations, he had us in mind, had settled on us as the focus of his love, to be made whole and holy by his love. Long, long ago he decided to adopt us into his family through Jesus Christ. (What pleasure he took in planning this!) He wanted us to enter into the celebration of his lavish gift-giving by the hand of his beloved Son.
>
> —Ephesians 1:3–6 MSG

The joyous intention of God in human history is that Jesus might be the firstborn of many brothers and sisters (Rom. 8:29), brothers and sisters who have been called by name by the Father and who are being transformed into the likeness of the Son of man with ever-increasing glory by the generative power of the Spirit (2 Cor. 3:18).

We were made to participate in the life of God, in fellowship with the Father, Son, and Spirit, as dearly beloved sons.[3]

But there is another character in the story line of God's beloved creation, a character whose intention is to disintegrate all that is good and beautiful and true. Satan knows that if he can dislodge a man from the place of secure sonship, he can not only stunt the restoration of the image of God in the man but also indirectly wound the heart of the Father (Zech. 3:1–2; Rev. 12:10). Satan is cunning and calculating in his methods and brutal and savage in his intent (1 Peter 5:8). And the primary target of his assault is the sacred seat of sonship from which we were born and to which we are invited to return. We don't have to look far in this world to see the sustained assault against the intimacy and connection intended between fathers and sons. And we don't have to look far in our internal world to see the disintegration of sonship as well.

Years ago I came across a very revealing story recounted by Gordon Dalby. He told of a nun who worked in a men's prison. One year she brought some

Mother's Day cards to distribute to any prisoners who were interested in sending cards to their moms. Word spread, and requests for cards began pouring in. The demand was so great that she reached out to Hallmark to see if they'd be willing to donate extra boxes of cards. That first year the warden drew numbers from a lottery to determine which inmates would receive the limited number of Mother's Day cards. With Father's Day quickly approaching, the nun got to work securing sufficient boxes of Father's Day cards, and the warden announced a free giveaway to all who were interested in sending a Father's Day card.

Not a single prisoner asked for one.

What are we to make of this story? What has happened to the God-intended bond between fathers and their children?

- Of U.S. students in grades one through twelve, 17.7 million (39 percent) live in homes absent their biological fathers.[4]
- According to 72 percent of the U.S. population, fatherlessness is the most significant family or social problem facing America.[5]

While the condition of fatherlessness is where most men find their souls, this wasn't the reality in which Jesus lived.

I remember sitting with John Eldredge, several years into my faith journey, and seeing through him what would become the most compelling portrait of the gospel I'd ever encountered. Through John's teaching on masculinity, I saw for the first time how Jesus is the embodiment of both unfailing compassion and masculine courage. He is at once gentle of soul (Matt. 11:28–30) and as relentless as a Navy SEAL in his warrior heart (Ps. 24:7–10).

I was starting to see the emasculated Jesus I had been handed for so many years. Could it be possible that Jesus embodied all the essential qualities that make the heart of a man come alive? And could it be true that the restoration of our hearts, as men, has been made available to us? The next day I cleared my calendar, skipped school, and headed up to the snowy high country of the Colorado Rockies, armed only with my Bible. I hiked in and hunkered down on the shore of an alpine lake. There I sat, confessing to the Spirit that I needed fresh eyes, cleansed of the religious veil, so that I could see Jesus—not as I'd been taught but as he truly is in heaven. I walked through his life as portrayed in the gospel of Mark, from beginning to end, dropping all my presuppositions as best I could. I took the stories and the man at face value. I immersed myself in the reality of his life. And I've never been the same.

Jesus lived as a son. In any and every moment, he modeled for us what it looks like to live as a son. What love looks like, in human form, played out in his relational integrity and wholeness of heart. In total dependency and union with his Father. When we look at the mission of Jesus through a religious veil and see him as simply a merciful means to eternal salvation, we miss sonship entirely. The place of sonship was the foundation of Jesus' life, and it both attracted his students and filled them with ache and longing.

"Teach us to pray" (Luke 11:1). Although these words lead us into what has become known as the Lord's Prayer, Jesus' teaching on the heart of prayer has been all but lost to us under the barrage of religiosity. But it begins this way: "Our Father." If we would pause, allow our hearts to enter the scene, and become a student of Jesus alongside his other disciples, we would encounter a son inextricably united with his Father. The Scriptures are filled with glimpse after glimpse of Jesus' union with his Abba.

"I and the Father are one."

—John 10:30

"Whatever the Father does the Son also does."

—John 5:19

"This is life; that you might know the Father."

—John 17:3[6]

The disciples were in awe. Jesus' life had a quality of eternity as he rested in the strength of his Father. His life flowed with ever-present anticipation and expectation of goodness now and goodness to come, knowing that he was the delight of his Father and that satisfying goodness was being prepared for him (Isa. 42:1).

It was this very life—this vibrant, intimate, and abundant life in and with the Father (John 7:38)—that his disciples wanted to know and experience for themselves. It was from this space that they turned to their teacher and said, "Jesus, teach us. We want what you have. We want to know this life." Jesus consented, paused, and turned toward them, saying, "Father . . ."

He could have stopped there with this one word—*Father*—and it would have been sufficient. You see, the human soul is always searching for the Father.[7] The reach for the accessible Father was the beginning and the end of Jesus' prayer life. Better said, his whole life. Jesus revealed ultimate reality through these words: "I came from the Father and entered the world; now I am leaving the world and going back to the Father" (John 16:28).

Here is the central idea. Whatever else we observe about the life of Jesus, we know this to be true: at every moment, Jesus modeled what it looks like to live as God's Son. It was the bedrock of his life that allowed him to become the cornerstone of restoration for all of mankind. It's amazing to think that even Jesus needed to receive the validation of his Father before he launched into his life's mission. I wonder what it was like for him to hear those words from his Father: "Son, you are the real deal. You have what it takes. I delight in you" (Matt. 3:17, my paraphrase). His Father's constant validation was a holy reservoir from which Jesus drew strength for the rest of his days.

What might it be like, deep in our masculine soul, to live in an atmosphere of abundance? To live with an abiding expectation of goodness now and goodness around the corner? To know a profound sense of robust well-being, a sense of being provided for, protected, and fed? To experience a union with God that nothing could dissolve? What would it be like to be so restored as a son that we could become our true self? To become the kind of king, like Paul, who over time was able to live energetically rooted in God, even in the midst of hunger, shipwreck, and torture?

> Now that I have been so immersed in the true nature of God and his
>   kingdom,
> now that I have thoroughly put to death the self-sufficiency and self-
>   preservation of the false self,

now that I have been resurrected and restored to my true self,
now that I have become in my essence what God meant when he meant man,
now that I have become uniquely who God meant, when he meant me,
now that I have trained and become practiced in living a life in experiential
union with God himself,
now that it is no longer the separate-I who lives but the very breath, strength,
and life of God-with-me who lives in me,
I am ready for anything, anywhere.

Imagine what it would be like to receive that validation from the Father, to have that reservoir from which to drink daily. To be integrated in our masculine soul. To live in ever-increasing union with the Father.

We would become *unstoppable*. Pause for a moment and let that sink in. Truly.

I suggest that it is available. And I submit that this reunion with our Father is the primary work that God is up to in your life and mine.

What's Not Working?

It is a simple yet profound question. And I was blown away to see what surfaced when I finally gathered the courage to give this question serious consideration.

It wasn't until several years into being married, having young children, pursuing my vocation, and navigating ever-deeper waters of life that I began to be more honest with myself about unanswered questions in my soul. I noticed a growing impatience with struggles my wife was facing. When circumstances afforded a pause, I observed fear and doubt and pressure rising within me from the depths. *What's not working?* It was late on a Friday night after a rough week in my marriage and in my work that I found myself writing this question on a blank page in my journal. With a pen in one hand and a beer in the other, I was surprised to see an extensive list materialize.

I came face-to-face with all I was carrying and the terrible emotional weight of the idea that life was up to me in nearly every arena of my life. For perhaps the first time I became honest about the negative impact I've had in my most precious relationships as I habitually moved against people, disengaging from honest, heart-to-heart relationships to control outcomes and avoid shame. I saw the constant reaching—for exercise, for beer, for food, for caffeine, for sex, for relief from an unnamed pain rather than for the restoration my soul longed to know.

It was hard to put a name to it, but I felt behind. This sense of being behind touched every category of my masculine report card. From fitness to finance, relationships to responsibilities. From my marriage to my general hopes for maturing. (A good friend confessed, as we discussed this dilemma, that he even felt behind in his yard work.) Try as I might, I simply couldn't escape this reality that permeated so many areas of my life. As I looked deeper, fear of failure seemed to be ever present, always with a sense of scarcity and a feeling that things were not going to work out, whatever those things might be.

In it all, I could tell that what wasn't working was my ability to be present. So often caught up in the regret of the past or the worries of the future, I had become what A. W. Tozer called a practical atheist: believing God exists in the past and in the future, but for all practical purposes, a genuine reality of and connecting with God doesn't exist. I was never at rest. Always focused on the next thing. Always moving, trying to make life happen. And it wasn't working.

If we would stop and allow enough pause for our soul to rise to the surface, giving the question of what's not working honest consideration, perhaps we would become more aware of our pain. Pain is a symptom of a deeper ache and longing in our soul. Peeling back the layers and getting to the deepest layer of all the "not working," we might arrive at the core dilemma of the masculine soul. It is something we must name as fatherlessness, the reality of not experiencing the abundant and generous life being made available to us as a son.

The only tragedy greater than the profoundly deep fatherlessness our soul experiences is that we have come to accept that sense of fatherlessness as normal.

It is critical to recover the reality that our masculine soul is eternal. It comes from the Father—from an atmosphere of perfect intimacy, love, and affection—and will one day return to the Father (John 16:28). This eternal reality is written on our hearts (Eccl. 3:11), and the ache and longing we all feel testifies to that from which we come and that which God is seeking to restore as Father. Regardless of the quality of fathering you did or did not receive from an earthly father, we all carry the design, the fall, the assault against sonship, and the possibility of its restoration deep within our souls.

Remember with me for a moment the perfect intimacy that existed between Adam and God at the birth of mankind. Adam knew he was God's favorite son. He delighted in the goodness of God and brimmed with life and strength as he learned day by day how to rule, to take dominion over all that had been entrusted to his care. And then came a day—and in that day, a moment—when he was faced with a decision. Eve had taken life into her own hands. She had fallen, and now he had a choice. And in that moment, he chose Eve over God.

"Adam, where are you?" the Father called out. The perfect intimacy of a father and a son had been both surrendered and stolen. A father was looking for his lost son. Now, of course, as we touched on in the introduction, the Father knew where Adam was; he is all-knowing. But the question was an honoring one. It was Adam who was lost and now out of touch with where he was, or better said, *who* he was. Adam answered, "I heard you in the garden, and I was afraid because I was naked; so I hid" (Gen. 3:10).

Adam's story is every man's story. Somewhere in our stories, the intimacy between Father and son was severed. Sin created a break, and the accuser has had a field day ever since, setting out to prove that fear and shame are nonnegotiables. He has set out to destroy the image of sonship and our identity as God's favorite son. Every man knows fatherlessness at some level, and so we go it alone.

Atlas and the Condition of Fatherlessness

My dad grew up on the precarious edge of the lower working class. His father, a man who spent his childhood being passed between many foster homes, spent his adult years first as a self-proclaimed junkman, recycling salvaged metal, and later as a tile man.

Decades ago my dad recounted a story, the images of which have never left me. One of his childhood joys was collecting spare change in a large glass bottle. When my dad was eight, his father went broke—again—and was forced to declare bankruptcy. One day my dad came home from school, and his parents asked for his change jar. They literally broke the bank and, with the sum of my dad's entire change collection, were able to buy three bus tickets to relocate from Pennsylvania to Florida in order to rebuild a life through a loose connection with a distant relative.

Looking back, I wonder if something very deep and traumatic transpired that day for my dad. What sort of message takes root in the soul of a boy enduring this sort of trauma? Left with no redemptive interpretation, the heart of the boy has little choice but to learn a fateful lesson, perhaps something like, *Now it is up to me.* And perhaps even deeper, *I am worthy of love when I provide financially for my family.*

With every wound comes a lie; with every lie, an agreement; and with every agreement, a vow. Like most of us, my dad has worked ceaselessly for decades, motivated by a deep and steadfast love for his family but also no doubt by a wound—and through that wound a lie that suggests this is the only path for life and love.

After completing medical school, my dad married my mom, had four children, and became a successful surgeon, building a private practice through the hard work of going door to door with business cards in the steel factory communities of Pittsburgh. A town hero in many ways, he eventually traveled the country and parts of the world as one of the first physicians to teach laser surgery. In my childhood memories, he is a man of few words, but no one I have ever met worked harder to provide for his family. Simply put, he became my hero and was the strongest man in my world.

My best childhood memories are of the very rare summer evenings when my dad would finish surgery early enough to meet us at the local swimming pool right before closing. My dad was made for water: as a young boy, he dove for sand dollars to sell in local tourist shops; as a young teen, he cleaned pools to help support the family; as an older teen, he worked as a lifeguard on the beach. At the pool, he would take a swim with me holding fast to his strong shoulders. I remember watching him swim the length of the pool underwater in a single breath. I remember feeling like surely he could go for hours; I rested in the joy of this nearness and the strength I saw within him.

And vacations—as a kid, my dad had known "vacation" only as an out-of-reach ideal enjoyed by wealthy people who were different from him. As a father, he worked seven days a week, but he made the sacrificial decision that in order to provide for us what he'd never had, he would fight for a seven-day vacation every year. As I look back, day six of vacation holds the very best memories of my entire childhood. Day seven started with the dreaded words "Party's over," as the stresses of the real world flooded back. I would watch it in my father's body language. Ah, but day six was the treasure of my boyhood. My dad was funny, free, playful, present. For eternal moments, we got the best of him, and I wanted for nothing.

Everything changed when my grandfather died. I was ten years old and attending my first funeral. I was sitting next to my dad when he began to weep. It was an awkward and fearful moment. I had never in my life seen my dad cry. It seemed that he didn't even know how to, as he did a weird sort of convulsing motion. I didn't know what to do. Out of instinct, I put my arm around him to comfort him for the first time. No words ever followed, and I had no outside source to interpret all that happened to my soul that day. While it took decades to put it into words, some deep fissure erupted in my masculine soul, and an agreement took root. *The strongest man in my world is not strong enough.* As I watched the strongest man in my world break, my anchor released, letting the current take my soul out to sea, and I responded with this unspoken vow: *I will become the strongest man in my world.* So began my story of fatherlessness.

Shortly after the funeral, I came across, for the first time, a picture of Atlas—the Greek mythological figure sentenced to hold the weight of the world. It answered in a broken way the deep masculine question in my soul—the central ache of a man to be enough. It was a perfectly cunning ploy of my Enemy. *I am a man now. I must be the strongest man in my world. If anything good is going to happen, I'm going to make it happen. Life is up to me. I'm on my own.*

While I could not have put those words to it at the time, three decades later my soul was able to paint a vivid picture of the crime scene. In some sad and broken way, it had felt good to have a mission. I couldn't know at the time it was simply my shattered soul making agreements with lies and making vows that would fuel my drivenness and push for success for decades to come.

In many ways, my story is every man's story. How about you? Where has the sense of fatherlessness taken root in your story? This is merely the first step of a thousand-mile journey of recovering a father-centered reality.

God, where do I feel behind in my life? What do I say to myself when something doesn't work out the way I want it to? What do I say when I fail? How do I feel in the presence of older men?

These questions might help you begin the excavation process. Invite the Holy Spirit to lead you into the deeper places of your soul and story and, with curiosity and expectation, consider where these patterns of reacting to circumstances and feelings in particular situations began.

How Have You Learned the Father?

George MacDonald posed this question in his brilliant book *Unspoken Sermons*: "How have you learned the Father?"[8]

If we were to be honest and dive into our own inner world (and that of most men), we would discover that the story of fatherlessness is not the exception but the norm. If we were to pause, let that soak in, and be honest, it might help us unearth a core assumption obscured below the surface of our masculine heart. What comes to mind, emotionally and unedited, when you think of your full experience and observations of "father" in our culture? Look at the examples of many of the men you grew up around—coaches, teachers, fathers of friends, the men in your masculine heritage—in these specific places in your story. I'm asking you to pause and take stock honestly. Write down the first ten words.

For more than a decade, spanning five continents, I've asked thousands of men this question concerning what words come to our hearts when we hear "*father.*" The responses vary a bit, but the essence is startlingly consistent. Yes, there are some positive words, but the vast majority are words like these:

distant
unemotional
angry
absent
stressed
quiet

violent
abusive
fearful and worried
at work
independent
always on his phone
without friends
checked out
silent
self-sufficient

Here's why this is so significant to grasp: the primary place we establish our core beliefs about God as Father is how our father responded to us when we did something wrong. This is why MacDonald went on to say that it's better not to have known the Father than to have learned him wrong.[10]

The single greatest factor that will shape our freedom, our strength, and our ability to become a king is receiving a spirit of sonship and allowing our understanding of our true Father to be reformed in every facet where it was harmed, lost, or learned wrong.

Have you noticed that religious principles can take a man only so far? What are we to do with all our unanswered questions? No doubt, this book will answer a few, but in the process, it is intended to raise many more. Christianity is not merely a set of principles for living. It is an invitation into an interactive life and a kingdom, a reality by which we walk with a loving Father and are able to not only navigate life but also thrive as a son who is known, is being fought for, and is maturing and being made whole and holy through the loving pursuit of his Dad.

Surfacing Fatherlessness to Heal

This is why the Father relentlessly shines light on the condition of fatherlessness in each of our souls. I recently headed out of town to facilitate a retreat for a select group of leaders. Just as I was leaving cell reception, I received the call from my wife. You know that call. "Something is wrong with the transmission in the minivan." This was the critical moment. We all have knee-jerk reactions, unedited thoughts that rise up. As for me, these four habitual thoughts arose:

Why does this always happen?
I never should have left town.
We can't afford this.
I'm not sure what to do.

Have you noticed how quickly these sentences pop up in our mind if we are willing to listen? Agreements with lies bubbling up from the orphan within us? Do you see the layers of fatherlessness being expressed from deep in the soul? So many times when we experience hardship, we interpret it either as God holding out on us or as proof that we're on our own. What if the Father is pursuing us in our wounding? What if our Father is constantly bringing to light the fatherless places in us *in order to heal us*? In my story, this second great conversion of my life into sonship began with the Father surfacing the conditions of fatherlessness beyond what I thought I could bear.

Recovering Wholeness

I wasn't strong enough.

After my collapse, as I lay on the scorching asphalt outside the Home Depot, almost viewing myself as an outside observer, thoughts raced through my mind. Images of my wife in a hospital, my son in his car seat happily waiting for his dad, and me in this pile of utter disorientation and despair. And then I sensed a Presence. It was a Strength and a Presence I had never known. These words pierced my heart:

Son. Get up. We can do this together.

Somehow I found my way to my feet. Through what can only be described as supernatural intervention, something—*Someone*—came to my aid. I was miraculously able to wipe my tears, gain my composure, get in the truck, and drive my son home. I managed to function through the day until I could get him bathed and ready for bed. We were snuggling together on twin mattresses pushed side by side on the floor of my childhood bedroom. While I was falling apart inside, my son was enjoying the trip of a lifetime, as he received the intimacy of shared adventure with his dad. In the quietness of the summer evening, Joshua leaned over, looked me in the eyes, nose to nose, and said, "Daddy, we are brothers."

Something in me knew that while it was cute, it wasn't technically true; I was his father, and he was my son. But immediately I felt the nudging of the Holy Spirit. *Stay with this. Don't miss this.* I paused, lingered, and asked my son, "Joshua, how are we brothers?"

He responded rather matter-of-factly as a three-year-old can, "Daddy, God is my Father, and God is your Father, so that makes us brothers."

I was speechless. Gentle tears bathed my face as my shattered, orphaned heart began to receive a revelation of God as Father, and to receive his affection and care, in a way I had never known. God spoke to me through my son, and my life would never be the same. Joshua was right.

I looked Joshua in the eye and said the most powerful words I've ever said. "Joshua, I'm sorry. Please forgive me. I've always tried to be the strongest man in your world. But you are right—we are brothers. And we need our Father more than anything else. Let's pray and ask God to Father us."

And so we began. "God, we are your sons. We ask you to Father us today." It's been more than a decade since that warm summer evening, and in all these years, we have not gone a day without asking God to be our Father.

The next several days, as Cherie continued in the treatment program, I was caught up in the early sacred experiences of becoming my Father's son again. As Joshua and I moved through the geography of my youth, we felt the love of our Father as he poured out his affection, his provision, and his gifts for our hearts in response to our asking to come home as sons. We rode bikes as though we had found ourselves together in my childhood all over again. Down to the corner store to buy candy. Through the meandering path to the swimming pool. Joshua rode on my shoulders, just as I remembered riding on my dad's. We explored the creek behind the house, catching crawfish and salamanders. We played Cowboys and Indians and roasted marshmallows over moonlit campfires.

This was the very geography God was harnessing to heal the fatherless places in me and to begin initiating me in sonship. Act by act, moment by moment, my masculine soul began to heal. And as I healed, I loosened the Superman cape I hadn't even known I had been wearing around my neck for so many years. The Father began to show me that in an effort to be a good man, to be Atlas, I had taken on a whole host of identities in the hope of saving Cherie's life. In my unfathered places, I'd attempted to be not only her husband but also her father, her counselor, her girlfriend, and more. As the Father began to heal my heart, I realized I was simply unqualified for all of those roles except for husband. I began an entirely new level of repentance, as a son, truly entrusting my wife, for the first time, to the care of her Father.

Deep in my masculine soul, I began to embrace the revelation that ultimately I had no capacity to save my wife or my marriage. I began to acknowledge that in fundamental ways the fates of both were beyond my control. Instead a new question was being birthed.

What kind of man do I want to be?

I could feel this newfound strength rising up, a consecrated yes, not as an orphan but as a son: "I'm in. No matter the circumstance and no matter the outcome." It was suddenly clear that I could become the man I wanted to be in my marriage only by first becoming a son and receiving the provision, the protection, the care, and the abundance of a loving Father.

While the restoration of strength has taken time, almost overnight Cherie began to notice peace and joy returning as a direct result of my choosing to become a son. Some enormous pressure I'd unknowingly put on myself and on her began to lift. I had no idea that my commitment as Atlas to always come through was one of the central pressures that had her heart pinned down in despair. As an orphan, I had become the kind of person who was hurting the person I love most. Out of my newfound identity as a son, and out of my growing reservoir of settledness and strength, her heart experienced a newly recovered space to breathe and slowly begin to heal.

Being more than a decade removed from those days, I look back in awe at how the heart and soul of my wife has become alive and free and beautiful in every way. She has become the greatest hero of my life. And it was all birthed in the harrowing and risky choice of us both entering into deeper relationships with the living God, me becoming a son and her becoming a daughter.

The journey of becoming a son began that day when my son spoke words of life into my soul, and it has continued every day since. What was then simply a risky ask to be fathered has turned into years of being grown, cared for, invested in, and strengthened by the Father through dozens and dozens of men. The journey of sonship is not a one-time event but an ongoing process, as Jesus modeled, of maturing in oneness.

When the son is ready, the Father appears.

The map of my soul is being redrawn. New habits are being formed that allow me to live more and more out of being a son of the greatest Father ever known. And it is that Father who makes himself available today, and every day, to each of us.

> The hardest and gladdest thing in the world is to cry out, Father! from a full heart. The refusal to look up to God as our Father is the one central wrong in the whole human affair.[10]

The first doorway we must travel through on our path toward becoming a king is to choose sonship. It is a choice.

Are we willing to become our Father's sons again?

Will you open your heart to unlearn the Father as you have learned him and instead learn him as he truly is? The Father is pursuing you. He is opening up his heart and his kingdom and his treasures to you. He is asking, *Son, are you ready to become who you were born to be? We can finish this together.*

If we are ever to become the kind of men to whom God can entrust his kingdom, the journey must begin in the most unlikely of places. We must choose a spirit of sonship, taking the place set before us as the greatest gift of God's heart, receiving the identity against which every war has been waged by our Enemy, who knows who we are and fears who we could become.

In many ways, to consent to being a son is the hardest and the easiest of the narrow gates through which we must enter. It is easy, because all it requires is a genuine turning of our souls to receive the lavish love of the Father. Yet it is the hardest, as it will require us to begin forsaking the many other places in which our wounded hearts have sought the independent and self-sufficient life for so many years. It will require relearning everything, throwing out our former map and receiving a new one that outlines a reality more dangerous and more joy-filled than we have ever dared to dream.

With these words of George MacDonald, I invite you to join me on this wildly adventurous narrow path: "Since we are the sons of God, we must become the sons of God."[11]

Father, I confess I am your son, and you are my Father. I ask you to Father me. By day and by decade. You have my yes.

If you are among the few who would consent to this narrow way and risk giving your soul over to this new reality, then to you I say wholeheartedly, "Welcome." Let us receive this big idea and continue our quest to becoming a king. For you might not expect what's around this next bend in the ancient path.

3

BECOMING TRUE

There are many people who think they want to be
matadors, only to find themselves in the ring with
2,000 pounds of bull bearing down on them, and
then discover that what they really wanted was to
wear the tight pants and hear the crowd roar.

—Terry Pearce

It caught me completely by surprise. A friend sent me a photograph[1] of an
extensive construction site in a densely populated city center flanked by
towering structures. Enormous excavators appeared like larvae in the bow-
els of a compost heap, nearly engulfed by the chasm that would eventually
contain the foundation of a new skyscraper. The hole for the foundation
was deep, extending deeper than I ever would have envisioned for this sort
of building. As I studied the photo, I could make out a host of men at the
bottom of the chasm, doing the hard and steady work of removing debris and
preparing the land. The Father was giving me an invitation and a metaphor.
And I could feel the false man in me recoiling.

It wasn't until nearly a decade later that my experience was described
by words I came across from Mike Mason: "A thirty-year-old man is like a

densely populated city; nothing new can be built . . . without something else being torn down."[2] In the journey to recover the ancient path, we come to the sobering reality that we cannot build before we have properly excavated. To become a king, we must give our strength to the sacred work of excavating before we can participate with God in the process of building in his way and in his time.

While this ancient truth was knocking at my door, I had yet to become the kind of man who has ears to hear it or a heart to receive it. I was spending most of my energy tinkering with my outer world, trying to change other people so that I could feel better, trying to make life work. All the while, I had largely chosen to ignore my inner world—the world to which God most deeply wanted to draw my attention. The external world is easier to access, to measure, to evaluate. The inner world takes time, curiosity, and, above all, an honesty we often won't consider employing until the pain is more than we can bear.

Pain

"I want to die."

It just came out. I was sitting in the counselor's office in the presence of a kind, older man—a man who, I felt, understood me more deeply than did anyone who had ever known me. "I want to die." But I quickly realized that wasn't quite true. There was something more true: "There is *a man in me* who wants to die." Through this pain, I had finally come face-to-face with the false self in a life-and-death wrestling match.

The most dangerous dimension of the false self is that it often works for us, providing false nourishment, satiating the need for identity and validation apart from God. In my youth, I chased the feeling of power through relationships with women and through positions of leadership; these were my medications of choice. President of my class nearly every year and on to student body president in high school and even dorm president at my university. Wherever I went, I found myself in charge. To the outside world it may have looked like strength. In hindsight, as I look below the surface, I can see that it was a young man unconsciously taking his question—the desperate need for masculine validation—to everyone but God.

It wasn't enough; it never is. And it was killing me.

Understanding People

If there is one central idea from which this entire conversation flows, it's this: our masculine heart, the truest us, created in the image of God, is always—at every moment—being expressed and operating through either the true self or the false self. It is critical to understand this idea, because it is the beginning of the lifetime process of becoming aware of which self is active, dismantling the false self, and restoring the true.

Anyone who spends time with me will quickly discover I am a very intense person. This intensity has been the fuel for some of my most courageous and admirable experiences, and it has gotten me into some of the deepest trouble of my life. For years, my intensity led me to personal exhaustion and, even worse, relational damage. I tried to repent of it. But try as I might, I could not. Through years of soul inquiry, I've come to understand that my intensity is a central way in which I bear the image of God. Part of God's nature is a deep intensity; we see it in Jesus as he flips the money changers' tables and moves toward the castoffs of society. It is a portion of himself he has deposited in me. And repenting of the image of God in us is a futile endeavor.

However, what has also become clear is that my intensity leads to both self-harm and harm of others when it is employed by the false self (the part of me that pursues a self-sufficient life that leads to death). In contrast, when it is expressed through the true self, in union with God, it leads to the kingdom coming in me and through me. Every moment, this God-given gift of intensity is being expressed through either the true self or the false self. Any strength expressed through the false self becomes a liability.

Some friends of mine and I founded a small brewery called Sons of Thunder, and we recently threw a Christmas party to introduce our latest brew, Wonderworker, a tribute to the true Saint Nicholas. I created artwork, captured story, made guest lists, decorated, ordered T-shirts, arranged live music. Looking back, I see my intensity at play in the service of both the true self and the false self. In my true self, I was available to partner with God to bring joy and redemptive story to a group of friends. But in much of it, I operated out of my false self, pushing too hard, running over the ideas of others, and living under the chronic self-indictment of *Whatever I do, it's never enough.*

The more I become aware of how the image of God is being expressed in these two ways, the more I can address the false and operate as the unique man God meant when he meant me. Not only to decrease the harm that my intensity (in my false self) brings to myself and others but also to bring a measure of joy and strength (in my true self) to those I love.

What Were We Made For?

Two of our core needs are for loving relationship and meaningful work. In *Addiction and Grace*, Gerald May shared his observation from twenty years of counseling and walking with people. He suggested that every human's story comes into congruence around this central need: to love, to be loved, and to move ever closer to the Source of love.[3]

We are relational beings at our core. We were born out of the heroic fellowship and intimacy of the Trinity. Simply put, relationship is who and what we are. Love in relationship was meant to be the foundational energy and context of our beings. The bestowing of validation and identity from the heart of God to us is intended to be the headwaters of love flowing into our lives.

The early chapters of Genesis offer a glimpse into life and relationship as it was intended. Adam and Eve "were both naked, and they felt no shame" (Gen. 2:25). Exposed and vulnerable without shame. Free, alive, and relishing a union with each other and with God that knew no limits. Oh, friends, what it would be like to be that free. Yet, as in most great stories, that original design was shattered. Through both the grasping of Eve and the passivity of Adam, separation from the living God entered the world.

Moments before the fall of man, identity and validation were undisputable—seated in the Father's love, in union with Jesus, and under the intensely adventurous and joy-filled leadership of the Holy Spirit. We were God's favorite, and we *knew* it. Not a knowing like dates and facts for a history test but a *knowing* as a captain knows a ship on wild seas or a woman knows a man in unbridled and holy sexual intimacy. It is a knowing of the deepest sort. *Ginosko* knowing, as captured in the Greek—intimate, interactive heart knowledge.

Before the fall, Adam enjoyed and rested in love and validation. He had self-esteem and self-worth that sustained and strengthened him for the meaningful work the Father was training him to do. In union with God, he and Eve knew they were everything they needed to be to partner with God and contribute creatively to his creation. They had everything they needed to rule and subdue as well as cherish and steward creation. Adam knew, *I have what it takes.* Eve knew, *I am a life giver.* They were united as one with God; nothing was impossible.

After the fall, identity was called into question; Adam began an incessant search to answer the question, *Who am I?* Shame rolled in like the tide. Anxiety was born, and the reaching to fill the ache of the masculine soul apart from God began. It began as a reach for a fig leaf to cover all that was exposed and vulnerable. For the first time, man had no rest in knowing he was the beloved son, God's favorite. "I am" was replaced with "I'm not," and hiding was the only way to respond to the unnamed anxiety.

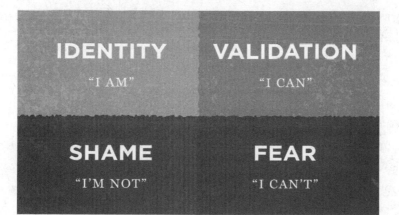

Through the fall, validation was called into question. Fear spread like a heavy fog. "I can" was replaced with "I can't." For the first time in human history, Adam doubted his strength. For the first time, Eve doubted her capacity to bring forth life and beauty. And thus began our desperate search for love in the form of validation and identity apart from God. Wholehearted authenticity, courage, love, vulnerability, intimacy—all evaporated. Shame grew. Anxiety filled the air. Hearts were unsettled. And both Adam and Eve turned to the false self to deliver them.

The False Self

Mostly what you meet when you meet a man is his false self—his version of Adam's fig leaf—behind which he hides from fear and attempts to avoid anything that generates the feeling of dread and death. The false self can be understood as the sophisticated construct developed out of separation from God to avoid pain and shame and to provide identity, power, and meaning. It is a reaction to fear. Ultimately, the false self attempts to disengage from authentic and loving relationship with others, with self, and with God in order to self-protect. Our false self provides the illusion that we can make life work apart from God. It seeks an artificial peace and meaning by avoiding shame and fear, instead of a true peace and purpose through trust and love.

I want to unpack the false self more, because a deep and cultivated experiential knowing of both the true and false selves is essential in the journey of becoming a king.

The False Self Is Habitual

Much of the person we bring to any circumstance is a set of preprogrammed reactions. Most of what we do is not well thought through; it's programmed and predictable. Ultimately, our capacity for habit is part of our God-given design. Thank God that every time I drive my car, I don't have to consciously tell myself, *Right foot on the accelerator; hands at ten and two; check blind spots.* Our capacity for habit and unconscious action is part of God's provision for us so we can live creative and dynamic lives in a complex material world. The false self is our capacity for habit and unconscious thought, feeling, and action—gone wrong. Or better said, our self gone independent—free from a genuine, real-time connection with God. The false self is like a computer program coded by a broken world, our sin nature, and our Enemy. It persistently and habitually reacts to external stimuli in a way that may have nothing to do with God, even though our creedal statements profess belief.

"Morgan, I'd like to get a cat."
"Morgan, I had some unbudgeted expenses this month I need to tell you about."

My wife knows exactly what I'm going to say, right? We all have them—certain phrases, questions, and circumstances that cause our false self to go into habitual reaction mode. It's the opposite of our souls being rooted in God and being informed not only by his counsel and direction but also by his life coursing through us to allow us to transcend our brokenness and rebellion.

For example, when my wife says, "Hey, Morgan, I'd like you to cancel your next adventure trip you have planned with your friends," I can feel my body react as an expression of something being threatened deep within. Before thinking, before prayer, the false man within me has, out of habit, already rejected the comment and answered no, without exception. On the other hand, if my wife says, "Hey, there's an opening on the calendar; why don't you just take a day of solitude? Head out on a joyful adventure of your choice. Do what would be best for you," I don't have to think about it or pray about it; I have a reactive, predictable response. That is the habitual, programmed, reactionary false self. Its reference point is self, not God. Maybe I'm not supposed to go to the wilderness on this trip. Maybe we are supposed to host our extended family next month. Perhaps we are not. We were designed to thrive in an interactive, conversational relationship with God. To become the kind of man who can consent to God's leadership and guidance in the everyday fabric of his life is one of the great indicators of becoming a king.

One of the saddest statements I ever hear about the human experience is when someone says of an older man, "Oh, he's just set in his ways." What this means is that he has perfected the self-life. He has cultivated an elaborate and sophisticated manner to make life work apart from God and to avoid pain; he has become static. It is what sets apart the elderly, someone who's grown old in the maturing of his false self, from an elder, someone who has matured in his true self and its ever-growing union with God.

The False Self Is Self-Referencing and Self-Stabilizing

As Thomas Keating explained, the center of gravity of the false self is itself.[4] The false self is like a bicycle wheel that's balanced only when spinning. As soon as it slows, it becomes imbalanced until it falls down. In contrast, the center of gravity of the true self is God. It is therefore able to rest and doesn't need a constant state of doing in order to be at peace. The false self can't stop its active self-orienting and self-provisioning. When the motion stops, the false self will collapse. Thus the false self expends an incredible amount of energy to stay in constant motion rather than resting in the constancy of a dynamic, relational, loving God. The result is an exhaustion of soul that, if we are honest, we know far too well.

The Pursuit of the False Self Is Futile

The false self seeks preservation through means that simply can never deliver. In Western cultures, most guys can make life work well enough through a good bit of young adulthood that the false self continues to serve them. Yet the brilliance of God is that the false self becomes less and less capable of producing the life we seek.

The false self is a careful construct crafted largely to avoid shame and fear and make life work apart from God. As we are being formed, external problems often help reveal places within us that need to be tended to. The brilliance of God's design for masculine initiation is that the more we truly want life as it was meant to be, the less efficient the false self becomes in producing what feels like life. As men, we become very sophisticated in faking it in most relationships. But thankfully, as we grow and move deeper into relationships such as marriage, the false self begins to get exposed, because, as Mike Mason suggested, a wife is wonderfully "in the way, like a tree growing in the center of the living room."[5]

Over time the man who wishes to truly become a more wholehearted king is invited by God to pass through an increasing death of the false self, only to find a greater life in the process. The false self can no longer produce the life it promised, and the man is left with two choices: to die or to be reborn. The choice of death takes many forms. Sometimes it is literally a suicide, but far more often it's simply the death of quiet desperation or sanctified resignation.[6] Many men will kill their hearts, get busy, and let their masculine souls go to sleep. They will keep going through the motions—paying bills, attending church, building careers, raising kids—all the while slowly deadening their hearts. While medicating for the pain, they lose touch with desire. And in losing touch with desire, they lose the very place where they can encounter and live in the lavish love of the Father.

Look around at the men in your world. It's a pandemic, really: the anger boiling just under the surface; the addiction to some artificial life, in vicarious living through video games, fantasy football; the cynicism, the despair. Yet there *is* another way. Life gives way to death so that death can give way to a greater life. The story is written all throughout the teachings of Jesus. Remember, "Unless a kernel of wheat falls to the ground and dies, it remains only a single seed. But if it dies, it produces many seeds" (John 12:24). And this life that emerges through the process of passing through a death is the foundation of so many of the great stories intended to buoy our hearts and carry our hope.

We were meant to be reborn into a new life, a true life. The pain and loss of the false self and its death were meant to compel us to lean into the vibrant and accessible life of Jesus, the abundance of the Father's heart, and the leadership of the Holy Spirit and, in doing so, become the man we were meant to be. We were intended for intimacy, relational integrity, and wholehearted courageousness—all of which are available only in and through the death of the false self and the restoration of the true self.

Repentance and Recovery

If Jesus' mission was to once again make the kingdom of God available to all of creation through the deliverance and restoration of the human race, how do we partner with Jesus to receive his deliverance and recover the *imago Dei* (image of God) in us? Jesus proclaimed repentance as the first step to entering the kingdom of heaven: "Repent!" "By God's action and initiative, the kingdom of heaven is now open to you again!" "The kingdom of heaven is right here." "Repent and enter the kingdom of God."[7]

What does repentance look like when it comes to the false self and our need for identity and validation? Dallas Willard defines repentance as "rethinking our thinking" and "reconsidering our considerations."[8] Under the action and direction of God, we reconsider our preprogrammed reactions, holding each response accountable to a God-centered reality. We put to death the false self and choose to be born again.

Impact

Cherie and I were at odds again. We were noticing some of the unnamed patterns of relating that had operated during all our years together and set us on a course of destruction. Small things would trouble us—little foxes, the Bible calls them (Song 2:15). In my anger over a frustrating day, I would go to silence. Or in my deep struggle with financial fear, I would make aggressive moves toward control over our budget. We observed that even small hurts had become patterns of habitual harm inflicted upon each other. It was time for help.

I was sitting with a counselor (again), sharing the resentment building between Cherie and me, when he suggested, "How we relate with other people, particularly those closest to us, is one of the greatest indicators of our spiritual maturity." It isn't our doctrine or our service, our ability to come through or to provide. Nothing speaks more deeply than the quality of our relating with God and with others.

What is my impact on Cherie and the other people closest to me? How do I hope she experiences me? What do I fear her experience is of me? I took an honest inventory and came to a startling conclusion: my relating was a mess; so much was still entangled in my false self and my searching for love and validation rather than offering a genuine, loving strength. In the rubric of relationships, there's no relating more central to the human experience than relating with our spouse.[9] This disruption of being exposed in the poor quality of much of my relating led me to soberly take honest inventory for the first time—well into our second decade of marriage—regarding how I genuinely relate with my wife, looking at what my impact is on her. *What does my style of relating evoke in her?*

Looking back, I could see the invitation the Father had been extending—to choose a narrow way to dig deep into my soul and do the excavation necessary to become ever more whole and holy. God is always at work in our story to integrate the shattered pieces of our soul. It is only in becoming increasingly wholehearted and living into deeper union with God that we are able to become the men we were meant to be. I have a hunch that's why it took years after Cherie's health struggles for us to come to the moment we found ourselves in more recently.

We were back in the loving shelter of our marriage mentors' counseling office, for what I considered a tune-up. Finally, no drama, no rescue or major issues to work through. We were there because we were choosing to invest in our marriage for some maintenance—so I thought. I sat relaxed on their couch, and for the first fifteen seconds, everything was going great. Until they asked Cherie kindly, "How are you doing?"

Then her tears. My internal alarms went off. I immediately went into self-preservation mode. *Are you kidding? She was just fine thirty seconds ago. We were just fine. What is this about?* But I have learned enough, grown enough, to pause, breathe, stay present, and trust God in this process. So I chose to settle in and come to the center of her sharing, as her friend, and listen.

She began to tell our story from a perspective I had not heard before, a perspective I don't think she had ever articulated, even to herself. She described those months, many years ago, of moving from health into the emotional unraveling that led us to a treatment center. As she described her experience, she spoke of seeing herself in the context of our marriage as a little, delicate, beautiful bird trapped in a cage. She was the bird. I was the one who'd put her in the cage and wielded the key—the only key—to the lock.

At that moment there were two men inside me in the room. The false self in me was ready to walk out for good. *This is unfair, unjust, even cruel. All the energy I invested in trying to love her, rescue her, help her, and now I'm the perpetrator. This is BS. I'm done.* My false self was at his end. But there was a truer me, a more integrated me, a more being-made-whole me. And I, united with the Father, finally had eyes to see, to *own* the impact of my false self on the one I love the most and had hurt most deeply.

In the guise of rescuing the beauty, leading my family, and acting as the head of the household, I had systematically smothered her heart, rendered her all but voiceless, and put her in a cage so she could no longer fly. The damage had been done. Even if I had unlocked the door and thrown away the key, I didn't know if she would have had the capacity or the desire to come out while I was near. The true me, the more intact me, was crushed with sorrow. I had broken my wife's heart and was unable to see a redemptive road map for this story. There was no precedent I could lean into. As with most of the journey, everything God was asking felt far from suburban and deeply frontier for my masculine soul. I had hurt the one I love the most. Repeatedly.

Sixteen years earlier, I had vowed to love Cherie and to forsake all others. But that day in the counseling office, I realized I'd broken my covenant a thousand times over, choosing myself—my own self-preservation, my own agreements with fear and shame—over truly loving my bride. My broken heart had been accessed yet again, and it was being beckoned and invited to be made even more whole.

The impact of our false self is devastating to those we love most. We can fake it with others—at work, at church, just about anywhere else—maintaining a brilliant disguise that can work effectively for decades and fool even the closest of companions. But for those with whom we share a roof, it is not easy to hide. Not for long. It was only through the earlier soul work Cherie and I had done that we could see and then safely tend to these profoundly deep pockets of trauma in our marriage.

Awareness

The context of the journey of deliverance from the false self and restoration of the true self is unique, but the process is universal. It begins with awareness. The first step to becoming true is becoming aware of the false. *Who am I in my false self? What version of myself do I present to the world as a mask to self-protect? What is my effect on people? What do people feel when they are around me?*

You'll want to get to know the false self and get very familiar with him. We must become students of the person—the self—we have become. We must watch the false self at work and see how he expresses his self-protection by avoiding shame and acting out of fear through his predominant style of relating. We must become keen observers of his impact on others and how that relates to the story of their souls, so we might allow God to continually expose the parts of our heart and our soul that have yet to be integrated into wholeness. Only by coming to know the false self can you engage in the slow and steady process of putting him to death so that the true man might be resurrected in his place. It is only in consenting to the excavation of the masculine soul that we can become the kind of man and the kind of king within whom God can build a lasting kingdom.

To put to death the false self and invite God to restore the true self is the gate along the narrow path that can lead us deeper to coming to know the man God made us to be. Let us venture around the next turn along the ancient path and wonder together about this hidden treasure that can be found only through participating in God's excavation of our masculine soul.

4

BECOMING THE MAN YOU WERE BORN TO BE

We are all under the same mental calamity;
we have all forgotten our names. We have
all forgotten what we really are.
—G. K. Chesterton

Ridley Scott's film *Gladiator* is based on the true story of the Roman Empire in 180 AD, after the death of Marcus Aurelius. At the heart the film is a conflict between evil and good over the issue of power. Commodus, the representation of evil, seeks the throne of his father for the sake of self; Maximus, a general in the Roman army, is willing to oppose him for the sake of others. The story line goes like this:

The general becomes a slave.

The slave becomes a gladiator.

The gladiator defies an emperor.

The kingdom is restored, and a great goodness returns to its people.

Fearing he will lose the throne, Commodus commands that Maximus be murdered and orders the rape and burning of his wife and son. Yet Maximus's great heart, connected to his true identity, surpasses evil's efforts to annihilate him. Later in the film, Maximus transforms a platoon of slaves into an elite band of brothers, and they prove victorious in the Colosseum against overwhelming odds. In the stillness following the gladiators' victory, Commodus enters the arena, flanked by armed guards, in order to determine the identity of this gladiator, whose helmet conceals it.

"Gladiator, do you have a name?"

Maximus replies, "My name is Gladiator," and turns his back on the emperor.

The emperor responds in anger, calling out the identity he has bestowed on this man. "Slave! You will remove your helmet and tell me your name."

Maximus pauses, knowing that his fate and the fate of the entire Roman kingdom rest upon his response. He breathes deeply, then turns and removes his helmet. As tens of thousands listen in awe, Maximus unveils his face and reveals his true identity.

"My name is Maximus Decimus Meridius,

commander of the armies of the North,

general of the Felix Legions,

loyal servant to the true emperor, Marcus Aurelius,

husband to a murdered wife,

father to a murdered son.

And I will have my vengeance in this life or the next."

The true name of Maximus emerges, superceding the name Commodus had given him. The people rejoice, chanting, "Live! Live! Live!"

Commodus is so deeply ruled by his relentless need for validation, to have his soul's question answered by the people, that he gives way to their demands. The people rise up in celebration as the identity of the true hero is revealed. Lucilla, sister of Commodus, says, "Today I saw a slave become more powerful than the emperor of Rome." There is something Maximus knows, some reservoir he draws from when all hell breaks loose. And it changes the world.[1]

As our souls become whole and, over time, we go through this metamorphosis into trueness, we are opened up to the greatest treasure given us by the heart of God: the restoration of our identity. As Gerard Manley

Hopkins wrote, "What I do is me: for that I came."[2] On this treasure hunt, we discover the person God intended us to be since before the creation of the world (Eph. 1:4), since before the fall of man. And through partnership and participation, we are invited on a rare and remarkable journey to become that man. It is the most holy journey we will take. To become who we are known as in God's kingdom. To come to know what God sees when he sees us. And through partnering with him, offering our consent over time, we step onto the narrow path beckoning us to become precisely who we were meant to be when he meant us.

"We were built to count, as water is made to run downhill. We are placed in a specific context to count in ways no one else does. That is our destiny."[3] God's primary mission is our *becoming*, and he is making his intentions known to us through every whisper in every day. The modern-day parable of Maximus moves our heart because it borrows its power from our story. We have all become someone we are not. Behind this fig leaf and the construction of a false self, the person we truly are is hidden deep below the surface of our life. Salvation, while essential, is simply not enough to solve this dilemma. It is a doorway out of the false and into an epic adventure in the masculine frontier, a daring journey of dismantling, restoration, and becoming who we were born to be.

Every man has a question in the center of his masculine soul. We bring that question to every possible place except the only One who can provide everlasting life to our soul. The Scriptures are intended to lead us back to the headwaters to recover who we truly are:

> You made all the delicate, inner parts of my body
> and knit me together in my mother's womb. . . .
> You watched me as I was being formed in utter seclusion,
> as I was woven together. . . .
> Every day of my life was recorded in your book.
> Every moment was laid out
> before a single day had passed.
>
> —Psalm 139:13, 15–16 NLT

Jeremiah reminded us, "Before I shaped you in the womb, / I knew all about you" (Jer. 1:5 MSG). Literally, God *knew* you before you were created. He had holy plans for you. In the Scriptures, "knowing"—knowing God's heart and knowing who we are, our name—is the Hebrew word *ginosko*; it's an intimate heart-knowledge. This word was applied as a Jewish idiom to describe "knowing" in the context of sexual intimacy. That's a different kind of knowing, a deeper kind of knowing—a soul knowing. You need to know who you are, and you need to have encounters with God that transform the whole man. It is this theme we see echoed in many of the great stories.

Encounter and Process

In Tolkien's *The Lord of the Rings*, Lord Elrond comes face-to-face with Strider, a brave but mysterious loner who hangs on the fringes of the the civilized world. Elrond, the king of the elvish people, unveils the sword of Narsil and turns to Strider, man to man, soul to soul: "Put aside the Ranger. Become who you were born to be."4 So begins the long and heroic journey of Strider becoming Aragorn and being restored as the king of Middle Earth.

Saul, a fierce and violent crusader set to destroy the people of God, puts off his false self through a series of supernatural encounters and takes upon his true identity, Paul. And he leads God's people into freedom. Jacob, whose name means "the deceiver," spends most of a lifetime living out that fateful identity. Then he wrestles with God. He literally seizes upon the living God in a blow-by-blow, all-night battle, crying out, "I won't let go until you bless me!" (Gen. 32:26, my paraphrase). God wounds Jacob in the hip, leaving him with an injury that strips him of the last vestiges of self-sufficiency. God gives him his true name, Israel, and from the strength of this revelation, Israel is able to walk with God and fulfill his destiny. Abram, at the ripe old age of seventy-five, has an encounter with God and becomes Abraham, the father of many nations. And at the age of one hundred, he completes the process of becoming his name. Simon betrays Christ, not once but three times. Later as he lives out the full stature of his given name, Peter, in partnership with the power of God, three thousand men and women come to faith during the feast of Pentecost (Acts 2).

Do you recall the film *The Matrix*? The entire story line is borrowed from 1 John 4: the whole world is under control of the evil one. Thomas Anderson has found himself as a cubicle jockey, working in a high-rise office building, pushing papers and furthering bureaucracy. But deep in his masculine soul, another world beckons. He has tasted reality and is brought to a decision point, where he can choose either the blue pill, which will take him back to the life he's known, or the red pill, which will show him, in the words of Morpheus, "how deep the rabbit hole goes." Thomas Anderson chooses to be saved. He goes through a rebirth and baptism and is then trained as an apprentice to become a warrior to free the people from the matrix and the power of evil. He is no longer Thomas Anderson but Neo, meaning "the new man." As he is growing and maturing, the day finally comes when he faces an agent. These dark and demonic warriors have woefully intimidating supernatural power, and no one has ever withstood an agent. As Morpheus and Trinity watch, Neo faces his enemy.

"Morpheus, what is he doing?" Trinity asks.

"He is beginning to believe."[5]

What is Neo beginning to believe? He is beginning to believe who he truly is, who he is known to be in God's kingdom. He is becoming the man he was born to be.

This is the critical idea we must not miss. In order for us to become who God meant when he meant us, we must seek to encounter God and receive the name he wants to bestow upon us. Yet we must also engage in the slow and steady process of apprenticeship to become our name. In the words of George MacDonald, since we are, so must we become.

Our New Name—The White Stone

In the book of Revelation, John brought this central reality for our masculine soul: "To him who overcomes, to him I will give . . . a white stone, and a new name written on the stone which no one knows but he who receives it" (Rev. 2:17 NASB). When a man encounters the living God in the depths of his soul, he is given a new identity, a new name.

George MacDonald was a Scottish poet, a man C. S. Lewis referred to as his master. In *Unspoken Sermons*, he offered a brilliant teaching I've gleaned a lot from, called "The New Name." In it, MacDonald reflects on Revelation 2.

> The giving of the white stone with the new name is the communication of what God thinks about the man, to the man. The true name is one that expresses the character, the nature, the being, the meaning of the person who bears it. It is the man's own symbol, his soul's picture in a word, the sign which belongs to him and no one else.[6]

And who is it given to? The one who overcomes. The Father wants every man to know he is an overcomer. You are a victorious one. That's part of your name in heaven.

> For Zion's sake I will not keep silent,
> for Jerusalem's sake I will not remain quiet,
> till her vindication shines out like the dawn,
> her salvation like a blazing torch. . . .
> you will be called by a new name
> that the mouth of the LORD will bestow.
>
> —Isaiah 62:1–2

> GOD put me to work from the day I was born.
> The moment I entered the world he named me.
>
> —Isaiah 49:1 MSG

In the book of Ephesians, Paul used superb language when he wrote, "For this reason I kneel before the Father, from whom every family in heaven and on earth derives its name" (Eph. 3:14–15). Eugene Peterson paraphrased this giving of a name as "parcels out . . . heaven" (Eph. 3:15 MSG). In a name, you're receiving a parcel of heaven, unique to you.

Paul wrote in the book of Romans, "We see the original and intended shape of our lives there in [Jesus]. After God made that decision of what his children should be like, he followed it up by calling people by name" (Rom. 8:29 MSG). God has called you by name. Your name. "After he called them by name, he set them on a solid basis with himself. And then, after getting them established, he stayed with them to the end, gloriously completing what he had begun" (Rom. 8:30 MSG). That's what God is up to with us: gloriously completing what he has begun.

You'll notice that in Scripture, when a man encounters God, he is often given a new name, handed a parcel of heaven, told what is written on his white stone. It is the manifestation of the soul's journey from the false self to the true self. A man's name is the soul's picture of who and what he is intended to become. And the process of initiation is the journey a man must take with God if ever he is to become his true name.

God is constantly inviting us to put off the false self and begin an ever-deeper journey of knowing and becoming who we were meant to be. If we are ever going to become the man God meant when he meant us—since before the creation of the world—we need to recover some particular lost treasures. We need to know who we truly are. At the center of God's saving work, his restoring work, is a restoration of our identity, our name. He is whispering to us the answer to the soul's deepest question: Who am I?

We Cannot Live Beyond Our Identity

Les Misérables is Victor Hugo's nineteenth-century novel that has been adapted into the well-known Broadway musical and also for film. One of its main themes is the transformation of identity of Jean Valjean, the central figure in the story. By his middle years, Valjean becomes a uniquely powerful man who uses his power for the well-being of others, contending for the vitality of an entire community as a mayor and factory owner and offering his strength in self-sacrifice to save the lives of others. Yet to appreciate the self-giving man who Jean Valjean becomes, we must first know his story, just as we must know ours.

During his childhood, Valjean's family endured terrible destitution and loss under the oppressive social conditions of early nineteenth-century France. When the children of his older sister are on the brink of starvation, Valjean breaks into a bakery to steal a single loaf of bread in order to help them survive. Under the force of a penal justice system, he pays dearly for his crime. He is arrested and convicted and eventually serves nineteen years of imprisonment and hard labor.

Even in its injustice, Valjean's imprisonment provides his broken heart with an identity. Those years, those chains, and the bitter messages they speak about who he is, about life and human relationships, and about what God is like erode his strength and harden his heart with fear, despair, and hatred. The woundedness takes root, and Jean Valjean embraces a lie about the essence of his nature.

This lie is overturned through the intervention of a faithful bishop. The sequence opens with Jean Valjean restlessly sleeping on a hard bench along a cobblestone street of a small French village. His clothes are threadbare and tattered, and a ragged hood covers his weary, hardened face. He has just been released from prison and placed on parole, and the only identification he has is a yellow passport, the document that permanently identifies him as a convict.

After Valjean is roughly expelled from the park bench by authorities, a passerby counsels him to go to the home of the local bishop, a man known for his kindness and hospitality. In hunger and exhaustion, Valjean finds the bishop's home and knocks on the door, his desperation overpowering his expectation that he'll surely be turned away. Much to his surprise, the bishop does not rebuff him; instead he invites Valjean to have supper with him and stay the night in his home. As the embittered Jean Valjean stands at the bishop's door, opened wide to him, we witness this dialogue in the film adaptation:

Bishop: Come in.

Valjean: Look, I'm a convict. My name is Jean Valjean. I've served nineteen years hard labor. They let me out four days ago. I'm on parole. I have to go all the way to Dijon by Monday or they'll send me back to prison. Here's my passport. I can't read, but I know what it says. "He's very dangerous."

Bishop: You're welcome to eat with us as my guest.

Valjean: I'm a convict. You saw my passport.

Bishop: I know who you are.

Here it is: the face-off between the false identity that Valjean has embraced and the truth of who the bishop sees him to be as a fellow bearer of God's image. Valjean cautiously accepts the invitation and takes his seat at the bishop's table for his first home-cooked meal in decades. As he drinks the last of his wine, he catches the keen and steady gaze of the bishop, then looks down at his empty plate. With a wry laugh, he makes this passing comment: "And tomorrow, I'll be a new man." He then retires as a guest of the bishop to the warmth of a real bed.

In the darkness of the night, the message of his wounds collides with the unexpected kindness of the bishop. Agonizing dreams recalling his nineteen years of imprisonment haunt his broken heart. He wakes up in a panic, the memory of his deprivation more vivid than the quiet of the peaceful home around him. He then does the only thing he knows to do: reject the hope of kindness and the possibility of a new life and rely instead on his hardened independence to survive. He crawls out of bed, determined to steal the bishop's silver cutlery and run away into the night. Jean Valjean cannot live beyond his adopted identity, who he believes himself to be.

Meanwhile, the bishop wakes in the night and hears noises coming from the kitchen and dining room. He comes upon Valjean in the act of stealing, and Valjean takes a full swing at him, knocking him unconscious and making his escape. The next morning, local officials apprehend Valjean. When they discover the silver he is carrying in his ragged sacks, they bring him back to the bishop's home.

It is in this scene that we encounter the surprise of God's love and the length to which the bishop will go in order to rescue and restore the heart of this man. The scene opens with the bishop and his sister in the garden as his sister laments the loss of the silverware. We see the bishop's bruised eye, inviting us to consider the bishop as a symbol of one who sees clearly and yet endures assault for his vision of Valjean's redemption. Soon there is the sound of boots on the ground as a group of policemen march into the bishop's garden, gruffly dragging the hooded Valjean along with them.

> **Police chief:** I'm sorry to disturb you, but I had my eye on this man.
>
> **Bishop:** I'm very angry with you, Jean Valjean.
>
> **Police:** What happened to your eye, Monsignor?
>
> **Bishop:** Didn't he tell you he was our guest last night?
>
> **Police:** Oh, yes, after we searched his knapsack and found all this silver. He claimed that you gave it to him.
>
> **Bishop:** Yes, of course I gave him the silverware.
>
> Bishop looking at Valjean
>
> **Bishop:** But why didn't you take the candlesticks? They are worth at least a thousand francs. Why did you leave them?
>
> Bishop to the police
>
> **Bishop:** Mr. Valjean has to get going. He's lost a lot of time.

Surprised by the bishop's support of Valjean's story, the police reluctantly release him from his handcuffs. The bishop dismisses the police officers and gives back to Jean Valjean his knapsack full of the stolen silver—but now with the added silver candlesticks. As the scene comes to its climax, the bishop stands soul to soul with Jean Valjean and pulls back the dark hood from Valjean's head and face. With the eyes of faith, we see God removing Valjean's shame, bitterness, and false identity.

> **Bishop:** Don't forget. Don't ever forget—you promised to become a new man.
>
> **Valjean:** Why are you doing this?
>
> **Bishop:** Jean Valjean, my brother, you no longer belong to evil. With this silver, I've bought your soul. I've ransomed you from fear and hatred. And now I give you back to God.[7]

As with Jean Valjean, life has given each of our broken hearts an identity. We each have our personal and self-destructive version of a yellow passport. We, too, may not be able to read it clearly, but the soul knows what it says. It shapes us every day.

Who have you become? What have you come to believe about who you truly are? It is one of the central questions to which we must give deep and honest consideration.

Here's why:

We cannot live beyond the identity we have embraced.

Let that soak in for a moment. This is why so many well-meaning attempts to free the hearts of men from bondage ultimately fail. We hear it echoed through the halls of churchianity all the time: "I'm just a sinner saved by grace." It's a death sentence. You see, if we cannot live beyond our identity, then when our identity starts with "sinner," try as we might, we will never be free. Not for long. That pornography addiction, that medicating with alcohol, that compulsion (from success to exercise to cupcakes)—whatever your prison may be, you will not escape it. What's sad is that "a sinner saved by grace" is the identity so commonly spoken over people in religious circles.

Scripture, though, is very clear in offering a different perspective on our identity. Do you notice how Paul addressed the people to whom he was writing, letter after letter?

- To the *saints* of Ephesus
- To all the *saints* in Christ Jesus in Philippi
- To all in Rome who are loved by God and called to be *saints*
- To the *holy and faithful* brothers in Christ in Colossae[8]

Oh yes, Paul went on to deal with some profound soul issues—in some cases, positively wicked stuff. But he began with speaking to the people's true identity. *Our* true identity. These were not mere sinners. These were saints, holy men who had been formed and created uniquely in the image of a whole, strong, integrity- and life-filled God. Yes, they faced great battles. Yes, they contended with sin, which warred against their true nature. Yet this was neither the end of their story nor the seat of their identity. These struggles did not define them; they were merely the context of the story in which these saints were being restored and returned to who they were meant to be since *before* the fall.

Let me say it again: we cannot live beyond our identity. Actions reveal beliefs 100 percent of the time.[9] Tozer suggested we must look far below our creedal statements and doctrinal beliefs to uncover what we truly believe about reality and ourselves. It's what you *do* every day, in and out, every moment, that reveals what you really believe about reality.[10]

A name is a terribly powerful thing. What is on your yellow passport? You have been given a name, an identity. What identities have you lived out that are not true about who you truly are? "I am weak." "I'm an orphan." "I'm disqualified." "I'm inadequate." "I'm an imposter." "I'm an addict, a failure, a victim."

Here is the damage and the danger of a gospel of sin management, of this sinner-saved-by-grace identity: we cannot live beyond being a sinner. "I'm just an addict." No! Being an addict of any kind is simply not the truest thing about who you truly are. You are a son. You are a good man who has perhaps taken his ache and longing for love and validation to dark and deadly places. Perhaps your reach to medicate has taken you to pornography or to other addictions. That is not your sentence. That is not your fate.

Do you believe you are just a sinner saved by grace? If so, you will never live beyond that identity. You'll never live victoriously, not in the long run. The promise of the gospel is far more than sin management. Breakthrough, restoration, and healing of the soul of man are very much available through the power of Jesus' life, death, resurrection, and ascension. There is so much more than we have been led to believe. The masculine journey is an ongoing process of putting to death the false self, the yellow passport, the name, the identity, so that the true self might be reborn. It's death of the old and birth of the new.

You Are a Masterpiece

I remember walking into Saint Peter's Basilica in Rome many years ago. The *Pietà* caught me by surprise. I was a college student who'd just begun an entirely new life in God. It was a 180-degree turn from my old life, and I was at square one in learning of the Way. I found myself on a shoestring budget, backpacking across Europe, looking to recover the story of the gospel for my young and thirsty heart. Having grown up Catholic, I decided to go to Rome to see if there were any true remnants of this life-giving gospel tucked away in this ancient land.

Inside Saint Peter's Basilica, I started to approach Michelangelo's *Pietà* but was stopped in my tracks. It was Mary, the mother of Jesus, holding the broken, beaten, and bloodied body of her crucified Son. The *Pietà* is carved out of one piece of marble, and as I looked at it, it seemed so filled with life, it was as though Mary were alive and I could watch and feel as she wept over the body of her Son. There was a group close by with a tour guide speaking English. I unashamedly positioned myself so I could hear his narrative. He was sharing that when Michelangelo carved the *Pietà,* what he experienced was nothing less than an interaction with the Divine. Michelangelo said that deep in this single block of coarse marble, he saw Mary and Jesus. And with fervor and awe he carved and carved, first with hammer and chisel, then with fine and delicate tools, until he at last freed them from the confines of the stone. It was a masterpiece. There is none like it in the world. Unique and utterly reflecting the image of God.

In Paul's teaching to his apprentices in Ephesus, he made this bold and beautiful claim: "We are God's masterpiece. He has created us anew in Christ Jesus, so we can do the good things he planned for us long ago" (Eph. 2:10 NLT). Modern translations often lose the essence of this verse. The Greek word *poiema* is often translated as "handiwork." Sounds like the kind of art project your kid brings home from Sunday school or first grade. Special in its own right, but not exactly what comes to mind when you think of a masterpiece. The intention of the heart of God is far deeper and more vast. *Poiema* means masterpiece. Think of a great piece of music that sweeps up the audience into a grand story that transcends, for a few moments, the reality of their days. That's what God meant when he meant us. The wounds in our life are very real. The sin, the addiction, the person we have become. But they do not have the last word in their attempts to lay claim to our identity. It was never intended to be so. We were meant to be transformed. We are being invited, beckoned, and led.

The wounds are meant to be healed so that the scars can become the stories of heroism that strengthen the soul and save the world.

In the early days of my story, leadership defined just about anything to which I applied myself. I was always rallying a group of guys around something adventurous or heroic. In my earliest memories, it was gathering the neighborhood boys to build bike jumps in the woods behind our homes, or rallying kids to play out the heroic adventures of warriors under the cover of night. As I grew older, it took the form of starting businesses and leading organizations. As I mentioned earlier, when I was in eighth grade, multiple requests from students and faculty led me to run for student body president. And that successful campaign, for a time, seemed to answer some deep question in my searching soul.

I was a young and uninitiated boy, gifted in leadership but desperately searching for an answer to my question through the affirmation of men. Leadership was my medication of choice, and I binged on it, cofounding an auto-detailing business when I was sixteen, and choosing to lead every step of the way. The world cheered me on. But inside I was merely feeding the poser, hiding behind a fig leaf of self-sufficiency, shame, and fear of not having what it takes. I did possess a true gift, the nature to lead, but out of my brokenness, my masculine heart was mostly being expressed through the false self and my search for validation.

Then came a crash and a conversion. I'd won the game, succeeded in every way a person could—leadership, straight A's, a trophy girlfriend. And I was dying inside. Though I wouldn't have been able to put words to it, I could feel the divided soul within me: a public life and a private life. I was in a downward spiral, which I hid from the entire world. I attended a prestigious university, part of me fiercely committed to making life work apart from God. I intended to keep fueling the deep search for love and validation through the pursuit of more leadership opportunities and worldly success. The other part of me, the true man, was asking for attention and care. He knew—or at least hoped— that there was another path. I chose to open my heart for the first time to the possibility that God had a better story, a way for my soul to be whole again, a place where I might find a real rest, a place to crash from my exhaustion, a place of still waters to restore my weary soul.

And then I met Linsey.

It was late in the evening at a fraternity deck party. Well on my way in medicating the pain, I was caught by a woman's glow. She was different from anyone I had ever met. I'd had enough beer to approach her and say what I was thinking, before I could edit myself. "What's a woman like you doing hanging out with guys like us?" And she laughed. I'll never forget her laugh: kind, loving, caring, and true. So began a friendship. Little did I know I was being apprenticed into the kingdom. All I knew was, she was providing me access to a safe place, one that was not dependent upon her or me—the one place I could "come as I am." Most nights, she would listen to my escapades and woeful stories of searching for life and love in so many places. God gave her his heart to see the man I truly was but had yet to become. Linsey took a risk and, over time, shared and modeled a life of walking with God. After one of those rich and lingering conversations, I found a place of solitude out in the wild and wrote down a prayer to give my false self to God and invite his life to restore my life, to unite my heart with his, and to recover my true name.

So began a long and steady process of deepening union with him and more integration into the man God meant when he meant me. It was the greatest risk I had ever taken—to let go of control, of outcomes, to surrender my old way of making life work apart from God, to forsake drinking at the cisterns of leadership, women, and financial success and turn toward the heart of God to recover who he made me to be and destined me to become. I felt not unlike Mr. Anderson in *The Matrix*, choosing the red pill and being stripped of everything I knew, pulled from one world and reborn into another. The next stronghold of my false self, who was going to become a rich president of a leading company, was reflected in the key interviews I had lined up with Fortune 500 companies in my senior year. And then I was given an invitation to an obscure leadership program tucked in the foothills of the Colorado Rockies. It had little prestige outside of its small community. While it spoke of training leaders in families, in society, and in God's kingdom, its accreditation as an undergraduate program signified a step backward. But although the false self was pleading with me to stay the course of self-sufficiency and success, this obscure program had the scent of everything I sensed God was up to in my life. I'd traveled enough miles to know the old ways were death. I had to risk this new life.

I packed up my truck and moved west. There I began to recover who God meant when he meant me. It was only in giving God my consent to have his way, in walking away from all of the less wild lovers, that I could become the kind of person who could begin to receive his revelation of who I truly am. One day I picked up a brochure promoting a leadership program built around John Witherspoon. Out of all the words on the brochure, one sentence seized my heart. It said of Witherspoon, "He was a man who shaped the men who shaped America." In that moment, even before I had room in my theology for God to speak, I heard his voice. He said to me, *Morgan, this is who I made you to be. You are a man who shapes the men and women who shape my kingdom.* I felt warm tears on my face as I tucked the brochure into my pocket. It wasn't until later that I learned Witherspoon was a signer of the Declaration of Independence, a president of Princeton University, and a man who taught regularly on a kingdom view of reality. He was one of the forerunners of both the idea of America and the advancement of God's kingdom in his generation.

As I write today, more than two decades later, the brochure sits next to me on my desk, tucked in a journal with other profoundly intimate words the Father has spoken to me of my names in heaven. It is a great risk to speak of words as intimate as these, but I'm choosing to share them with you believing that he has parceled out heaven, a treasure like this but even far greater, for every one of his sons. It is only in seeking that we find, in knocking that the door is opened.

As I commited the next decade to the slow and steady process of becoming, a genuine transformation began. For the first time, I chose the lowest seat at the table,[11] believing as Francis Schaeffer suggested that to have the power of Jesus' life, we must follow him by living the way he lived. By choosing excavation over building, allowing God to build my character rather than spending my energy on the building of my own kingdom, over time the Father began to supernaturally place me in kingdom leadership roles. Though I wasn't orchestrating it, I increasingly found myself in roles as teacher and strategist. I was beginning to become the kind of man God could trust with shaping the men who shape his kingdom. My name, whispered decades before, became the most powerful fuel for me to endure the process a man must go through to be broken down and rebuilt. This journey into becoming our name, our true self, is one our Father is beckoning us toward at every juncture.

Recently we were exploring, as a family, this big idea of identity. Cherie was leading Joshua, Abigail, and me through prayer as we took some time to listen to God regarding a name he might have for us in the kingdom. For context, Joshua was in full transition into the middle school years, where the atmosphere and pull of culture is homogenous—everyone wears the same thing, does the same thing, acts the same way—and he felt the draw to be like everyone else. As we were praying, Joshua reached for a sticky note and began drawing. I thought he was just distracted and drawing a picture. Knowing these things must be pulled and not pushed, I let it go, and we moved on. Later that week I was doing laundry and found that note in Joshua's shorts. It said, in big, distinct letters, "One of a kind." I went up to Joshua and asked, "Hey, what's this?"

"Oh, that's a name the Father gave me. He said I'm *One of a Kind*."

We rescued the sticky note and taped it above his bunk bed so that the last thing he hears every night and the first thing he hears when he rises is his Father's voice, against all those other accusing voices.

You know who you are, son?

You are one of a kind.

You are Joshua Morgan Snyder.

God is weaving a tapestry. He is restoring your name, your true identity. The stories you love and the roles you long to play—they are telling you something about reality. It is far more than wishful thinking; it is destiny, a homecoming. He uses stories and history, Scripture, strangers, pictures, nature. He'll continue to woo you, continue to speak to you, if you choose to have ears to hear.

"Your true name is one which expresses your character, your nature, your being, the meaning of you, the one and only one who bears it. It's your soul's picture in a word, the sign which belongs to you and no one else."[12] There is a man God is recovering. He sees you in the marble. He has chisel and hammer.

He is working to release you from everything weighing heavily on you. To set you free to be all that he meant when he meant you.

To become our name is to bring, in ever-increasing measure, our strength—not our question—to the world. To choose the narrow path of becoming a king is to cultivate a deep, risky, and wonderful knowing of our true name in the kingdom. In doing so, we take our question to our God alone, so that we might bring the name he has given to us and his image he has deposited in us to a broken and battered world. "Let him call me what he will. The name shall be precious as my life. I seek no more."[13] It is only from a steadfast knowing of who we are that we can respond and participate with God's building of a life in us centered on fulfilling the destiny for which we were made. It is through this narrow gate alone that we can proceed along the ancient path of becoming a king. And yet, for each of us, that process of becoming our true name must first be formed and forged through becoming a generalist.

5

BECOMING A GENERALIST

There is something about the outside of a horse
that is good for the inside of a man.
—Winston Churchill

The central narrative of the masculine journey is the restoration of the whole human person, as a man, through deeper integration and union with God. If we are to become the kind of man, the kind of king, to whom God can entrust his kingdom, we must risk venturing through the narrow gate of becoming a generalist.

It's our Father's intention for us to become the kind of men who can say with confidence these words from Hopkins: "What I do is me: for that I came."[1] But that unique expression of God—that *poiema*, that masterpiece he intends to bring forth through the heart of each man—must first be established on the foundation of what masculinity means, in its essence. A man must first become what I have termed a "generalist," so that he can have the firm foundation for the true self that is being recovered. As a by-product of the industrial and technological age, one of the great unspoken tragedies of our time is the atrophy of what it means to be a man.

In 1784 Benjamin Franklin made these remarks about the Native

Americans which colonists came to regard as "the savages of North America."
A commissioner from Virginia made known to the Indians of the Six Nations
a fund was created for youth education. He said,

> If the Six Nations would send down half a dozen of their young lads to that
> college, the government would take care that they should be well provided
> for, and instructed in all the learning of the white people.
>
> The appointed Indian representative for the Confederation for the
> Iroquois tribe responded, "Our ideas of this kind of education happen not
> to be the same with yours. We have had some experience of it; several of our
> young people were formerly brought up at the colleges of the northern prov-
> inces; they were instructed in all your sciences; but, when they came back to
> us, they were bad runners, ignorant of every means of living in the woods,
> unable to bear either cold or hunger, knew neither how to build a cabin, take
> a deer, or kill an enemy, spoke our language imperfectly, were therefore neither
> fit for hunters, warriors, nor counselors; they were totally good for nothing.
>
> We are however not the less obliged by your kind offer, though we
> decline accepting it. And to show our grateful sense of it, if the gentlemen
> of Virginia will send us a dozen of their sons, we will take great care of their
> education, instruct them in all we know, and make men of them.[2]

What does it mean for a man to become educated? What does it take
in this day and age to *make* a man? I was recently talking with a young man
raised in Alaska who found himself relocated to the heart of a city in Arizona.
He was describing an unnamed ache in his heart. He shared that in Alaska,
a man was required to be rather capable in a wide range of circumstances, as
there are simply few other resources available in the remoteness of their village
to solve problems. He said that every boy learns how to work with his hands
and fix snowmobile engines and homes and about anything else that can break.
A man needs to be able to listen to his wife and engage his kids and provide
a wide array of skills and care that would otherwise be outsourced to experts.
The young man was reflecting that in his new urban environment, so few of
his skills that were essential in his former world were now even relevant. And

in his eyes I could see the questions surfacing: What does it really mean to be a man? What was it God was wanting to share with the world of himself, uniquely through each man but universally through all men?

If we hold to the idea and promise that we, as men, are created in the image of God, then we must give honest consideration to the types of qualities that are meant to be formed in us and employed in the service of heroic love on behalf of all others. Now, these are of course deep waters. And let me be clear: I'm not suggesting these qualities are mutually exclusive and reserved only for men. However, it would do us well to recover foundational treasures we have lost that were meant to bring strength and life to many.

Men were made to come through. To rise to the occasion. They were made to engage, to act. To offer a strength in love and sacrifice so that others can flourish. They were made to bring a strength that, woven together with vulnerability and beauty, could bring forth life beyond telling. Men were made for action. To protect, to provide. To come through in a manner that allows others rest. To provide for others protection and places, both physically and soulfully, to be known and, above all, loved. Men were made to fix things. Whether it is a broken mower or a broken heart. They were made for war, so that others might experience peace through their sacrifice. There are qualities that are so quintessentially masculine that they are difficult to name, yet they are found to be at the epicenter of every man's story in his battle to become. Where women might tend to find their greatest fears to be related to abandonment, a man's greatest fears are mostly rooted in failure and often manifest themselves in either passivity or unrestrained aggression.

Before a man can pursue the specifics of his vocation and his name, he must recover the masculine within him that every man was intended to share. He must be able to work with his hands and his heart. He must contend with adversity, failure, exposure, and fear in its many forms so that he can pass through and become rooted in his identity first as a bearer of God's image, as a man, so that in all things and in every way, what he brings to any situation, whatever that situation may be, is his masculine strength.

To become a generalist is to name the universal qualities God has set within our masculine soul and to partner with him in the restoration of every one of these qualities so that wherever we find ourselves and whoever we find ourselves with, the world can rest knowing that what it will encounter and benefit from is, first and foremost, a man.

One of the great losses of the Industrial Revolution and the information age is that men have primarily become specialists; they have skipped over the critical stage of developing into a generalist.

Wendell Berry said it best in *The Unsettling of America*:

> The Industrial Revolution created an army of specialists. Work was removed from the sacred and the ritual, the liturgy, and community. Now for the most part, [work] is a means to an end; it's a commodity of exchange. As specialists, we're trained to do something that makes money, and with money, we can buy seemingly everything. Everything that we need: food, clothing, shelter, entertainment, even sex. We were never meant to buy sex, or food, or shelter. Not as simply the lowest common denominator as a means of exchange. The once sacred has migrated to a commodity, and part of man has atrophied.[3]

There are parts of us that have atrophied and are now a shadow of what was intended. And, guys, we feel this ache in our soul.

Castration by IKEA

I've felt the loss of the generalist and the ache of something missing within my masculine soul whispering to me much of my adult life, dissonant with something I've tasted and know to be true. But this loss, this ache, shouted the day a coworker asked my friend Allen and me to assemble a set of IKEA shelves for her office. The instructions were as simple as I've ever seen in a package. Yet, internally I blew a gasket when I looked at them. Not because of the instructions themselves but because of the *unspoken message* in them. They were a metaphor for the current condition of most men lacking the process of becoming a generalist.

Imagine with me, if you will, five simple sketches depicting the directions, with "men" who don't have the sort of tools you'd expect for them to be able to handle a task as heroic as assembling numbered, ready-made, predrilled, step-by-step furniture.

Picture one: A cartoon rendering of a eunuch standing alone, smiling, with a thought bubble featuring two simple tools: a hammer and screwdriver.

Picture two: The happiness quickly evaporates into despair as the eunuch tries unsuccessfully to pick up the box of prefab furniture pieces by himself.

Picture three: Happiness returns as a second eunuch arrives on the scene. Now both are smiling as they remember for the first time since kindergarten that two are stronger than one.

Picture four: Once again, the first eunuch plunges into peril and dread as he stands with an open box, instructions in hand, and with a thought bubble filled with what most people imagine is really going on inside a man who begins any project: one simple, oversized question mark.

Picture five: All is well, because he has found a phone tethered directly to IKEA headquarters. Like an oversized umbilical cord, it reaches to the experts at this kind of sophisticated work, always at the ready to save eunuchs from impending self-harm (or at least the perils of oversized question marks lurking in their thought bubbles).*

Be brutally honest. Take a look at those directions. The problem here isn't IKEA; I trust they have no ill motive in their attempt to provide assembly instructions, no intention of emasculating. Yet IKEA is responding to a fear that has haunted us all of our lives. Do you notice the fear or frustration that rises up within you when something requires your strength and you come face-to-face with a situation that surfaces the soul's question, *Do I have what it takes?*

---

*   For a full illustration, go to BecomeGoodsoil.com/Castration.

There's a reason IKEA has made the instruction manual this way: it works. One look at IKEA's sales numbers tells us that their strategy to require no real skill in the assembly of their products is a bull's-eye on the target of our culture's demand. IKEA's success is partly an answer to the question for the current state of masculinity.

Hello, Trouble

By way of contrast to our castrated IKEA buddy, I want to point to an alternative. Years ago I came across a brilliant video, created by Gerber Knives, called *Unstoppable*. It is a series of images of men in places of wilderness in which their strength is required. It's a brilliant montage of men doing real things with real knives. Encountering peril in the field and practical necessities in working trades and soul-filled adventures and conquests. An ocean fisherman pulling up a net. A rancher in a dusty old corral cutting open a bag of grain. A boater freeing a rope wrapped around a propeller. The video is honoring and evocative to the masculine soul because each image represents some step toward ruling and exercising a sort of fierce mastery within a man's particular kingdom. Powerful images of rescue, perseverance, adventure, and risk. Different men, different circumstances. All of them contending. Armed with a pocketknife, they face their worlds and whatever is thrown their way with a strong and steady confidence.

Our souls can't help but respond. Videos like this that embody men engaging in battle, adventure, and risk-taking evoke something deep in every man I've encountered. Overlaying these powerful images—men in movement, engaging courageously and rising to take on any challenges life throws their way—is a strong, weathered, masculine voice.

Hello, trouble. It's been a while since we last met.
But I know you're still out there.
And I have a feeling you're looking for me.
You wish I'd forget you, don't you, trouble?

(I will not.)
Perhaps it is you that has forgotten me.
Perhaps I need to come find you,
remind you who I am.**

Take a moment to let your heart respond to that. What would it be like for your soul to know *that is who you are?* Armed. Ready. Solid. The kind of man who can face real adversity with problem-solving strength. A man who will not be deterred by trouble, chaos, or calamity, one who lets those formidable circumstances provoke something true in his soul to come out and be made known.

Notice, too, if there's another voice in your heart that says, *That could never be me.* Listen closely, because that second voice is a lie. It is the deceiver. The Gerber video is a mythic picture of the spiritual reality God is after in your heart, in the heart of *every* man.

A man and a knife. That man could save the world. At least, he was intended to.

A man was intended to walk ever deeper into a blend of fierce mastery and determined love, both qualities growing in the context of deepening union with his heavenly Father. In fact, fully restored masculinity is part of God's answer to the trouble on earth. A wholehearted man walking in intimacy with the heart of God was meant to be one of the most powerful weapons to bring forth life as it was meant to be. A knife can become a physical expression of this spiritual reality. It's not as much about the knife as it is about what comes through the knife when it is wielded as strength in love. When you pull it out, it's as if you were saying, "I may not have the answer to the question at hand, but I am here. I choose to show up, to risk, to engage for a greater good."

Remember, it is mythic. The gospel is always being revealed to us to awaken, to disrupt, and to entice. Not all of us are meant to captain a fishing boat or break a wild horse. But we are all meant to rule and reign and bring a fierce mastery and a goodness to some realm that God has entrusted to our

---

** Find the video at BecomeGoodSoil.com/HelloTrouble.

care. We are not meant to surrender to conformity, despite what those IKEA instructions suggest. We are meant to live into our masculine courage.

This isn't a new thought. Though *The Abolition of Man* was written decades ago, C. S. Lewis could have easily written it after his first visit to an IKEA store. While it is one of the most challenging books I've ever read (and still have mostly not grasped), I believe that some of Lewis's insights into the fall of masculinity are particularly helpful on this point. He wrote, "In a sort of ghastly simplicity we remove the organ and demand the function. We make men without chests and expect of them virtue and enterprise. We laugh at honour and are shocked to find traitors in our midst. We castrate the geldings and bid them be fruitful."[4]

A man was meant to engage. To act. To be whole and strong. God, our Father, is relying on this untapped potential deep within your masculine soul. As a matter of fact, he has put all his chips on restored humanity to bring the kingdom to fullness. He's betting on you. However, through a collision of historical and cultural forces, as well as the wages of sin and the determination of our Enemy, so much of what was intended to be the heart of a restored man has been lost, stolen, and surrendered.

How can we live out our masculinity when our organ has been removed? The castration has come in many forms. One of them is the loss of a context in which to encounter a wide range of experiences and develop a broad array of practical skills, all of which help to shape us into becoming a generalist equipped to engage the troubles of this world, and their uncertain outcomes, with settled confidence. To become a generalist is to cultivate the craft of pursuing intimate, tactile knowing of a little bit about a lot of things. We've relinquished the opportunities to be tested, trained, and matured, which were intended to recover what was lost within us. To become a generalist is to take them back. Remember, the outside of a horse is perhaps one of the very best things for the inside of a man.

The recovery of essential and substantive masculinity was central to what Jesus was after when he declared that "the Son of Man has come to seek and to save that which was lost" (Luke 19:10 NASB). This verse has gotten neutered into a kind of eternal-Band-Aid-salvation prayer, but I would argue that the scope of Jesus' redemptive intention was to go deep and wide. What if by "the lost," he meant not people in general but all the parts of humanity that were lost and broken in the fall? The word translated as "save" is the Greek word *sozo*, which means "to save from suffering and disease, to make well, to restore to health in every way."[5]

What if the context in which Jesus offers his life is not a one-time eternal ticket out of hell but rather a day-by-day and decade-by-decade apprenticeship in kingdom living? The world, the flesh, and the evil one are insistent in their intention to take us out as men: to destroy the image of God in us, to create a path for us to atrophy into a sort of androgynous entity called a person, losing our masculine hearts in the process. Paul urged us with this counsel on how to live in the kingdom of God as men: "Keep your eyes open for spiritual danger; stand true to the Lord; act like men; be strong; and whatever you do, do it with kindness and love" (1 Cor. 16:13–14 TLB).

Through the incarnate life of God, in Jesus, we are offered another way. He has come to put a knife in your hand, to train you as a warrior and as a man. For most men it is literal. For all men it is a metaphor invoking the reality of the ancient path.

A Case for Carrying a Knife

Where do we begin allowing God to restore the pragmatic expression of our masculinity? It might start with carrying a knife. Literally. On you, every day of your life. It's easy to blow off that invitation. Some might say that carrying a knife is barbaric or simply nonessential these days.

We live east of Eden. Most of the needs for a pocketknife, in practical terms, have been removed. But the knife symbolizes a man whose heart and strength are becoming intact. It's an extension of the man and the deep intentions the Father has set in our soul. A man who has not outsourced his world and his masculinity to hired hands. A man who is capable of facing life's deepest challenges and coming out more whole. A man whose soul is rugged and tender, brave and kind, daring and playful—like Jesus.

In the process of becoming a generalist, years ago I began carrying a pocketknife every day. At first it felt archaic at best or even absurd, as there seemed to be very few contexts in my modern suburban life that required a pocketknife. But in time I found myself using it day after day, in countless situations. I confess, some of the first applications were an embarrassing realization of how much I had lost as a modern man. For heaven's sake, on some days the only use for my knife was taking the shrink-wrap off store-bought beef or breaking down another cardboard box left over from a delivery. But the pocketknife became an outward symbol of an inward process that, at the time, I could barely even name. I carry it every day now, and more than a decade later I have a collection of well-worn pocketknives that carry with them story after story of masculinity restored. As I found uses for the knife, God found opportunities to strengthen the generalist within my soul. To call me out into the uncomfortable, the unknown and uncertain. To prompt me to take risks and offer and become. God has used it to help recover and restore deep places in my masculine soul. It's become an extension of me. My phone used to be the first thing I reached for each day. Now it's my knife. Every draw is an exercise in wholeness, in integrity, in becoming solid through and through. It's one more small step toward whatever God meant by his command to Adam and Eve to exercise fierce mastery over their world (Gen. 1:28). Flicking that blade and using it to solve a problem, drawing from this masculine strength within, is partnering with a Father who is ever pouring into me the resources necessary to prevail. With every use, it has a way of healing my masculine soul.

The other day, the kids were in the back of my truck with some friends, creating something with all the gear in my gear box, when one of the boys said, "We need a knife!" My little six-year-old, Abigail, smiled and responded with easy confidence, "Oh, my daddy always has a knife!" For a moment, all was right in the world. Things were as they should be. They asked for a knife, but what they really wanted was a man, a father. My kids ask almost daily, "Daddy, can I borrow your knife?" In those moments, I experience a deep wrong being righted. The ship that was listing is finding its balance; the solid stature is revitalizing a strength once atrophied and now rising yet again from within me.

For me, the literal act of carrying a knife has been affirmation of the Father with no limits. Whether it's sliding my knife into the pocket of my bike jersey, tucking it in the tool pocket of my Carhartts, or securing its clip in my board shorts before a swim, it's working. I'm taking back something surrendered long ago. It's working for me. It'll work for you.***

Soul Sourcing over Outsourcing

How is your kingdom?

This might be the central question one apprentice of Jesus would ask with sincere curiosity of another, the central question a man must ask himself (and those he cares about) on this trek to become a king through the narrow gate of recovering the generalist. As we discussed in chapter 1, we've all been entrusted with a kingdom—the place where we have say, the range of our effective will, where what we want done is done. It starts simply with our body, with our mind, with our will, and quickly expands to people, relationships, and resources under our care. Choosing to walk through the narrow gate of becoming a generalist begins with becoming aware of the present-day condition of the relationships and the realm entrusted to your care.

- How is your soul?
- Are your relationships thriving and growing?
- How are your resources being stewarded?
- Where do you feel afraid and unequipped or overleveraged?
- What parts of your kingdom are you outsourcing, how much, and why?

It takes great courage and provides great data to make an honest assessment of your kingdom, through both a self-assessment and the feedback of those around you.

*** Want to take up a custom knife or bestow one on a friend? Find out more at BecomeGoodSoil.com/Knife.

All things are not equal when it comes to the masculine soul. To avoid hard work that requires an agency and competence beyond our training and outsource it to hired hands might be economically justified, but it can result in a devastating loss to masculine initiation. When we become specialists and focus on doing our one thing and in turn participate in an economy in which goods and services become mere commodities exchanged for dollars, something sacred and essential is lost. Better said, something essential is surrendered in our soul, at great unspoken cost to our personal kingdom. A man needs to know how to fix a toilet, manage a budget, and care for the heart of a woman. These aren't interchangeable widgets. They are the things that initiate the whole of a man.[6]

To begin repenting of the efficiency of specialization and turning toward becoming a generalist, we must consider replacing the habit of outsourcing with the practice of soul sourcing. This is one of the great hidden crises of our age. Masculinity goes haywire when it's not integrated. Just scroll through the latest online news feed to see that story lived out. Power is terribly abused, yet the answer cannot be, as Lewis points out, removing the organ and demanding the function. So what does it take to recover what's embodied in this idea of soul sourcing?

Ceding Mastery

A supreme book on masculinity is Walt Harrington's modern classic *The Everlasting Stream*. It's a must for your library. Walt was born the son of a working-class milkman. He climbed the ranks of society, became an elite journalist for the *Washington Post*, and spent time with the world's most powerful and influential people. Yet listen to Walt's description of the way he viewed his professional accomplishments from his father's perspective, and what Walt himself longed for as he entered fatherhood.

> It took my father time to feel proud that I was a journalist. I mean, I didn't
> even know how to replace my own car muffler. When I came to own a house,
> I wasted money on plumbers to fix leaky faucets and electricians to repair

broken light switches. I hired a nursery to lay down the landscaping and a gardener to trim and tidy it all up twice a year. Even if he could have afforded it, my father would never have ceded so much mastery of his world over to hired hands. But I had done what young men in America are supposed to do. I had risen in society. I had eaten dinner with the president of the United States. Funny, but despite all my social ascents, my simple and deepest hope came to be that I could teach [my son] some of what my father had taught me about being a man.[7]

Harrington was offering a lifeline for the masculine soul through the recovery of agency. *"Even if he could have afforded it, my father would never have ceded so much mastery of his world over to hired hands."* Walt's father was convinced there is value in cultivating a mastery, in knowing how to tend to the multifaceted aspects of his life. This innate knowledge and skill was worth more to him than the number of zeros on his annual income or the who's who of society. Even if he'd had unlimited funds to hire others to take care of his domain, Walt's father wouldn't have done it, because he valued something else more.

I know something of Walt's story. Among the many blessings of my childhood home, one of the losses and great aches was a culture that had ceded much mastery to hired hands. Only in the last two decades have I taken steps on the same journey Walt took, reclaiming what was lost in my masculinity through the try-and-fail, risk-and-explore, prioritize-learning-over-success path of becoming a generalist.

The world loves to champion the pursuit of our unique calling, vocation, gifting, and contribution to the world. The market is flooded with specialists, and from an early age we are encouraged as men to determine what we will be when we grow up and to set our face like flint toward that one external goal. But what if, before we can ever walk out the particular expression of God in us, we must first walk out the *general* expression of God in us? We bear the image of God, as men. Being a generalist is the foundation upon which we then become wholehearted specialists. What we share in common and become in common is more important than our unique expression of strength and love; they're the footers and the concrete slab upon which we build the house. And as Lewis pointed out in *Mere Christianity*, "There are lots of nice things you can do with sand; but don't try building a house on it."[8] To outsource our masculinity is to surrender the very foundation of our self, upon which we were intended to lead and to love.

Garrison Keillor wrote a very funny essay in *The Book of Guys*. Realizing one day that he was not being honest about himself as a man, he sat down to make a list of his strengths and weaknesses.

USEFUL THINGS I CAN DO:

Be nice.
Make a bed.
Dig a hole.
Write books.
Sing alto or bass.
Read a map.
Drive a car.

USEFUL THINGS I CAN'T DO:

Chop down big trees and cut them into lumber or firewood.
Handle a horse, train a dog, or tend to a herd of animals.
Handle a boat without panicking others.
Throw a fastball, curve, or slider.
Load, shoot, and clean a gun. Or bow and arrow. Or use either of them,
      or a spear, net, snare, boomerang, or blowgun, to obtain meat.
Defend myself with my bare hands.

Keillor confessed, "Maybe it's an okay report card for a *person*, but I don't know any persons. . . . For a guy, it's not good."[9]

Recovery of the generalist is vital to the masculine journey. We must receive the initiation, training, and validation in those arenas that all men were meant to operate in. Here are some of those arenas, by way of example.

- Handle a tool, a weapon, and a book with integrity of hands and heart.
- Handle a woman's heart with care, for her own sake.
- Bring order to chaos.
- Plant and cultivate something living.
- Build something physical, with our own hands.
- Fix things.
- Put food on the table with our own hands rather than with our dollars.
- Survive in life-threatening situations.
- Provide basic first-response medical care.
- Be integrated in soul, living in union with God.

This journey of recovering the generalist aspect of our masculinity is unique to each man and requires years of intimate consent to a kind, strong, brilliant, and patient Father, who is more than willing to train us in the way we should go. It's what he loves to do, and he's overjoyed when he's invited to do it.

In these encounters with the Father, not only will we recover parts of ourselves that have been lost, but we will also rediscover an aspect of him that has also been lost in our day and age. We get to learn the Father as he truly is, not as we have learned him to be. Our culture has lost touch with God's strength, wildness, prowess, and daring. One of the several deadly assumptions we've come to make instead is that God is soft. Dorothy Sayers said it this way:

To do them justice, the people who crucified Jesus did not do so because he was a bore. Quite the contrary; he was too dynamic to be safe. It has been left for later generations to muffle up that shattering personality and surround him with an atmosphere of tedium. We have declawed the Lion of Judah and made him a housecat for pale priests and pious old ladies.[10]

We've neutered and declawed our image of God, and in turn, this has been done to us. Our restoration as men—and the recovery of our heart and strength—begins not in our unique calling and gifting but in something far more foundational; our restoration begins in us simply *as men*. How will you start to regain strength in the places of atrophy? What waters will you venture into that you might have dismissed as unimportant, below you, or intimidating? What have you outsourced that you might need to take back for a season or a lifetime? How will you set aside your greatest competencies and risk venturing into and actively engaging in areas of your deep fears?

Creating a Context

"What does a man need to survive?" I posed this question years ago to my young son as we were headed out on an adventure.

After careful and honest consideration, he responded, "A wallet and a phone."

It was brilliant. And painful. Brilliant because of his perceptivity about our culture, painful because the culture in which my kids are being raised gives the false perception that his response is true. Aldo Leopold, in *A Sand County Almanac*, offered a thought that implied part of the antidote to a world without men. "There are two spiritual dangers in not owning a farm. One is the danger of supposing that breakfast comes from the grocery, and the other is believing that heat comes from the furnace."[11] Something in us recoils. Right. These spiritual dangers have become institutionalized norms in our technological age. Anything you need you can order online, even get it shipped for free in one day via Amazon Prime. All that's required is a few clicks. Yet in this age of über-convenience, something inside us grows soft, atrophies, and dies.

How do we avoid the spiritual dangers Leopold described? Dang, it's hard. After all, most days it feels like heat does come from the furnace and our breakfast does come from the grocery. And on any given day, doesn't it feel true that what we really need to survive are a wallet and a phone?

We've been steadily creating a context for masculine initiation and restoration in our family culture for nearly two decades. And in many ways, it's far more available than we've been led to believe. For example, we've been heading out to the national forest to chop wood and split it for the fireplace. To help make it fun for the kids, we've cultivated rituals like bringing a Thermos of hot chicken broth and packing the camp stove for making ramen noodle soup under the canopy of Colorado timber. It's a challenge to shoehorn this connection with the natural world into our little suburgatory, cookie-cutter context, but it's working. We've got a cord of hand-split firewood beside our home, and we've had some remarkably rich family time in the evenings, sitting fireside, exchanging the glow of the TV for the enticing glow of dancing firelight. In fact, these contexts are becoming part of the liturgy of our family.

I didn't grow up in any proximity to a hunting culture, and even into my midtwenties I knew little about bringing food to our family's table in any reasonable capacity with my own hands. Now, nearly two decades later, by choosing to venture into the places where I felt inadequate, I have recovered essential parts of my masculine soul. And by doing so, after years of tracking elusive creatures in the wilderness of Colorado, my family has experienced how breakfast can come from participating in the whole of a process rather than a very limited part of a hidden and disengaged process where our role is that of a passive purchaser at a store.

Yesterday was one of those great days. My buddy harvested a stunning bull elk. I encouraged him to consider processing the meat with our own hands in the Snyder family home instead of the local butcher shop.[12] He took me up on it, and we went to town. All hands on deck. Together, in community with our wives and kids, we worked with great care to take this wild animal from the field to the freezer. Eight hours later, steaks, roasts, burger, and filet were vacuum-sealed and ready to provide food for the family for the year to come. As I walked into the garage in the last light of evening to grab some celebratory beers, I saw what was left: four mostly meatless leg bones suspended from the ceiling, and a regal skull and antlers on the floor. It was a sacred moment. I could feel the Father's affection and delight over our risking—our risking to work on the whole of a thing and allow our souls to rejoice in the integration of our food and another part of what it means to be human, and our risking to press into the frontier of our masculine soul and take back what has been lost and stolen. From the harvesting of the game to the processing to the laughter and engagement of our wives and kids in this redemptive communal experience, we were experiencing intimacy and shared adventure and, together as kingdom apprentices, we were immersing ourselves even deeper into the kingdom among us.

Last night, with elk steaks hot off the grill and a roaring fire from freshly split Colorado aspens, something was healing in my friend and me and in our kingdoms. We avoided—at least for a moment—the spiritual dangers of which Leopold warned. For a moment, something was restored, strengthened. Our food hadn't come from the grocery; our heat hadn't come from the furnace. And it was good, really good.

What about you? What is your frontier for engaging in soul sourcing and connecting to the process of becoming a generalist? It might literally be carrying a knife and learning how to use it. Let me name some other categories that might help you. Start here. Where do you feel exposed, awkward, incompetent, out of place?

- **Work on the whole thing, rather than parts of things.**[13] Integrating in the whole of a thing engages the masculine soul in ways that are not accessed through engaging in only isolated parts of a thing. In this day and age, often the path of recovering the generalist is seeing a project through from start to finish. Engaging in every detail, not only for the end result but for what God does through the process. Perhaps it's a home improvement project or some initiatives that facilitate adventure with people you love. Get curious. Look behind the curtain, inside the wall, or under the hood. Roll up your sleeves and take a risk. It will pay off.
- **Cut your own grass.** Whatever it is you pay hired hands to do— plumbing, taxes, auto repairs, your wife's manicures—try it on yourself. Not forever; there's a season. It may not necessarily be wise or effective for you to do your own landscaping forever, but if you do eventually outsource it, you do so from a place of competence, agency, even mastery,

not from a place of convenience, ease, or avoidance. You outsource it once you've had the experiential knowledge of it. There is simply no substitute for intimate heart knowledge that comes through direct experience.

- **See a counselor.** Let me say it even more directly: if you have not invested one-on-one time with a counselor, it's time to do it.[14] It will take great courage to go, but these are essential miles for the masculine soul. Imagine the impact on your wife alone for you to model a willingness to consider what must first be torn down so that room can be made for other things to be built within the soul of a man.

- **Take mastery over your budget.** Finances quickly reveal the heart of the matter. I spent time last month with a friend who owns a big venture capital firm and regularly buys and sells multimillion-dollar companies. After several transactions created enough concern that their personal cashflow could be at risk for the first time in his life, my friend found himself in tears in honest disclosure. Fearfully and out of a very young and timid place in his soul, he said, "I actually have to live on a budget for the first time, and I don't know how." He wasn't talking about the venture capital budget; he was talking about the family budget for things like groceries and internet and garbage service. He didn't know how, and the scared little boy inside was deeply afraid to be exposed to his wife—that even though he has millions, he can't handle the budget for groceries. His courage and his willingness to move into that frontier, to open his heart to being fathered in new ways, makes the difference. Money is a flashpoint, and a budget or lack thereof is often a direct expression of the deeper things. For the man who has to be the one who controls the money to become a generalist, he'll need to relinquish the reins for a time, or even further, invite his wife into the partnership of leading together. For the man who avoids the budget and simply hands it over to his wife, he'll need to take the risk of jumping back in, letting it be messy, and taking a risk to allow the unfinished places in his soul to surface. In the end, it's never about the money. But the context of finances for the heart of a man very often has within it some particular on-ramp to the ancient path of becoming a generalist.

Some of you guys might have to clean up and take your wife or your daughter out to a formal meal. Others need to put on a pair of Carhartt coveralls and go cut some firewood. Initiation is unique to each man. Some of you guys need to go into the world of the heart and spirituality and intercession and learn deliverance, tackle some demons, bring the work and authority of Christ. Others of you have to back off all that spiritual stuff and just do some things with your hands. Every man has a frontier where he feels inadequate and unsteady.

One of the biggest steps for me was entering into my little daughter's world. My son and I share many of the same interests. But my princess, Abigail, is an entirely different species. Her grandma started offering her manicures and pedicures during family trips. One day Abigail turned to me and asked, "Daddy, will you give me a pedicure and a foot massage?" I was caught off guard. *Uh, I don't know how to do that. That's weird.* It was unknown, and I felt awkward and incompetent, but I didn't simply react by hiding and dodging. In that small but steady pause I'm learning to take before I respond, the Holy Spirit nudged me. *Say yes.* So I said, "You bet. I'd be delighted to." Risking this frontier with my daughter recovered something for my masculine soul in what it means to love and cherish the feminine. What started with foot massages went into manicures, and eventually I even created a Pinterest account to learn how to create flowers on her nails! But think about this for a moment: Who gets to wash his daughter's feet on a regular basis? She doesn't know that with every foot massage, I'm given an opportunity to bless her soul and foster the intimacy of a father and a daughter. Remember, to become the generalist is always a risk in engaging the frontier in confidence that God will work in a particular way to restore the *whole* man, from the inside out.

I received an email recently from a friend who shared a winsome story of how he has personalized his quest to begin to take steps toward cultivating fierce mastery in his world. He lives in an apartment in a major city on the West Coast. He sent me a picture of several pots he put together in which he's started to grow vegetables and a small tree. He described the process of moving from a digital, technical space to getting dirty, carrying heavy pots, providing water, and not knowing how it will all turn out. He wrote with excitement about the thought of providing for his family with food cultivated by his own hands. Something slowed down in him in that act of holy defiance. Something healed, and something strengthened. And that something is the center that God is after in each of us, to restore us as men.

What is frontier for you? Every one of us has something awkward and uncomfortable, a place of incompetence. Go there. As God restores the whole man, when you come and face the trouble, you will feel utterly different. It will still feel unknown, still dangerous, but it's there you will practice becoming the kind of man who, like Paul, can say, "Whatever I have, wherever I am, I can make it through anything in the One who makes me who I am" (Phil. 4:13 MSG).

This isn't a masculine caricature. You don't have to live in Colorado. You don't have to be a hunter. It is a recovery of *essence*, of masculine design. Even if you don't have a clue as to what it would look like for you to begin recovering your masculinity, it is available. The frontier of becoming a generalist is unique to every man, yet equally daunting, equally risky, and equally rewarding in the process of restoring the masculine soul and becoming a king. Ask the Father to bring it, ask him to create contexts meaningful to you. Ask Jesus to be in it with you. And ask the Holy Spirit to guide you into the next step.

A man and a knife *can* save the world.

You are that man. Now you must become who you were born to be. And because of that we must now learn how to engage in warrior training.

6

BECOMING A WARRIOR

Before my father died, he said the worst thing about growing old was that other men stopped seeing you as dangerous. I've always remembered that, how being dangerous was sacred, a badge of honor. You live your life by a code, an ethos. Every man does. It's your shoreline. It's what guides you home. And trust me, you're always trying to get home.
—Lieutenant Rorke Denver, *Act of Valor*

Nine months after SEAL Team Six took out the world's most wanted man, Osama bin Laden, they completed another dramatic and secret mission: rescuing Jessica Buchanan, an American aid worker, from the hands of Somali pirates. In response to her plight, two dozen SEALs parachuted into southern Somalia, killed all nine heavily armed kidnappers, and liberated Buchanan, as well as a second aid worker—all without any American casualties.

The heroic acts in the final moments of this remarkable rescue reveal something of the culture and character of the Navy SEALs. Here are Jessica's own words: "At one point . . . this group of men who've risked their lives for me already asked me to lie down on the ground. Because they're concerned there might be [more armed terrorists] out there. They make a circle around me and then they lie down on top of me, to protect me. And we lie like that until the helicopters come in."[1]

To the world, it was extraordinary. To the Navy SEALs, it was another day's work. It's what they do. Because it is who they have become.

I was connecting with a United States Marine Corps officer as he reflected on his combat training. He said they've learned through trial and error that the only way to properly train and be fully equipped for war is with live ammunition. It's the way of the marines, and it is the way of the kingdom of God.

If you have traveled this far along the ancient path to becoming a king, you don't have to be told it's going to be a fight. That's why so much of the masculine journey is warrior training. God must restore the warrior if we are to become the kind of man and the kind of king who can be entrusted with the leadership of his kingdom.

While becoming a warrior will take on expressions and applications unique to each man, the essence of the process transcends culture, profession, and context. We are being formed and forged in God's image, as men.

Let's take our place at the feet of great warriors who have marked out a path to becoming a warrior. Yet as we stand at this bend in the path, we remind ourselves that war is never the point. The goal must always be love.

A wise elder once said that we fight what is in front of us so we might protect what is behind us. Our enemies (the evil one, the fallen world, and the flesh in the heart of every person) are aggressively waging war against our heart, the hearts of those we love, and the hearts of those entrusted to our care. Our passivity will only increase the casualties. We must turn with increasing measure to our Father to be trained as a warrior, to become the kind of man who not only has the heart to give his life heroically but also has the skills and strength to do it effectively.

What Story Are You Living In?

As one of my mentors put it, the interpretation you use to understand your reality and your role in it will be the single greatest force in shaping what becomes of your next decade. In the words of Dan Baker in *What Happy People*

Know, "The stories we tell ourselves about our own lives eventually become our lives. . . . The choice is ours."[2] Our life will be significant in proportion to the stories we choose to interpret our reality.

What stories are you using to interpret your reality?

In the novel *Peace Like a River,* Jeremiah Land, the father figure in the story, put it this way: "We and the world, my children, will always be at war. Retreat is impossible. Arm yourselves."[3]

Yet in this powerful story, the weapons Jeremiah uses are not physical firearms but the even more fundamental weapons of courage, wisdom, strength, endurance, self-control, prayer, faith, love, and sacrifice. He wages war heroically against death, cruelty, and violence, but in the power of One far greater than himself.

While many Bible translations render the Hebrew name for God, Jehovah Sabaoth, as "the LORD God Almighty," it is more accurately translated "the LORD of Angel Armies." We can conclude that the Creator filled the spiritual realm with the kingdom equivalent of Navy SEALs for a reason.

The writer of Hebrews defined the nature of faith as "confidence in what we hope for and assurance about what we do not see" (Heb. 11:1). That which is unseen must not be irrelevant to our lives. In fact, as Dallas Willard taught in *The Divine Conspiracy,* "the most important things in our human lives are nearly always things that are invisible."[4]

The world, the flesh, and the evil one tempt us to settle for the smaller story: a narrow quest to arrange for the happy little life. Yet something deeper in us knows that a life arranged only for a sense of comfort, security, and personal happiness is far too small to hold the expanse for which the masculine soul was designed to thrive. We must remember Peter's urging: "Be alert and of sober mind. Your enemy the devil prowls around like a roaring lion looking for someone to devour. Resist him, standing firm in the faith, because you know that the family of believers throughout the world is undergoing the same kind of sufferings" (1 Peter 5:8–9). If we are to interpret our lives and understand the times, we must recognize the unseen war being waged for our soul as a man and let this be a central theme of our apprenticeship in warrior training for our unique place in the kingdom of God.

In *Waking the Dead*, John Eldredge made the point,

Until we come to terms with *war* as the context of our days we will not understand life. We will misinterpret 90 percent of what is happening around us and to us. It will be very hard to believe that God's intentions toward us are life abundant; it will be even harder to not feel that somehow we are just blowing it. Worse, we will begin to accept some really awful things about God.[5]

God's story is a love story, no doubt. A story of thrilling goodness, intimacy, and beauty. Yet we live quite east of Eden. It is a love story set in the midst of war.[6] And though we are elaborately provided for by Jesus' death, resurrection, and ascension, we must still battle to recover the treasure for which we were made: interactive relationship with God and others from a healed and whole heart.

We are asking Jesus to help us see into the unseen, and he assures us that if we ask, we will receive. As we ask, the Holy Spirit will pull back the curtain, and we'll never be the same. As we increasingly choose to believe, we will begin to see reality as Jesus sees it. To live the life Jesus lived, we must hold to the same beliefs that he held to regarding the nature of reality. Seeing as Jesus sees will change everything, *for the good*.

Training for the Fight

Where can we go to learn to resist and dismantle evil and fight for love as did Jesus, the warrior? Let's again look at the U.S. Navy SEALs for specific counsel and leadership. The Navy SEALs live out in the natural realm what men are called up into in the spiritual realm. Right here. Right now. Right where we find ourselves to be. Just as every great story borrows its power from the greatest story of all, the trial-tested strategies for the SEALs' survival and success borrow power from the truths of apprenticeship in the kingdom of God.

In Navy SEAL culture, this keen awareness of the story is called situational awareness. Cade Courtley, former Navy SEAL platoon commander and author of *SEAL Survival Guide*, defined situational awareness this way:

The ability to identify, process, and comprehend the critical elements of information about what is happening to the team with regard to the mission. More simply, it's being aware of what's going on around you. It's the ability to see the real world and react to any situation without hesitation and make split-second decisions that could have global ramifications.[7]

Though our battle is first and foremost an unseen one, all training is done with live ammunition. We need look no further than to our own story to see that the damage of evil is real and there is much at stake, including the life of our soul and the souls of those we love.

Survival as 101 of the Abundant Life

Our buddy Dave just figured out his wife has been having an affair, and it's blown up his world. Call me.

I picked up my phone after a day of writing and found this text from a close friend. The text message immediately following from another friend read, *My son is in crisis, again. I don't know if we can survive this story again. It cost us everything. I don't know what to do.*

It's a pretty typical day. I know many good men for whom the abundant life is quite out of view and who are just trying to survive. I confess that even now there are significant battles I face that cause me to wonder when the dust will settle or where to at least find the pause button.

Let's be clear on this matter. Without a doubt, the invitation of the gospel is to life so prolific and generative that we are meant to be bursting at the seams. I love this paraphrase of Isaiah's words:

> You'll see all this and burst with joy
> —you'll feel ten feet tall—
> As it becomes apparent that GOD is on your side
> and against his enemies.
>
> —Isaiah 66:14 MSG

Yet what do we do with the fact that, many days, failure haunts us and we can barely keep our head above water? How do we find this abundant life when we're simply trying to hold on?

One mentor put it this way: "Anything above crisis is living well." While this idea has been a lifesaver on rough days, reading that sentence can also provoke despair. Is the best I can hope for in this decade living just an inch above crisis?

Perhaps we need to hear it differently. What if I interpreted the trial as training, and the context as a son being trained to be a warrior? What if I first felt the validation—men who've gone ahead of me through the crucible of this decade also had their boats struck by tidal waves—then felt the relief of the honesty, and then felt myself leaning into the Father for his counsel?

While we long for a thriving life, it takes great humility to admit that in some areas we're barely surviving. From a place of sonship, rooted and established in the love and affection and life of God—seated at the right hand of my Father, united with Jesus, my older brother and greatest hero, and empowered by the Holy Spirit—I can receive the humility and courage to start back at square one with the basics of survival in the areas of my life where I'm drowning.

Sometimes getting back to the basics is the best way to move forward. Let me say it simply: survival is the level one of the abundant life. A fierce commitment to soul survival can lead over time to the abundant life. We must pause and start with the basics. What is in our power to do today to begin becoming the warrior? It was Saint Francis of Assisi who is attributed as saying, "Start by doing what's necessary; then do what's possible; and suddenly you are doing the impossible."

I want to suggest some very practical steps we can take today to reorient our direction toward becoming the warrior:

- Combat breathing,
- Union as the way of the warrior,
- Recovering our identity, and
- Identifying the particular plan of evil against your life.

Combat Breathing

Four seconds in.

Four seconds out.[8]

And it will save your life.[9]

In the midst of live ammo and life-and-death combat, SEALs know that everything must be done to lower the heart rate and focus the mind. The proven effectiveness of combat breathing is rooted in this kingdom reality: God designed our breath to sustain us, moment by moment, and to be a pathway back to the present and a connection with his heart in any situation.

Our life in God begins with our breath. Start with survival. Simple. How quickly we forget—or better said, are seduced out of—this lifesaving center! If you recall the story, God reached down into the earth, the soil he created, then breathed his breath into the soil and we became breathing beings. He designed us for dependence so that every breath might remind our soul that it's his breath sustaining us. He did this so our life might always be found in him.[10] Dallas Willard put it this way: "You're a soul made by God, made for God, and made to need God, which means you were not made to be self-sufficient."[11]

Our inherent neediness is the aspect of our lives that our false self resents most. It's also the environment that best allows our true self to live and grow: utter dependence on the life of God. C. S. Lewis reminded us in *The Screwtape Letters* that only the present moment is flush with eternity and the presence of God.[12] Our Enemy fears our rootedness in the present moment and the union with Jesus available here; he will do whatever it takes to keep our hearts pulled into either the past or the future, to cut us off from the present moment.

Research into the physiology of the breath and body is bringing to light more of the why behind the power of deep, intentional breathing. Such breathing turns off the sympathetic nervous system—the launchpad for the stress hormones cortisol and adrenaline and the "fight, flight, or freeze" response—and ignites the parasympathetic nervous system, the producer of the neurotransmitters responsible for calm, well-being, and a clear head. Ole Hallesby articulated how the saturating provision of the air around us reflects the saturating provision of the grace and presence of God. The oxygen our body requires envelops us on every side; to receive it, we need only breathe. Likewise, "the 'air' which our souls need also envelopes all of us at all times and on all sides. God is round about us in Christ on every hand, with his many-sided and all-sufficient grace. All we need to do is open our hearts."[13] And breathe.

Pause with me. Here and now. Give yourself the gift of sixty seconds of centering in the present moment, as if your life depends on it. Breathe. Sink into natural breathing, slow it until you find a rhythm of four seconds in, four seconds out.

(Inhale.) God, I breathe your breath into me.
(Exhale.) God, I breathe out everything I need to release.

How did it go?

With every breath, we have a gateway back to the narrow path. We're invited, breath by breath, to experience the reality of breathing in the Father's sustaining strength and life. Combat breathing is one of the great secret weapons for our warrior training, wherever we are, whatever our circumstances. Four seconds in, four seconds out. It's a bulletproof way to get back to center and find our life rooted in God in the present moment. If it's the abundant life we're after, we must cultivate the warrior's practice, relying on the regular cadence and moment-by-moment sustenance of God's inextinguishable life.

Union as the Way of the Warrior

Hopefully, you're coming to see that the power of God was intended to flow in ever-increasing measure in us and through us. We were designed for dependency. There is no stronger man and king than the king whose heart is fully rooted in, established in, and united with the living God (2 Chron. 16:9). We can mature in our true self only through union with God.

Recall some of Jesus' final recorded words on earth:

The goal is for all of them to become one heart and mind—
Just as you, Father, are in me and I in you,
So they might be one heart and mind with us.
Then the world might believe that you, in fact, sent me.
The same glory you gave me, I gave them,
So they'll be as unified and together as we are—
I in them and you in me
Then they'll be mature in this oneness,
And give the godless world evidence
That you've sent me and loved them
In the same way you've loved me.

—John 17:20-23 MSG

So we can pray,

Father, I choose union with you above all things. I ask you to reestablish my life in yours. You are the vine, I am the branch. I ask you to graft me back into you [John 15:5–7]. Show me where I have separated from you. I ask to become one heart and mind with you, Father, through the life of Jesus, that you would be in me and our partnership would mature in deepening oneness. That I would be one with you as Jesus is one with you.

Recovering Our Identity

In chapter 4, we explored the centrality of identity in the process of maturing the masculine soul into kingship. Identity may play its most strategic role right here in becoming the warrior we were made to be. Your Enemy knows who you are and fears who you will become in God's kingdom. The only one who underestimates your life is you.

Even Jesus, in order to fulfill his mission as a warrior, needed to know he was the beloved Son, the apple of his Father's eye. He needed to know who he was so he could live *from* that place in the face of unrelenting opposition. That's why we have this most remarkable scene in which God the Father broke protocol and spoke out loud the words every son longs to hear from his dad: "Son, you are the delight of my heart. You have what it takes. I love you with all my heart. I am with you. Let's do this together" (Luke 3:21–22, my paraphrase).

These life-giving words of identity came just moments before a forty-day all-out assault by Satan and the kingdom of darkness against Jesus. The evil one took ruthless swings, coming with multiple strategies and deceptions, all aimed at assaulting one place: the position of sonship, *of identity*, in the heart of God.

> *If* you are the Son of God, tell this stone to become bread.
>
> —Luke 4:3, emphasis added

> *If* you are the son of God, . . . throw yourself down.
>
> —Matthew 4:6, emphasis added

The evil one knew that if he could dismantle Jesus' belief in his identity as the Son of God, Jesus and his kingdom could be defeated. Yet for forty days, Jesus did not give way. He stayed in belief, against every possible assault and every opposing circumstance. He refused to surrender the truth that he is a Son and that his Father's fierce heart and strength and kingdom are at work in him, for him, and through him.

The same is true of our story, which the Enemy knows better than we know it ourselves. His single greatest place of spiritual assault is against our identity: both our identity as a son and our identity as a man uniquely bearing the image of God. The loss of this identity will be our sure defeat, and the staying power of it our greatest victory. The Enemy knows that if he can take out the son, he can get the man. If he can get the man, he can take his kingdom. Check the news on any day, and you'll see a fresh story of this reality playing out. It is here where we must take our stand as warriors in training. We must choose to become. Against all odds, we must ask the Holy Spirit to reveal the personal strategies the evil one has orchestrated to dismantle the place of sonship and the identity God is working to recover in us.

Identifying the Particular Plan
of Evil Against Your Life

What is Satan's plan for your life?

It's a profound question, one I never considered until God snuck up on me two decades ago. I was sitting with a sage who was teaching about God having a personal plan for our lives. I sensed the Holy Spirit asking, *If God has a personal plan for you, what personal strategy and tactics does Satan have to take you out as a man?* In an instant, my soul had clarity about three driving motives that, though unnamed, had been baiting my false self for years.

Becoming the president of my own very successful company.
Amassing great financial wealth.
Marrying my high school sweetheart.

Wow. For a moment life was crystal clear. I realized how much energy I had invested in those three desires, how much the fig leaf of a life structured outside of God pinned hope on these three dreams to make life work. None of these goals are evil in nature, but in the story God had for me, and with the state my soul was in during those years, these three motives could have hijacked my becoming who and what God intended. This revelation came to my soul decades ago, and with each passing year, I've gained more insight into Satan's unique strategy to steal, kill, and destroy, based on the particular landscape of my soul and the unique place God has put me to participate in his kingdom. The same is true for each of us as we're being restored and forged as his warriors.

For each of us, deep wounds in our masculine soul bring messages, and we forge deep agreements with these messages, lies that shape every one of our days. And then from those agreements we form vows. Out of a childhood wound, I made this agreement in my soul: *I am on my own.* And from that agreement, I made this vow: *I won't need anyone, and I will be the strongest man in my world.* Only through God's revelation of these deep agreements and vows (and the Enemy's schemes for them to become my destiny) has Satan's plan been foiled, because I've been able to choose to live into a deeper reality of a life fueled by God and not by my own scheming.

What is the Enemy's plan for your life? It's an important question for each of us to ask and keep asking.

There are daily strategies, cultural strategies, and geographical strategies set up by the Enemy to "steal and kill and destroy" us (John 10:10). And then there are brilliantly and deviously crafted personal strategies that take into account our stories, our woundedness, and our most vulnerable places. The goal of these strategies is to destroy us before we ever become whole and holy, unstoppable forces of good in a broken world. That's why Peter implored us to be on the alert—the Enemy prowls like a roaring lion seeking to devour us (1 Peter 5:8)—and Paul urged us to be aware of Satan's schemes (2 Cor. 2:11).

Much of the treasure hunt for the restoration of our masculine soul is hidden in the story of our family of origin. Have you noticed the themes that so often run through family lines—passivity, infidelity, betrayal, violence, addiction? There is more going on than meets the eye; there are personal strategies and tactics that work against us over time. The Enemy learns how to weave a story line that can cause division with distinct parts of our hearts. But he is not equal in power to God. He can be exposed if we will pursue a deeper awareness of how he's operating. He overplays his hand.

And you can be victorious. This is immensely helpful to understand. Yes, we must be trained. God is raising up kingdom warriors, his kingdom equivalent of Navy SEALs. He's creating a culture of seasoned warriors, trained with live ammo, to see this battle through to its end.

Consecrating and Enforcing

Now that we are oriented as warriors in training, perhaps two of the most effective weapons we can employ to invite the kingdom of God more deeply into the kingdom entrusted to our care are the consecration of God's kingdom and the enforcement of it.

Jesus is the King of kings. As a king in his kingdom, you've been entrusted with a portion intended for your care. We each have a kingdom where we have say.[14] Our kingdom begins with our body and soul and extends in increasing measure to include more and more of what God chooses to entrust to our care. (Even children have a kingdom. That's why I needed to instruct my daughter this morning to pick up the jammies she left in the bathroom.)

On the eve of Joshua's greatest test as a warrior, he turned his soul toward God to ask for his counsel. As instructed by God, he said to the people of his kingdom, "Consecrate yourselves, for tomorrow the LORD will do amazing things among you" (Josh. 3:5). To consecrate is to bring our kingdom under the rule and reign of God's kingdom. It is to will in our kingdom the very things that are good for God. By consecrating his kingdom, Joshua was able to make way for the full work of God. It's essential that we cultivate a maturing practice of bringing every dimension and aspect of our kingdom under God's rule so we might be both protected from the Enemy's schemes and open to every aspect and dimension of God's life being made available to us. As Francis Schaeffer suggested, "The size of the place is not important, but the consecration in that place is."[15]

Father, Jesus, Holy Spirit, all I am and all I have I give to you. I declare your goodness over my kingdom. I consecrate my kingdom to your kingdom. I consent to you and your leadership and give you say over everything you have entrusted to my care. I give you my body, soul, heart, mind, will, and imagination. I lift my soul to you and you alone. I bring my family—my wife and my children—under your care and covering, your rule and your reign. I consecrate our home, our vehicles, our finances, and all of our relationships. I consecrate our schools and our work, my life and walk and calling. Everything I have and everything I am I consecrate to you.

After consecrating we must turn toward enforcing. The kingdom of God operates on authority. To become a warrior requires us to learn to exercise our spiritual authority to enforce his kingdom in the kingdom he's entrusted to our care. We have been given the keys to the kingdom, yet very few men learn to tap into their power.

The death of Jesus Christ disarms the power and authority of evil.

When you were dead in your sins and in the uncircumcision of your flesh, God made you alive with Christ. He forgave us all our sins, having canceled the charge of our legal indebtedness, which stood against us and condemned us; he has taken it away, nailing it to the cross. And having disarmed the powers and authorities, he made a public spectacle of them, triumphing over them by the cross.

—Colossians 2:13–15

Jesus not only disarmed the power but also, through his resurrection and ascension, defeated death and gave us his full authority to conquer evil and to partner with him in calling forth his kingdom, in ever-increasing measure, on earth as it is in heaven.

"All authority in heaven and on earth has been given to me. Therefore go and make disciples of all nations [immersing them in the reality of the Father and of the Son and of the Holy Spirit[16]], and teaching them to obey everything I have commanded you. And surely I am with you always, to the very end of the age."

—Matthew 28:18–20

To mature as warriors, we must learn to walk in the authority of Jesus Christ, exercising his power to consecrate our kingdoms and to enforce his kingdom in the full realm he has entrusted to our care.

Father, through the death of Jesus, you have disarmed the power, authority, and rule of evil. Through his resurrection and ascension, you have established your authority over the evil one and his kingdom. Thank you, Jesus, for granting to me all the authority granted to you by our Father [Luke 10:19]. I enforce your kingdom. I enforce your rule. Father, through Jesus Christ, crucified, resurrected, and ascended, I enforce your authority in my kingdom on earth as it is in heaven. I agree with your intentions, and I give you full say over everything you've entrusted to me. I open the gates of my kingdom to your kingdom [Ps. 24:7].

From this place of authority, through consecration and enforcement, we can operate effectively as warriors to discern (1 John 4:1–6) the war set against our kingdoms through the world, the false self, and the evil one and his emissaries. From a place of consecration and enforcement, we can then bring ourselves into alignment and agreement with God and his kingdom.

Father, I agree with who you are. I agree with what you are doing. And I agree with how you are doing it. I break every agreement I have made with lies that contradict the truth and the reality of you and your kingdom. I break every agreement with every lie I have come to believe about who I am and about who you are. Father, "reveal who you are. Set the world right" [Matt. 6:9 MSG]. Father, may your kingdom come. "May your will be done on earth, as it is in heaven" [Matt. 6:10 NLT].

Wholeheartedness as the Greatest Weapon of the Warrior

One of the most remarkable aspects of Jesus' life was that the Enemy couldn't get to it. He tried with unrelenting ruthlessness, but Jesus couldn't be ravaged. "For the ruler of the world is coming, and *he has nothing in Me*" (John 14:30 NASB, emphasis added). This verse is key: there was no place *in* Jesus where the warfare could take hold. No one has had their identity as son assaulted more deeply than has Jesus. He fought hand-to-hand combat against the greatest Enemy creation has ever known. And he was victorious, because he fought out of the fullness of his life, as a wholehearted and integrated person choosing to live in moment-by-moment union with his Father.

Jesus both modeled and makes available a life we can have, the life that flows not only from an interactive relationship with the Trinity but also from a masculine heart being made ever more whole. This is our greatest weapon.

The fewer breaches in the wall, the stronger our defenses and the longer they will hold. Jesus announced the centerpiece of his mission when he reiterated the words from Isaiah 61:1:

> "The Spirit of the Lord is on me,
>> because he has anointed me
>> to proclaim good news to the poor.
> He has sent me to proclaim freedom for the prisoners,
>> and recovery of sight for the blind,
> to set the oppressed free."
>
> —Luke 4:18

The life, death, resurrection, and ascension of Jesus Christ accomplishes far more than salvation. Jesus offers this incredible promise that through him and in him we can have our broken hearts and our fractured souls restored to wholeness. One of the great secrets to becoming a warrior in God's kingdom is to take the ongoing restoration of our hearts very seriously. Through this ongoing process of inner healing, we increase our resilience to warfare and experience more and more of the abundant life we were meant to receive and offer heroically on behalf of others. From this foundation, we can then turn our hearts and strength to the central question of how, as we seek to become good soil.

7

BECOMING GOOD SOIL

*Our soul is like an inner stream of water, which
gives strength, direction, and harmony to every
other area of our life. When that stream is as
it should be, we are constantly refreshed and
exuberant in all we do, because our soul itself
is then profusely rooted in the vastness of God
and his kingdom, including nature; and all else
within us is enlivened and directed by that stream.
Therefore we are in harmony with God, reality,
and the rest of human nature and nature at large.*
—Dallas Willard, *Renovation of the Heart*

Abraham Lincoln was asked how he'd go about cutting down a tree. He's widely quoted to have replied, "If I had six hours to chop down a tree, I'd spend the first four hours sharpening the axe." There is a way things work, both with the orienting laws of nature and in the kingdom of God. Becoming a king is a return to a path and a process of agreeing with the way things work. The anecdote told of Lincoln is a reminder that the most effective path to attaining the life we desire has less to do with brute effort than with investing the proper time and care into preparing the tools we need for the slow and steady process of becoming a king.

In many ways the journey we've taken together thus far is meant to be a recovery of a map of big ideas that form the landscape of restoring the heart of a man. Now it's time to move in closer to familiarize ourselves with the finer texture and detail of this journey, including the general direction of the path and what perils and promises it might entail.

David wrote in Psalm 16:11, "You make known to me the path of life; you will fill me with joy in your presence." In this chapter, as we continue on the path toward restoring our heart, it's time for us to consider the conditions of habitat we need to establish and dwell within to thrive, to become within our souls as men the kind of deep and rich soil within which God's seeds can find abundant provision for deep and sustained growth and maturation. But first we need an introduction to our guide: Wisdom.

Choosing Wisdom as Our Guide

Our current context is not one that consistently exalts Wisdom to her rightful place; rather our age often exalts information and technical skill above the worth of Wisdom's long view. The habitat of our post-Christian, twenty-first-century Western culture is a worldview still greatly influenced by the modern era, a gospel of progress and the presumed supremacy of reason, information, instant gratification, technological advancement, and above all else, convenience.

For most of human history until recent generations, humanity cultivated wisdom through recovering a path to the good life at the feet of elders. The Industrial Revolution, the technology revolution, and now the information revolution have effectively offered their own gospel of progress that exalts information over wisdom. Here's the dilemma: a culture that values progress over wisdom will never be satisfied. The pressure to live for tomorrow and *the next thing* is relentless; the goal is a perpetually moving target. Rejecting the false gospel of progress and recovering Wisdom as our prized teacher and guide is essential to becoming a trustworthy king.

Let's go back into the story to reorient our heart. The book of Proverbs reveals that Wisdom was God's first work of creation. Before fashioning darkness and light, land and sea, or any living creature, God created Lady Wisdom.

> GOD sovereignly made me—the first, the basic—
> > before he did anything else.
> I was brought into being a long time ago,
> > well before Earth got its start.
> I arrived on the scene before Ocean,
> > yes, even before Springs and Rivers and Lakes.
> Before Mountains were sculpted and Hills took shape,
> > I was already there, newborn;
> Long before GOD stretched out Earth's Horizons,
> > and tended to the minute details of Soil and Weather,
> And set Sky firmly in place,
> > I was there.
> When he mapped and gave borders to wild Ocean,
> > built the vast vault of Heaven,
> > and installed the fountains that fed Ocean,
> When he drew a boundary for Sea,
> > posted a sign that said NO TRESPASSING,
> And then staked out Earth's Foundations,
> > I was right there with him, making sure everything fit.
> Day after day I was there, with my joyful applause,
> > always enjoying his company.
>
> —Proverbs 8:22–30 MSG

All through the book of Proverbs, Wisdom is personified as feminine, satisfying, generous, luscious. Seeking and finding her is the way to the good life. The recovery of a wisdom-centered view is being made available to us. It will require us to abandon our culture's playbook for how to succeed and win the game of life. It will require looking much further back into the time-before-all-time. It will require embracing profound paradoxes and deep disruptions that will steadily unearth the pillars upon which we've attempted to construct unsustainable kingdoms. It will require becoming even more a son and a student, trusting the relentless pursuit of a God who beckons us at each crossroads to follow him on the ancient path.

As we begin to see God providing Wisdom as our faithful guide, leading us powerfully down an ancient path, new ways of recovering life readily emerge, and more than that, a new way of *being* in God's great universe.

To align our heart with Wisdom's intimate guidance is to open our soul to feast on the rich fare it was made for. If we're willing to slow down and be yoked with Jesus, we can enter into a slow and steady process through which our living catches up with our knowledge, circumstances can surface places and parts deep within our masculine soul that have yet to be fathered and integrated, and we can, in time, become good soil.

One effective path to gaining wisdom is thoughtfully reading the text of nature. There we see the natural law of habitat: species thrive in habitats that correlate to their design. Wisdom, through nature, counsels us to take the role of habitat as seriously as life and death.

Five Habitats

As we look to cultivating a habitat of becoming good soil as an orientation for our journey to becoming a king, let's recover five ancient and time-tested truths that will help us form a strong foundation, a soil in which we can thrive. In my two decades of both giving consideration to the ancient path of restoration and sitting at the feet of sages who've helped me recover it, I've found these five habitats to be reliable and proven to bring recovery and restoration to the masculine soul:

1. The habitat of no shortcuts,
2. The habitat of embracing failure,
3. The habitat of choosing the lowest seat,
4. The habitat of living in the present moment, and
5. The habitat of speed of soul.

Let's turn these ancient stones over, one by one, and start to fiercely cultivate these soul-flourishing habitats in which we can thrive and become wholehearted kings.

1—The Habitat of No Shortcuts

I remember the moment as if it were yesterday: John Eldredge and I were in his truck, driving back from an elk hunt. We were young hunters, once again without any meat in the coolers after a week of hard backcountry hunting. In those early days, we had affectionately come to name our noble (and meatless) pursuits in the backcountry of Colorado "armed hiking." It's rare to see animals, even rarer to harvest one. It was the perfect setup by the Father for what was to come. John was the first of many older men I've turned to for counsel on recovering the ancient path to becoming a king.

After a long pause, he began the conversation with what felt like heresy. "There are no shortcuts in the masculine journey. No shortcuts in the kingdom of God." I could feel incredulity rise up in me. *This can't possibly be true.*

It has been almost two decades since that conversation, and slowly, as I went through one painful experience after another, as I observed my peers and culture, this piece of counsel has proven true. At that time, I believed that shortcuts to the life I wanted were available. Only through years of consent has "no shortcuts" moved from an unsettling disruption to a life-giving lighthouse in a turbulent sea. If we could embrace this one truth—there are no shortcuts—it would reorient how we experience God and interpret our initiation.

Few have said it better than Patagonia founder, Yvon Chouinard. In the documentary *180° South*, avid adventurist Jeff Johnson invites his heroes Chouinard and Doug Tompkins, founder of The North Face, to retrace their steps in their epic 168-day journey in Patagonia.

Taking a [wilderness] trip for six months, you get into the rhythm of it. It feels like you can just go on forever doing that. Climbing Everest is the ultimate and the opposite of that, because you have all these high-powered plastic surgeons and CEOs. They pay eighty thousand bucks and have sherpas put all these ladders and eight thousand feet of fixed ropes. You get to camp, and you don't even have to lay out your sleeping bag—it's already laid out with a little chocolate mint on top. The whole purpose of climbing something like Everest is to effect some sort of spiritual and physical gain. But if you compromise the process, you are an asshole when you start out and an asshole when you get back.[1]

Since the beginning of time, every age has faced unprecedented battles. Today's Western world lives and breathes a gospel of *now*. Instant gratification is the way of our culture; it is the norm, the expectation. This gospel has deeply infiltrated authentic Christianity, and the desire to have it our way and to have it now is toxic to becoming restored as a man of strength, integrity, and wholeness.

When we turn to the gospel, the story of God and his kingdom, we find a very different reality. Doesn't God seem profoundly comfortable avoiding shortcuts? We find Jacob required to labor seven years for the hand of his bride, only to be deceived by Laban and his own immaturity into a trap requiring him to labor an additional seven years (Genesis 29–30).

How about Joseph? Thrown into a well, sold into slavery, falsely accused, imprisoned. And when he finally saw a path out of the dungeon—if only fellow prisoners who were being released would remember him when they were free—we read these heart-wrenching words: "Two years passed" (Gen. 41:1 MSG).

How about in the book of Daniel, where we see a man prayerfully pleading for an intervention in his battle against evil? The text says that Michael, the great warrior of the heavens, was sent as an answer to Daniel's prayer but was delayed in a three-week battle against the prince of Persia (Daniel 10).

And we can't fail to mention Abram and Sarai, who were unable to have children. At the ripe age of seventy-five, Abram was told he'd be the father of many nations. Still, it wasn't until he was one hundred years old that the promise was fulfilled through the birth of his son Isaac (Genesis 15–17).

Jesus said it plainly: "Don't look for shortcuts to God. The market is flooded with surefire, easygoing formulas for a successful life that can be practiced in your spare time. Don't fall for that stuff, even though crowds of people do" (Matt. 7:13–14 MSG).

I appreciate A. W. Tozer's teaching on this in *The Pursuit of Man*.

In my creature impatience I am often caused to wish that there were some way to bring modern Christians into a deeper spiritual life painlessly by short, easy lessons; but such wishes are vain. No shortcut exists. God has not bowed to our nervous haste nor embraced the methods of our machine age. It is well that we accept this hard truth now: *The man who would know God must give time to him.* He must count no time wasted which he spent in the cultivation of this acquaintance.[2]

The core belief that there are shortcuts to the masculine journey has crippled the process of initiation and restoration in each of our lives. To allow our masculine soul to break the agreement with the idea of shortcuts is to start dismantling the hostile habitat and begin the slow and steady turn toward Wisdom's long view that leads to life. As I wrestled with this ancient stone, this truth that there are no shortcuts, I began to take honest stock of my life. Month by month, I realized that in many measurable ways I had been tempted by and had given way to shortcuts in my marriage, my work, my health, my fitness, my finances, my parenting, my spiritual life— the list goes on. Yet years later I see that some tectonic shift has taken place. By day and by decade, God has recovered this ancient stone for me, and I am slowly becoming the kind of man who no longer desires shortcuts. I want life. I want wholeheartedness. I want to become all God intended me to be. I want to stay the course of this decade of restoration. A decade of dismantling the false self. A decade of building character rather than building some personal kingdom. And I am willing to resist the illusion of shortcuts.

Father, forgive my unbelief. I yield to you today. I yield to the process, to the journey required to become all you intended for me and through me. I consent to the slow and steady way of Wisdom's long view.

2—The Habitat of Embracing Failure

It was Mike Tyson who said, "Everyone has a plan until they get punched in the mouth." The narrow path to becoming a man of noble strength and love inevitably involves a poignant list of failures as well as successes. There is a sacred shift that a man must make from being young and living mostly out of ideas he hopes are true to becoming the kind of maturing king who has formed a view of reality that can hold up to the brutal blows we take in this world. The world says failure should be avoided at all costs. Yet in the masculine journey, often failure is the only doorway through which we can access the deeper treasures we are intended to recover.

In a TED Talk on the power of failure, Brené Brown offered this:

> You know what the big secret about TED is? This is like the failure conference. . . . You know why this place is amazing? Because very few people here are afraid to fail. And no one that gets on this stage so far that I've seen has not failed. I have failed miserably, many times. I don't think the world understands that because of shame.[3]

Most men stop at failure. When we operate as orphans or from a place of self-sufficiency, we often cannot muster the strength to move *through* failure. Yet as we consent to the process of becoming a king, we will in time find ourselves, much like Brené Brown, among a fellowship of the like-hearted who have faced failure and have not given in—people who are willing to let failure be a faithful guide and a fuel for the better and deeper things waiting for us beyond failure's limited view.

It would do our heart well to remember the words Teddy Roosevelt delivered in Paris in 1910, known to most of us as "The Man in the Arena."

> It is not the critic who counts; not the man who points out how the strong man stumbles, or where the doer of deeds could have done them better. The credit belongs to the man who is actually in the arena, whose face is marred by dust and sweat and blood; who strives valiantly; who errs, who

comes short again and again, because there is no effort without error and shortcoming; but who does actually strive to do the deeds; who knows great enthusiasms, the great devotions; who spends himself in a worthy cause; who at the best knows in the end the triumph of high achievement, and who at the worst, if he fails, at least fails while daring greatly, so that his place shall never be with those cold and timid souls who neither know victory nor defeat.[4]

What matters most, what counts in Wisdom's long view, is the willingness to risk and enter the arena, to spend oneself on a worthy cause with courage and action, knowing that inevitably there will be moments of error, "because there is no effort without error and shortcoming," and that "daring greatly" is of high value, regardless of the failure or success of the endeavor.

In decades past, this value of daring greatly was, for me, merely inspiration and not yet an internalized value forged in fire. Life is different now. What I've come to learn is this: the apparent failures, over time, seem to bring more fruit than do the successes. I have a garage wallpapered with big-game hunting tags that went painfully unfilled, which meant years of no meat in the freezer. I don't have enough fingers to count my failures in everything from relationships to health to vocation. I have lists of failed real estate projects, business ventures, writing projects, and financial investments. And, to date, I have dismal college savings accounts for my kids. It gets deeper. I couldn't save my brother's life. I battled for eighteen months against his brain cancer. I fought to save his marriage, his career, his humor, his dignity; in the end, so much of it was sand running through my calloused fingers. The list goes on. Check marks in both columns—wins and losses—come only from taking risks, from choosing to live in a way that requires God to show up. True courage forms within us when we practice laying down our control of outcomes. As the SEALs' motto says, "Plan for success and train for failure."[5]

There are some deep truths about the masculine journey here we cannot miss if we are ever to become wholehearted kings. Better than asking, "Where are you succeeding?" we should ask, "Where are you daring greatly?" The thrill of victory and the agony of defeat—both are essential. Are you risking enough to be acquiring a healthy mosaic of failures? How have you *interpreted* failure?

Failures were meant to be one of our greatest teachers along the narrow path. The invitation of the kingdom is to depart from conventional wisdom. It's a radical reorientation, as our world lives in a damaging perpetual present tense. We have lost a deep understanding that the best things in life are worth waiting for. Like that first kiss my wife and I had, at the altar on our wedding day. The waiting was brutal, but the fruit . . . I would wait all over again. The waiting did something in me: it formed me and caused me to have to consider day by day, *Where do I believe life is truly found?*

Remember the words of John Ruskin: "The highest reward for one's toil is not what he gets for it, but what he becomes by it." It's the only thing we take with us from this world. It's what God gets out of our lives: the person we have become. Live in the day and measure by the decade. Few things have more power to help us cultivate a life-giving habitat of soul than unhinging our emotional life from outcomes and renouncing the idolatry of success as our measure as a man. As we practice the habit of letting go of outcomes and increasing risk, it isn't that the failures will hurt less; it's that they will hurt better.

3—The Habitat of Choosing the Lowest Seat

In the spacious context of taking Wisdom's long view and making friends with failure, let's turn to the next habitat for this decade of inner transformation: the habitat of the lowest seat.

I was young and ambitious and heaven-bent on changing the world. In my early years I had found myself leading most everything of which I was a part. Because I was so deeply practiced in leading, I was deeply disoriented when John Eldredge turned me toward Francis Schaffer and his counsel in an essay titled "The Lord's Work in the Lord's Way."

He offered it the first time he invited me to help form what would one day become a worldwide mission to restore the hearts of God's people. I was asked to help design and develop a men's retreat based on *Wild at Heart*, where men could go deeper into their stories and souls than they'd ever been.[6] And I was invited to do it from the lowest seat.

I remember the meeting and the words he offered to me as if it were yesterday. "I want you to consider giving yourself permission to be young." No one had ever said that to me before. Images and memories from childhood through young adulthood passed through my mind—being commended for my "maturity," being esteemed in the eyes of men for being "older than my years." It was a seductive ploy—there's a way that seems right to a man, the Scriptures suggest, but in the end leads to death (Prov. 14:12). God called my bluff. He shared this ancient stone in the process of becoming a king: take the lowest seat at the table until God makes it impossible to do so.[7] It wasn't what I wanted to hear. The kingdom is filled with paradoxes, and this one surely tops the list of improbable tasks for an eager young man.

The world says build, get out front, stay out front. Climb the ladder. Do whatever it takes to stay on top. Maximize. This is your best chance to exalt yourself. The kingdom suggests another way. Schaffer was alluding to Jesus' teaching that true masculinity is cultivated by choosing the lowest seat (Luke 14:7–11). And remaining there, in a sort of holy restraint, so as to follow in the way he modeled leadership.

John's invitation to take the lowest seat was simple but not easy. This was a radical invitation to try on a gospel whose offer was life, but a life counterintuitive to anything I had ever known. And over two decades, it's been a radical experiment in kingdom living, the fruit of which has been beyond description. It is out of this low seat that we are able to live in deeper integrity, and through that integrity we can grow into having both anointing and authority to offer God's kingdom out of both what we have lived and who we have become. This stands in contrast to noble yet feeble attempts to offer out of mere gifting and not from the honesty of miles on the odometer.

Whatever is built by self-effort must be sustained by self-effort. And self-sustaining has taken out many good men. But what is built by God is sustained by God. It is up to him, and he is fully capable of finishing what he has started. In the life of taking the lowest seat, from this place of integrity, flows kingdom authority. Taking the lowest seat at the table until God makes it impossible to do so is the only path to true kingship. The rewards are undeniable, but this is the hard and holy work of *becoming*, in which we must experience firsthand what it's like to watch Jesus' interactive work in us for the impossible to become possible. From that posture we can turn to a fourth soul-flourishing habitat.

4—The Habitat of Living in the Present Moment

I got home from work just in time to tag-team with Cherie and send her off to a regular monthly women's gathering. I took off my work hat and donned my dad hat, diving into the list of what we had to accomplish for the night. I finished preparing dinner as Cherie had graciously prepared both kids for upcoming spelling quizzes, hemmed Joshua's pants for his school concert the next day, paid out commissions for the kids' weekly chores (a few days late, as we'd had a commitment every night that week so far), and watched my seven-year-old rehearse her Constitution Day presentation.

On the outside, I might've looked pretty impressive as a dad; I'm often good at cleaning the outside of the cup. But on the inside, all that doing was motivated by exhaustion and a desperate need for relief. I was cranking through the to-do list, rushing the bedtime prayers and songs, all with my eyes on the prize: sitting down with a beer next to the fire after the kids were asleep. I had pegged that moment as the chance to breathe for the first time since morning. As I sat in the firelight, congratulating myself on the accomplishments of the evening, I felt my heart sinking, and with that sinking came quiet conviction.

I had missed everything.

I didn't really remember tasting dinner. I didn't really remember the joy on my daughter's face as she giggled about the funny twist in Oliver Ellsworth's fame. (He's the one who didn't sign the Constitution.) I didn't really remember what happened in the last chapter Joshua and I read together about the epic quest of Geronimo to defend vanishing Indian territories. I didn't really remember singing or praying with my precious little Abigail; I didn't remember the feel of her skin, and I didn't remember whether the moon was casting a glow into her childhood wonderland of a bedroom.

I was there. But I wasn't *there*—at all. I was becoming what a mentor had warned me about more than a decade earlier. A friend, now in his fifties, recalled a story of asking his wife time and time again to remind him of the countless activities he'd attended, supporting his daughter in her cheerleading and his son in his many football games. He was shocked to realize he couldn't remember any of them. He couldn't remember the first time Brianne drove away in her own car or the time Kevin led their team to state. He was there, but he wasn't *there*. Too tired, distracted by the many cares of his kingdom. He recalled the story to me through tears, as the kids are now grown and he is divorced and his wife has left. "My memory walked out on me." As I reflected on this heart-wrenching story, I sensed it was an invitation from the Father to look into my own story to see what needed to be excavated.

> *Father, you have my attention. At any given moment, how much of my capacity to connect with you and others in the present moment is being choked out by anxiety and commitments to my false comforters?*

His response came immediately to my heart. *Eighty percent.*

I was shocked. Not really by the number but by how deeply this percentage resonated with my experience of the evening and of much of my life in the preceding years. As I sat with God, a passage from C. S. Lewis's *The Screwtape Letters* came to my heart. It wasn't just any anxiety that was choking life in me; it was two very particular forms of anxiety: worry, which relates to fear of the future, and regret, which relates to fear of the past. In *The Screwtape Letters*, Lewis articulated the sinister work of our Enemy to use the twin thieves of worry and regret to short-circuit our connection with God. (Remember the ironic strategy in Lewis's narrative: it is the imagined correspondence of an older, wiser demon to his younger charge. In his letters, Uncle Screwtape refers to the Godhead as "the Enemy.")

To his young protégé, Screwtape writes,

> Humans live in time but our Enemy destines them to eternity. He therefore, I believe, wants them to chiefly attend to two things, to eternity itself, and to that point in time which they call the Present. For the Present is the point

at which time touches eternity. [In the present moment only] freedom and actuality are offered them. . . .

His ideal is a man who, having worked all day for the good of posterity (if that is his vocation), washes his mind of the whole subject, commits the issue to Heaven, and returns at once to the patience or gratitude demanded by the moment that is passing over him.[8]

Much of Satan's work can be exposed in this sinister strategy: to disengage us from the present moment and therefore shift us away from authentic and lifesaving union with God. But we need not fall prey; connection with God is *always* available. He desires to connect with you right now. Right here, in the very moment you're reading these words. Whatever else he is up to, he is always our fiercely loving and pursuing Father who is initiating and leading a rescue of our heart. His gaze is ever toward us, his favorite sons, that we might come into ever-deepening relationship with him. And his invitation is rooted in calling us back to the present moment where he *is*, the only place where we can encounter his voice, love, nourishment, and freedom.

Consider these words from Tozer in *The Pursuit of Man*:

For all our fears we are not alone. Our trouble is that we *think* of ourselves as being alone. Let us correct the error by thinking of ourselves as standing by the bank of a full flowing river; then let us think of that river as being none else but God himself. We glance to our left and see the river coming full out of our past; we look to the right and see it flowing on into our future. But we see also that it is flowing through our present. And in our today it is the same as it was in our yesterday, not less than, nor different.[9]

Start with a simple exercise. Honor your process of becoming—right here and right now—with a sixty-second exercise of coming into the present moment.

Pause. Slow down until you notice your breath.
Notice the natural rhythm of your breath.
Try to slow your breathing down ever so slightly. Slower inhale. Slower exhale.

As you breathe, count ten breath cycles.

As you continue to breathe, notice:

What do you smell? Breathe and tune in until you can answer.

What do you taste right now?

What do you hear? Listen carefully.

What do you feel?

What do you see?

Breathe. Through tuning in to your five senses, allow the Father to slow you down to the pace of your soul. Now attend to the atmosphere of the kingdom of God, the joyous, energetic, affectionate, generous, powerful community of the Trinity into which you have been wholly invited. Risk opening your soul afresh to the love of Father, Son, and Holy Spirit right here.

Right here, you can be present to God.

Pause.

Breathe. Three long, deep, steady breaths in. Three long, deep, steady breaths out.

Listen.

Can you sense a shift? What if the greatest gift you could give to your family, to your kingdom, is *you*, the truest you? It's that simple. And that profound. For my heart, being present includes a few simple and heroic steps:

Go slower.

Do less.

Love more.

These steps are flowing into choosing rest, prioritizing play, exercising stillness, and nourishing my heart with some great books, great worship, a few great friends, and some great outdoor adventures.

As we slow down, do less, and love more, we in turn give permission to those in our world to do the same.

5—The Habitat of Speed of Soul

"When we are busy, the Father is quiet." The words from my mentor Jim pierced my busy and hurried soul. It wasn't that my Father wasn't speaking; it was simply that I'd become so busy that I'd lost the ability to hear. Mostly good things filled my time, but all of it was too much.

In the years since, I've learned how common this theme is in the lives of good men. As one mentor put it, dogpile is a grand strategy of the Enemy. If he can't take a man out, he'll just get him busy, buried by good things, his good heart for people baiting him into too much and too many. It was a pattern of living like this that led me to being both practically unable to hear God's voice and increasingly vulnerable to spiritual attack.

We live in a time of unprecedented pace. Never before has so much been instantly accessible, from transportation to communication to information. Today's technology allows us to multitask as well as leverage time and energy at a pace and a manner that is incomprehensible. We must pause to ask and wonder, *What's the impact of this on a soul?* Connectedness enabled by modern technology, while having some benefits, has also created some devastating and incalculable harm to the soul. Every age has a primary spirit assigned to culture in general, and then people specifically, to take us out. We don't have to look far to identify the spirit of this age as relentless busyness. Richard Foster and others call it "hurry sickness,"[10] the perpetual *too much to do, not enough time*. We're baited to live at such a dizzying speed that intimacy is destroyed, and we're left with a culture of scarcity. Simply put, we are very practiced in the discipline of hurry.

Hurry sickness manifests itself in many forms, but the impact is the same. Look at the trend toward perpetual accessibility—we have become a people too easily available and perpetually engaged; media and the internet are constantly on. The inconvenient truth is that convenience has hijacked many values that used to hold much more soul centrality. Our souls know little of rhythm and rest. Moments that were meant to help us internalize reality have been lost, and we have grown uncomfortable with silence, solitude, stillness—the very contexts that were primarily intended to allow us to hear the voice of God speaking to us, guiding us, and affirming to us what is true.

Overload of commitments, activities, relationships—usually under the guise of being good things—has resulted in our lives exceeding the capacity of our souls. Dallas Willard was once asked what books he recommended, and he responded, "I suggest you read a few, very deeply." But we're so inundated with content that we simply don't know where to start. The effect is a sort of deadening of the soul rather than a true deepening of the interior life and an integration of the self through truly becoming an apprentice of God and his kingdom.

Progress has perpetually divided time into smaller and smaller segments. We've been trained and practiced in instant gratification, and it is shaping us profoundly. When the current of culture becomes the prevailing force in our life and we give consent to a gospel of now, we set our soul within a habitat that simply isn't in alignment with how we were designed to thrive. Besides doing a great disservice to the human soul, this gospel of now has caused us to interpret many of our disappointments as God not coming through for us. He works in a particular way, in a manner, but the spirit of our age has virtually eliminated our willingness as men to participate with him and agree with the *process* that becoming requires.

Busyness is the enemy of intimacy. The Enemy is having a field day baiting the hearts of good men to sacrifice the intimacy God intended them to enjoy with himself, with themselves, and with others. Remember, we are relational to our core. Relationships by nature are inefficient and don't do well when driven by urgency. Relationships suffer, souls suffer, and we are caught in a spin in which the spirit of this age causes us to settle for less and make agreements with living on very small portions of life. However, if we are able to see that this frenetic way of living isn't inevitable, isn't "just life," but rather is a calculated and strategic ploy of our Enemy that can be exposed and defeated, it is very possible to live in the midst of a culture like ours and find abundant life for our soul.

Choosing to cultivate, over time, a habitat for our masculine soul that aligns with these five ancient truths will signficantly help combat the particular destructive atmosphere in which we live in this age. Only then can we take steps toward breaking our agreement with this unsustainable way of living, so that we might recover life, both in our walk with God and in our maturing role as king.

On Margin

Years ago I was swept up into an interview of Dallas Willard by a couple of eager young men. I was struck by Dallas's posture: he was sincerely engaged yet slow to answer as he gave honest consideration to every question, forming responses he thought would be most helpful, from a place of union with his Father.

A young man posed this question in response to Dallas's urging to give serious consideration to the spiritual practices in their lives: "Dallas, my life feels out of control most of the time. The demands are never-ending. I simply cannot find the time for the spiritual practices. What do you suggest?"

After a long pause: "You will need to choose to take the time to consider why it is you do not have the time to practice the sorts of things you want to practice."

I was busted. What it exposed in me was an unwillingness to crucify my flesh and the part of me that demands a quick and easy solution to recovering the narrow path. The inconvenient truth is this: in our false self, we choose convenience over a life immersed in God's kingdom reality. The world offers convenience, yet the kingdom refuses to give way. It has bestowed too much dignity on the process and on us as image bearers.

But had that young man chosen to take the time to consider why he didn't have the time, the first reality he would have bumped into, which plagues us all, would have been a life without margin. Richard Swenson defined margin as the space that exists between our load and our limits—specifically, the discrepancy between the load we are carrying and our capacity to carry that load.[11] In a culture and an atmosphere without limits, what little margin once existed has simply vanished. It is one of the central strategies of the evil one in our age to take out the hearts of the next generation of kings in God's kingdom. Without a fierce resolve and intentionality to fight for limits—flowing from a deeper set of convictions about where life is found—we will be plagued by this prevailing culture that destroys relationships, topples kingdoms, and crushes the hearts of men.

Swenson suggested that margin is where we can expect the unexpected. As Dave Ramsey has said regarding budgeting, we are surprised every year that Christmas shows up again on December 25th. If we can be surprised by the things we can clearly expect, how much more do we find ourselves shocked by unexpected yet inevitable circumstances like a broken water heater or a broken bone? Consenting to margin allows the soul-budgeting to anticipate the unexpected and be prepared to offer strength and love in those situations that are out of our control and yet require our wholehearted strength of engagement, as men.

Margin is the consent for God to move in our lives in ways we have not planned for or expected. God is the Wild One. He is constantly ahead of us, intervening in our lives for a story of our becoming that we have yet to fully know. It is only in margin that we are able to cultivate both a receptivity to his movement and a masculine heart whose posture of consent is willing, as Jesus said, to work with him, watch how he does it, and learn from him (Matt. 11:28–30 MSG). Only through our consent to ruthlessly eliminate hurry can we mature in the process of recovering soulful living. We are not machines; we are men with a soul, being led and initiated through the process of becoming a king.

After having been mentored by Dallas Willard for many years, John Ortberg shared this story in his book *Soul Keeping*.

> I had moved to Chicago. Entering into a very busy season of ministry, I called Dallas to ask him what I needed to do to stay spiritually healthy. . . . There was a long pause—with Dallas there was nearly always a long pause—and then he said slowly, "You must ruthlessly eliminate hurry from your life." I quickly wrote that down. Most people take notes with Dallas; I have even seen his wife take notes, which my wife rarely does with me.
>
> "Okay, Dallas," I responded. "I've got that one. Now what other spiritual nuggets do you have for me? I don't have a lot of time, and I want to get all the spiritual wisdom from you that I can."
>
> "There is nothing else," he said, generously acting as if he did not notice my impatience. "Hurry is the great enemy of spiritual life in our day. You must ruthlessly eliminate hurry from your life."[12]

We were concluding a recent Become Good Soil leadership retreat, where elders offer pearls of wisdom from the ancient path set before us. As a hero of mine took the stage, he slowed his movement, making eye contact with each man in the room. Then, slowly and with great care, he began to speak words of life.

Do it slower.

Talk slower.

Eat slower.

Make love to your wife slower.

Do. It. All. *Slower.*

I could sense in the room the disruption of *hurry* being exposed for the harm it has caused. At the same time, the allure of hope was rising in the room—hope for the margin, rhythm, and soulful living our masculine heart yearns for and dared to believe was available. This simple act of doing it all slower is an example of a way to put into operation what will, in time, become a revolutionary break from the spirit that shapes this age, and a cultivation of our soul until it is completely transformed. Again, when we're busy, the Father is quiet. Often it is our inability to hear, not God's lack of speaking, that keeps us from hearing his voice. Simply put, we fail to become the kind of man who has the capacity to listen. Attempting to live at a pace and a rhythm that denies the life of the masculine soul will result in great loss or—worse—disastrous consequences. As one wise man said, "We reap in the next decade what we have sown in the last one." At this stage of the masculine journey, a man has enough miles to begin feeling the reality of consequences, for better and for worse. A life without care for the soul is simply unsustainable. To recover this ancient truth and begin to slowly start to cultivate good soil that won't compromise will bring untold transformation.

The Paradox of Cultivating a Habitat for Becoming a King

These five ancient truths are a way of putting into operation this hopeful mission of restoring the masculine soul and making the changes and taking the risk to become good soil.

In his brilliance and deep kindness, Jesus told the story of a generous farmer scattering an abundance of seed, offering a transforming insight into the nature of God's kingdom—both the extravagant sowing of the Trinity and what gets in the way of those seeds germinating and bearing fruit within us.

I read the parable again, chewing on it as aspen logs crackled and popped in the fire, and a question rose in my heart. You know how it goes; these conversations with God are more nuanced and intuitive than we can easily put into words, but my question was something like this: *Today, Father, what is the condition of the soil of my masculine soul?*

Let's come back to the story Jesus shared with his apprentices.

> "Listen! A farmer went out to plant some seeds. As he scattered them across his field, some seeds fell on a footpath, and the birds came and ate them. Other seeds fell on shallow soil with underlying rock. The seeds sprouted quickly because the soil was shallow. But the plants soon wilted under the hot sun, and since they didn't have deep roots, they died. Other seeds fell among thorns that grew up and choked out the tender plants. Still other seeds fell on fertile soil, and they produced a crop that was thirty, sixty, and even a hundred times as much as had been planted! Anyone with ears to hear should listen and understand."
>
> —Matthew 13:3–9 NLT

I have considered a great number of teachings on this passage, but one mentor really brought it home to help me understand the reality of the integration of the masculine soul.

For years I approached this story as four distinct conditions of the heart of four different kinds of people. Yet the revelation God brought is that *all four conditions exist in each of us in varying degrees at any given time.* The process of integration and wholeness of the masculine soul is the process of increasingly becoming a greater portion of the good soil within. Let's take some time to consider each soil condition and allow God to shine light on where we might be in this process of the slow and steady cultivating of good soil in our souls.

The hardened soil is prone to cynicism and is impenetrable in many ways. Our trauma, our woundedness, the warfare, our agreements— the seed just can't stick; there's no penetration. Untended pain and trauma often lead to this condition. The soul in this condition is unwilling and perhaps even unable to be open to receive the life God wants to bring it. What parts of your soul are the hardened soil?

The shallow soil represents the fruit of a soul that has suffered under the reality of our present age. Richard Foster suggested that "the curse of our age is superficiality."[13] It's the driving energy that keeps the hearts of men from rooting deeply. It is very important to note that, in this condition of soil, seeds are planted and there is the beginning of genuine growth. Jesus said these people had joy when they heard about God's kingdom (Matt. 13:20). But because they hadn't developed roots at the time of testing, they fell away. It's a state of constant immaturity. It's a version of masculinity built on a false belief that shortcuts are available, that there is a way to have the world *and* the kingdom of God. Its fruit is what we painfully see all around as the prominent condition of most kings and their propped-up kingdoms. It results in simply having more kingdom than the character of the man is able to sustain and operate from in love. What parts of your soul and your life represent the shallow soil?

The cluttered soil is represented painfully well by the "thorns and thistles" (Gen. 3:18). This portion of us is entangled and enmeshed in "the worries of this life" and "the deceitfulness of wealth" (Matt. 13:22). There's nothing quick, easy, or sexy about the process of becoming good soil, no shortcut to the hard work of painstakingly extracting each thorn and thistle from our soul. Eugene Peterson suggested that this recovery of the ancient path is the "long obedience in the same direction."[14] Slow and steady wins the race. That's the way of trees, that's the way of nature, and that's the way of the kingdom. Jesus said the seeds sown in cluttered soil take root and begin to grow but in time are choked out. The weeds are the worries, the duplicity of the false self, and the inability of a man to die to his old self so that he can be reborn. Weeds, it's been said, suck up valuable nourishment and moisture from the soil but bear no fruit. What parts of your soul and your life are best represented by the cluttered soil?

The good soil is rich, teeming with moisture and nutrients. The good soil, Jesus suggested, stands for the portions of us that—by cultivating, tending, and maturing—"Hear the word, retain it, and by persevering produce a crop" (Luke 8:15). Suffering produces perseverance; perseverance, character; character, a genuine wholeheartedness—and wholeheartedness produces inextinguishable hope (Rom. 5:3–4). It is this anticipation of good that fuels our becoming a king. In many ways, the five ancient stones we're attempting to recover all lead to this central idea in the path.

Years ago I asked my uncle, a third-generation farmer, about his understanding of a bumper crop. He explained that a bumper crop is an unnaturally large yield. When you have yields beyond thirty times the input, the only way to describe them is supernatural; the equation of input to output simply doesn't match. The promise of becoming good soil is that, in time, we will share in the joy of a supernatural harvest, both in us and through us.

I took a big risk when I ejected on a story I'd thought was life in order to follow the Wild One into a story of choosing excavation over building, lowest seat over center stage, and nearly two decades of the hidden years. It takes a lot of crap to make good soil; that's the way of nature and that's the way of the kingdom.

If you are reading this with a willingness to consent to the wildly unpopular and rarely chosen journey of becoming a king, you are becoming part of God's plan to bring a hundredfold yield. The kingdom is always hidden and revealed in paradox. The first shall be last, and the path to greatness is to become the lowest. To embrace this kingdom reality is to live on the frontier of the masculine soul, where few men choose to dream and to dare. It is to find yourself among a small fellowship of men who've chosen to honor God above all else, allowing the integration of their masculine souls and the recovery of who they are, who God is, and what his story is all about to be the driving force of their days and their decades.

You are that kind of man. Or better said, you can become that man if you so choose. God's Word is clear that when you choose the narrow path, the slow and steady, the no-shortcuts path to becoming a king, your life will yield a supernatural harvest. In a world of instant gratification, it feels like heresy to suggest that life is found in something slow and steady. And yet, as Jesus said, the test of a person or a practice is its fruit (Matt. 7:16). Consenting to a slow and steady process is a radical risk. But if it is fruit you seek, you can be confident that the narrow path will yield a harvest in you and through you of thirty-, sixty-, even a hundredfold.

The ancient path is traveled only by those choosing to mature through practice and through receiving the interactive life of God and his kingdom. It has a return on investment that beats anything this world has ever known. The results are supernatural. They can be trusted. The narrow path becomes the shortest path. God has set the path before us. Tested and found true by the hearts of a few men, generation after generation, who have given their consent to God's leadership and have been swept up into the prevailing goodness of God. Only through our consent to these ancient truths and to cultivating a habitat for becoming good soil can we courageously walk through the next narrow gate of becoming the deep roots for which the soil was intended. And that's where we must travel next.

Father, I choose to pause. To breathe. What are you saying, and how are you inviting me to participate with cultivating a habitat that is true for my masculine soul? Give me a picture of the current state of my soul. Show me the conditions of the soil within me. You have my attention. I choose to lean into your counsel, your heart, and your intentions in this place.

8

BECOMING DEEP ROOTS

Nothing more is required of us than that
which we can do in union with God.
—Cherie Snyder

Packed with a lift capacity of more than thirteen hundred pounds, my friend Bart's Kubota tractor is a wonder of a machine. He spent many childhood days watching earlier models of this earthmoving giant do heavy lifting. Five decades later he realized the dream of owning his own and, over time, has become a skilled operator. It's about more than dirt for Bart. It's soul therapy, a spiritual practice for him to get behind the wheel, move dirt, build roads, and, piece by piece, create a redemptive outpost tucked away in the Colorado Rockies—a location where many can adventure and strengthen their souls.

One day, the tractor quit working. Bart couldn't figure it out. He ran through diagnostics, did all the troubleshooting he'd learned over his many years of working with heavy machinery. Nothing worked. He walked back toward the cabin, asking God, *What's going on with the Kubota?* As he passed the fuel shed, it hit him. *This thing runs on diesel, and I just filled it to the brim with unleaded.* Bart didn't have a tractor problem; he had a fuel problem. No matter how great his tractor is, it will work only with the proper fuel.

We'd be wise to look at our soul in this same light.

Human beings are designed to run on the fuel of God and his kingdom. And the good news Jesus proclaimed is that the doors to the kingdom of God are wide open, the fuel of his life in endless supply. The with-God life is available, right here and right now.

But how do we go about entering this open-doored kingdom? What exactly are the effective means of living the with-God life? And what are the practical ways we can make God and his kingdom our moment-by-moment fuel?

The men through the ages who have recovered the narrow path suggest there is a way. It is a way of living by day and by decade that positions us to draw upon the life of God and, over time, become the kind of person who is overflowing with well-being. Dallas Willard first articulated for me the distinction between *trying* to live the with-God life and *training* to become the kind of man who naturally and essentially draws his life from union with God.

Now that we have courageously considered the role of habitat in our becoming, we can get even more practical with these soul-shaping questions. Whose apprentice are you, and what are you practicing?

In *The Spirit of the Disciplines*, Dallas offered some keen insights into the distinction between trying and training. He gave an illustration of a group of young athletes who become deeply enthralled, idolizing pro baseball players. Both on the field and off, they want to do everything they can to be like the pros they admire. Therefore when the young kids are on the field, they act exactly the way the pro players do. They wear the same uniforms, use the same equipment, and do everything they can to look and act just like their heroes. However, try as they might, there still exists a nearly uncrossable gap between the young fans and the pros they watch in the stadiums. And surely by now we all can see clearly the issue at hand. We all know that the pros became who they are on the field by all the constant training they consented to by day and by decade off the field. It's everything we don't see that forms the pro athletes into the kind of people we do see on the field. From nutrition to physical training, from mental training to skill development, it's what we don't see that counts the most.

What we find here is true of any human endeavor capable of significance to our lives. We are touching upon a general principle of human life. It's true for the public speaker or the musician, the teacher or the surgeon. A successful performance at a moment of crisis rests largely and essentially upon the depths of a self wisely and rigorously prepared in the totality of its being. . . . There is an art of living, and the living is excellent only when the self is prepared in all the depths and dimensions of its being.[1]

What did Dallas highlight here? What did he point to in the blueprint of reality? And what difference does it make in our quest to become the kind of king who is trustworthy to the core? Dallas highlighted this reliable and gracious natural law of being human: who we are in our inmost being and what we are capable of offering in a critical situation are mostly the by-products of who we have trained to become in our day-to-day lives. How we arrange our days and spend our time is central to becoming the kind of king to whom God can entrust his creative power. It is this slow and steady exercise—or better said, consistent practicing over time—that produces the kind of king God intends us to become.

What is the relationship between the kind of human Jesus was on earth and how he spent his time? An exhaustive look at Jesus' spiritual practices is beyond the scope of this book, but we can draw from several foundational truths expressed through his life.

We know he spent time in solitude.

We can infer that he spent time in study, given his upbringing as a Jewish man and his agility with the Scriptures.

We know he spent lots of time outdoors.

We know he spent time with his close friends.

We know he spent time fasting and feasting.

We know he willingly offers himself as our Teacher.

Therefore, is it possible that learning from Jesus how to spend our time could be a transformative variable within the context of an intentional season of our lives given fully over to the process of becoming?

Because the phrase "spiritual disciplines" sometimes connotes dogmatic religious activity that's heavy, awkward, and ill-fitting, I'm choosing to use the word *practices* when talking about the activities we purposefully engage in as apprentices of the narrow path. Practices are activities within our power to engage in that enable us to do what we could never do by direct effort or willpower alone.

The power of indirect practices is written into the text of nature. We benefit from the power of indirect practices all the time. For example, I may not be able to shift out of a terrible mood by sheer force of will, but taking a short run in the Colorado sunshine shifts my mood in a way that direct effort rarely can. I cannot show up at the starting line of a marathon and expect to run the whole thing by sheer force of will, but day by day I can will myself to train and trust that the reliable by-product of my training is that I will be able to finish the race. As it is with our physical health, finances, or relationships, it is even more so in our relationship with God and his kingdom. It is my intentional daily cultivation, or practices, that put me in position to be made whole and true. And it is here where I can expect and anticipate the power of grace. As Dallas taught us, a New Testament understanding of grace is, "God acting in our lives to accomplish what we can't accomplish on our own."[2] When we arrange our days around experiencing deep joy, contentment, and confidence in our life with God, we can count on the action of God to transform our character into the likeness of our Teacher.

What Are You Practicing?

Let's move into one of the most operational questions for the masculine soul in this process of becoming a king: *What are you practicing?*

In other words, how are you actively shaping the details of your days and your decades to orient yourself toward a life that takes on increasing qualities of eternity? George MacDonald gave us a vision for where we're going.

We are the sons of God the moment we lift up our hearts, seeking to be sons—the moment we begin to cry Father. But as the world must be redeemed in a few men to begin with, so the soul is redeemed in a few of its thoughts and wants and ways, to begin with; it takes a long time to finish the new creation of this redemption. . . .

His children are not his real, true sons and daughters until they think like him, feel with him, judge as he judges, are at home with him, and without fear before him because he and they mean the same thing, love the same things, seek the same ends. For this are we created; it is the one end of our being, and includes all other ends.[3]

When being an apprentice in kingdom living becomes our primary motive and the fuel for our days, we start to take seriously these questions:

What is in my power to do—*to practice*—in order for me to participate with God in transforming my inmost being and rooting me more deeply in his life?

What activities position me to receive from God what I cannot produce by willpower alone? How can I arrange my days as a student and son to cultivate deeper union with God?

Our consent to the narrow path and to becoming a king is the on-ramp whereby revolutionary ideas penetrate our lives through tangible and accessible daily actions. It is here where God can bring forth a supernatural bounty, and so we must turn our attention to establishing deep roots. After sitting with sages for more than two decades, I want to suggest three categories for our consideration that seem to be the most helpful themes in engaging in this practice with our masculine heart set on the goal of inner transformation:

- Practices of engagement,
- Practices of abstinence, and
- Practices of being weird.

As Richard Foster has brilliantly taught, a list of spiritual practices is never intended to be exhaustive or even particularly prescriptive. If anything, it is to serve as an on-ramp to experimenting and training through trial and error. Let's dive deeper into these three areas of practice.

Practices of Engagement

Much of our training as kings takes place in our small, daily, moment-by-moment choices. Practices of engagement are ways of choosing a courageous yes to the things in our power that we believe, over time, will keep us on the rare and life-giving path of becoming a king. The possibilities of these practices are wide and vast. My intention here is simply to provide a few practical illustrations that will serve as signposts along the narrow path of becoming.

The Practice of Play

Years ago my family and I headed over to my friend Sam's house for dinner. As we pulled in, we found Sam cutting his grass on a riding lawnmower. The scene would've been pretty normal, except for one thing: the *way* he was cutting the grass. Instead of efficient rows, he was making big, sweeping circles and swirls with his mower, cutting his front yard into a wild and whimsical display. I suppose it'd be great for paint and canvas, but it was kind of weird for a front yard. I racked my brain; maybe he'd had a few too many beers before our arrival? I couldn't figure out what was behind this. And his big grin made it even more perplexing. Part of me was embarrassed to even ask. Yet I've learned something in this decade of choosing excavation over building: questions lead to treasures, and good risks are worth taking.

"Sam, I'm stumped. What are you doing?" I asked a bit awkwardly.

He responded with a big smile. "I'm playing."

I was floored. I could not find a file for his response. I simply had no category.

This man is a big deal in his multimillion-dollar development company. *If I don't have time to play,* I thought, *he surely doesn't.*

Or do I?

With Sam's answer, my Teacher was pulling another string to unravel me.

Then, a few weeks later, a second disruption pulled a little more on that same string. My wife, Cherie, as a result of much of the healing and restoration work in which she engaged, now has come full circle to offer trauma-sensitive soul care to many. She has served professionally for many years as a Christ-centered movement and meditation practioner. With that, for years came a stream of catalogs featuring women's stretchy pants, flowing steadily into our mailbox.

Over time we began to notice a pattern in these catalogs: men and women laughing and playing together. In the summer catalog, they're whimsically drawing on a sandy beach. In the winter catalog, they're throwing snowballs.

For years, my internal reaction to the men in these pictures was the same: *Get a job! Go* do *something!*

I mean, be honest. Who has time to draw pictures in the sand?

I sure didn't.

Or did I?

My offense at these images pointed once again to my unconscious commitment to a false belief that my worth is dependent on my accomplishments. This leaves little room for joy.

Additionally, these playful images were appealing to something deep in the human heart. Prana and other clothing companies selling to women know what they're doing when they stage those photos; they know what works. What Prana has learned is that there is something very attractive to a woman about a man who is willing to play, or better said, is *capable* of playing.

And that man was not me. At least not back then.

Finally, another disruption pulled at that same string, until it unraveled. It came while I was reading *Unbroken*, Laura Hillenbrand's remarkable story of Louis Zamperini, a World War II pilot shot down in the Pacific. Zamperini survived four months floating in a life raft, only to be captured by Japanese soldiers and tortured for years as a POW. Louis was finally set free, only to find that the prison within his heart and mind had become more wretched than the confines of the POW camps. In his twilight years, he came to know the restorative power of the resurrected Christ in a real and intimate way. Hillenbrand showed a photograph of an elder Zamperini, carefree and saturated with joy. Of all his remarkable accomplishments, from competing in the Olympics to surviving multiple POW camps, this one disrupted me the most: Louis took up skateboarding, *at eighty-one*. The joy on his face is piercing. In spite of all the pain, the loss, the terror, Louis has found a life in the heart of God so deep, he is able not only to live *but to play*.

As I've sat at the feet of some seventy-five men over the past decade in order to mine what it means to really *live* in this time of consenting to the process of becoming a king, I've found that choosing to play is a disruptively consistent theme that runs through the wisdom they share, and choosing not to is one of the consistent sources of deepest regret.

"I wish I'd played more and found joy in all of it."

"I wish I'd worried less and played with my kids more."

"Joy could've been my accelerator, my fuel. There was so much joy for the taking, and I missed it."

"I was a good provider, a faithful husband. But looking back, I realize what I missed out most on was play. Now in the sunset of my life, I often think of how rich it would have been to know that at my eulogy my children would be able to say, 'My dad laughed often, played much, and always lived the message that life has the last word, even in the face of such deep challenge.'"

Researcher Brené Brown qualitatively evaluated the importance of play to human well-being. After a decade of interviews with thousands of people, she wrote this: "I learned . . . how things that I take for granted, like rest and play, are as vital to our health as nutrition and exercise." In her book on wholehearted living, *The Gifts of Imperfection*, Brené cited a renowned researcher and founder of the National Institute of Play,[4] Dr. Stuart Brown: "Brown explains that play shapes our brain, helps us foster empathy, helps us navigate complex social groups, and is at the core of creativity and innovation."[5] I was disrupted and enticed. And I needed a gracious first step.

So I bought flip-flops.

For years, guys who wore flip-flops bugged me. What can you do in flip-flops? Not much. And that's the point. Through introducing the value of play for its own sake, my Father was pursuing my heart and recovering his joyful, playful image in me. He was excavating yet another layer of my life—in which I was hustling for worthiness—and demolishing the stronghold of my conviction that my worth depended on my productivity.

Play is simple but not easy. It's exposing. Risky. As Brené Brown observed of our Western culture, "Spending time doing purposeless activities is rare. In fact, for many of us it sounds like an anxiety attack waiting to happen."[6] But there is gold to be found if we risk an expedition into unknown territory. Our capacity to play, to laugh, to chillax, and to simply *enjoy* being present is directly proportional to what we have come to believe about the heart of God. And perhaps directly related to how comfortable we will (or will not) be when we cross into eternity.

As I've begun actively trusting the centrality of play in God's story, I'm seeing it more and more. Solomon, one of the wisest men who ever lived, wrote in Ecclesiastes that there is a time for every activity under heaven and that God has made everything beautiful in his time (3:1, 11). Solomon observed that there is a time to laugh and cheer (v. 4). He urged us, "On a good day, enjoy yourself" (7:14 MSG). Solomon's exhortation to joy crescendoed with this:

> Seize life! Eat bread with gusto,
> Drink wine with a robust heart.
> Oh yes—God takes pleasure in *your* pleasure!
> Dress festively every morning.
> Don't skimp on colors and scarves.
> Relish life with the spouse you love
> Each and every day of your precarious life.
> Each day is God's gift. It's all you get in exchange
> For the hard work of staying alive.
> Make the most of each one!
> Whatever turns up, grab it and do it. And heartily!
> —Ecclesiastes 9:7–10 MSG

What's frontier for you in the practice of play? For me it started with buying flip-flops as an act of faith, and it has grown from there. As I was asking God for advance words to orient me for a recent family trip back east, I sensed this simple instruction: *Play.*

Coming off three months of intense, back-to-back missions, I was nearly disoriented by the counsel. Yet it was exactly what I needed. My Father's leading gave way to a week of sidewalk chalk, roller coasters, campfires, s'mores, fireworks, catching lightning bugs, swimming, playing games, riding bikes through puddles, eating ice cream, getting muddy, and laughing.

My kids loved it. And so did I.

Play has opened up a new place in my heart, and through it, a whole new curiosity about the nature of God's heart and the atmosphere of his kingdom. The practice of play is exposing the places in me that have yet to know a God who lavishes me with love and affection just as I am.

The Practice of Defiant Joy

For a bunch of overachievers, it was the worst business plan we could've imagined. And we couldn't be more joyful. All four of us were in the throes of consenting to this decade of becoming. All of us were serving in middle-manager-type roles in other men's kingdoms. We all had young kids, young marriages, and battles on every front. We had given God permission to let this decade be more about excavation than building and more about becoming than accomplishing. And through it all we began to realize that the currency we were lacking most was joy. So we began to wonder together: What could we do to fight for more joy?

We all deeply enjoy craft beer. Even more, we love celebrating the stories of heroic men who've preceded us and whose tracks we want to follow. So we started dreaming up a plan to create, alongside an award-winning brewmaster, recipes for brews branded around legendary men of ages gone by. Our plan was to fund the entire joy venture out of our own pockets and give it all away for free—for our joy and the joy of the men we love. In 2008 the Sons of Thunder Brewing Company was birthed, and we've been brewing and bottling joy ever since. The budget for our joy-venture is extraordinarily small, but the impact is exponential. We give away what can't be bought, and though it is a financial loss by design, it spreads joy like kingdom chicken pox. Every shirt, hat, and pint of delight we give away shares the love. The JoyBomb, which we define as an unexpected gift at an unexpected time, has become our symbol. And in an organization whose mission is to brew joy, whether it's beer or a craft soda like the "Oh, My Darling Clementine" we're currently working on for our daughters, joy abounds. When you don't have income or a staff, regular board meetings are simply permission for adventure and play, and a committment to see this message realized in and through each of our hearts as men.

Joy matters. It's a fuel (Neh. 8:10). And it is a currency of the kingdom of God (Rom. 14:17). Think of the meaning of the Hebrew word *eden*. The closest English translation is the word *pleasure*. Think of the nature of God that he would create the Sabbath for rest and delight. Think of the jubilant imagery of the Psalms and the writings of the Hebrew prophets, images of feasting and dancing, of being intoxicated by the river of God's pleasure, and of the trees of the field clapping their hands in response to the goodness and greatness of God (Isaiah 25; Psalm 30; Psalm 36; Isaiah 55). Think of Jesus' dedication to arranging his days  around the value of joy, so much so that he was accused of being "a glutton and a drunkard" (Matt. 11:19). Given the vividness of these images and practices, I have to ask, how did I miss the importance of practices of joy for so much of my early adult life?

How has the Father been trying to restore practices of joy for you? Joy, after all, is direct defiance of the kingdom of darkness. Your version of defiant joy will no doubt be unique. But make no mistake, joy matters. And the conversion to a joy-saturated life happens only over time. This decade is a crucible. Over time joy is intended to be an irreplaceable fuel to persevere through the often grueling terrain along the path of restoration and the mission to becoming a wholehearted king.

The Practice of Learning

Confession: I devour books. I have resolved to resist the cultural temptation to content-binge; rather I have decided to become the kind of man who returns to an important book and gnaws on it as a dog gnaws a bone. Chewing on a really good book is one of the most effective ways I reorient my soul away from the chaos of this world and toward the kingdom-among-us. I have cultivated the learner in me through practice, and it has become a primary means of regular soul strengthening. Take heart from the words of Charles Spurgeon as you dive into this practice.

> Master those books you have. Read them thoroughly. Bathe in them until they saturate you. Read and reread them . . . digest them. Let them go into your very self. Peruse a good book several times and make notes and analyses of it. A student will find that his mental constitution is more affected by one book thoroughly mastered than by twenty books he has merely skimmed. Little learning and much pride comes from hasty reading. Some men are disabled from thinking by their putting meditation away for the sake of much reading. In reading let your motto be "much not many."[7]

The long-term effect of education being institutionalized and primarily structured around specialization and a career is a gradual loss of the vision of learning as a fundamental way of being human and being masculine. Our false self urges us to cling to our expertise; we have a gravitational pull toward the false comfort of what we already know. Yet the soul is generative in nature, expansive in its capacity to learn, mature, and cultivate fierce mastery.

At the heart of becoming a king is the recovery of practices for lifelong learning. Not just for the content itself but also for the formation that happens within us as we seek to unlearn where we have learned reality wrong and set out with curiosity again and again to learn deeply and well.

Here's a way to experiment with this practice: choose to learn about something that has little to do with your profession or your usual interests. In the past month, I've been learning about ballistics through a science experiment my son is conducting. We've done everything from studying the underlying physics and doing the calculations, to building wood forms and conducting experiments, to consulting gunsmiths and local experts in the field. This experiment has broadened my understanding and promoted my growth, not merely in familiarity with the subject matter but also in my character, through the challenge, the perseverance, and the venture into the unknown.

Our profession and our formal education cannot form the boundary lines of our learning. If we are to pass through our initiation into becoming a king, whole-person growth through learning must become a foundational habit.

The Practice of Worship

We often think of worship as singing songs in a church building on Sunday mornings. John Eldredge has challenged this operating assumption: "Worship is what we give our hearts away to in return for a promise of Life."[8] We are worshiping creatures; it's in our nature. From technology to success to validation from our spouse to money, power, and sex, all day long we worship people, places, things, and ideas. Worship, when consecrated and brought under the care of and connection with God, can become an essential way of living that allows our heart to feast on God again and again and again.

Overflow from an inner reservoir of the life of God is the substance of the heroic and sacrificial life of a good king. Yet most of us live as dry sponges. We chase down solutions to problems without pausing to simply become saturated in the love and life of God. I want to be like a sponge fully saturated in the life of God. And a couple of songs in a Sunday morning worship service is simply insufficient.

If this overflow is going to be my daily experience, I must arrange my days in that direction; I have to cultivate the practice of worship. Dallas Willard suggested that of all the spiritual practices, worship is the most complete. It is an invitation to respond to God's divine affection. And in our response, our hearts increasingly come into alignment and agreement with the nature of God and the reality of his kingdom.

Take an honest inventory. How much is your soul being saturated—filled to overflowing—through a regular practice of worship? Let's face it, singing several songs on a Sunday morning isn't sufficient as the source of life for which God seems to make available as the promise of worship. What can you do to experiment with a deeper practice? One practical suggestion is to reclaim your drive time as an opportunity for intimacy with God. Rather than treating your vehicle as a mobile office, catching up on phone calls and emails, or simply medicating your soul's thirst with content-bingeing, what if you staked out your vehicle space as a place of intimacy? What if you took one song and immersed yourself in it again and again on repeat, until God was able to use it to access deeper places within your soul? If we want more, the more we have to risk experimenting with going after it in fresh ways.

My friend Jonathan David Helser has served as a mentor in the practice of worship for years. He suggests approaching worship as giving back to God what he has first poured into us. Let God first fill you—with his life, his heart, his words, his affection, his acceptance of you right here, right now, just as you are. Remember, when we talk of the practice of worship, we mean something far deeper than singing songs. What if it is first a response to receiving God's genuine affection and life? What if a freely chosen practice of worship became a river of life flowing into and saturating your masculine soul? Though the forms that worship can take transcend music and singing, the unique effectiveness of these two forms is evidenced in millennia of Hebrew and Christian practices. There is a vast supply of worship music, but I suggest aligning with those particular songs and artists anointed to bring God's life to you.

Through regular, heart-centered practice of personal and Spirit-filled community worship, I experience more of God and sense more of his heart coming *to* me and coming *for* me. And I experience the capacity to give my heart back to him with greater and greater abandonment. I experience union with him and a coursing exchange of love and affection. I experience what can only be described as a fundamental maturing from a culture of scarcity to one of abundance and overflow.

The Practice of Adventure

I nearly wet my pants. Energy from lightning ripped through the ground, and I could feel it, even hear a faint, eerie hum. The air was electrified, the sky ablaze, as the sun dropped behind the jagged peaks of the Flat Tops Wilderness Area. The sound of bull elk bugling in the early twilight crescendoed around me, seemingly from every direction. I was a neophyte bowhunter hurled into the major leagues. Highly exposed on an 8,900-foot peak that hosted only broken aspen groves and scattered ponderosa pines, I was miles away from shelter. The storm was imminent, the pregnant sky about to give way.

It's been said that discretion is the better part of valor, and having been formed in a risk-averse culture, I've lived that motto quite well. But that evening, as thunderclouds built overhead, wind swirled, and the sun painted fire in the sky, I found my heart responding to something deeper than conventional wisdom—some ancient beckoning. A sort of divine revelation perhaps? I hunkered down below a partially protected rocky outcropping and gave myself over to whatever might unfold.

And what did was cause for awe. Three giant bull elk emerged from the aspens, bugled back and forth, then hurled themselves at each other, the sound of their jousts and clashing antlers rivaling the crack of thunder overhead. The lead cow elk hustled the herd of calves and cows through the aspen grove and along the sagebrush hillsides, skirting the combating bulls. It was a rodeo of nature's greatest proportions.

As Eldredge suggested in *Wild at Heart*, "The masculine heart needs a place where nothing is prefabricated, modular, nonfat, zip lock, franchised, online, microwavable. Where there are no deadlines, cell phones, or committee meetings. Where there is room for the soul. Where, finally, the geography around us corresponds to the geography of our heart."[9] That night on a lonely mountain peak in the national forest, I finally discovered a geography that matched the internal landscape of my masculine soul. John Muir said it this way: "Everybody needs beauty as well as bread, places to play in and pray in, where Nature may heal and cheer and give strength to body and soul alike."[10]

Theodore Roosevelt, too, understood that nothing restores the heart of a man like encountering the living God in wilderness. It was in the Badlands of North Dakota that, as a young man, he sought refuge and comfort in the wake of the sudden loss of the two deepest loves of his life: his mother and his wife. He went west to heal and ultimately to become much of the man he was meant to be. In his later years, Teddy reflected on the impact of wilderness on his soul as a young man: "Do you know what chapter . . . I would choose to remember were the alternative forced upon me to recall one portion of it, and to have erased from my memory all other experiences? I would take the memory of my life on the ranch with its experiences close to nature and among the men who lived nearest her."[11]

Adventure is intended to be a primary atmosphere in which we live our life with God. No one is more adventurous than the One who created the lion, the waterfall, the sunset. Adventure is a doorway into the deep life of God. It is a context in which God entices and disrupts the many parts of our masculine soul that need to encounter him more deeply. To live in such a way that God has to show up, rather than viewing God as a convenient backup plan or insurance policy—that is the life in which the masculine soul thrives.

One of the greatest adventures I'm currently facing is the initiation of my young children into adulthood. This adventure is filled with unknowns, risks, questions, and fears. Yet it is also saturated with promise and possibility, as our family embarks on this journey in partnership with God and under his constant care and counsel.

Pause and ask God, *What have I done with adventure? Where is both simple and heroic adventure in my life? How am I inviting those I love and those who have been entrusted to my care into an adventure that requires you to show up?*

Let's choose to no longer neglect heroic adventure, to no longer go through life half asleep, to no longer be confined to a smaller story that isn't big enough to give the masculine heart room to grow.

Practices of Abstinence

Practices of abstinence strengthen our "no muscle" and help deliver us from the power of our attachments and the illusion of certain death should we cease to allow them to have their way. We come to realize that the false self dies only when we choose to move away from the false sources of life. The life of the true self is indestructible and can withstand any deprivation.

Practices of abstinence are a path to the freedom of the indestructible life of Jesus. What do we refrain from? What normal or legitimate things do we abstain from for a time? Again, we must be careful of religious trappings and religious vernacular. This is from the heart; it's integration of the soul we are after.

Some of my closest allies and I have cultivated a practice of fasting together most years, for the month of January, from a wide range of food and drink we can turn to for life more than we would like: alcohol, sugar, beer, caffeine, dairy, beer—you get the point. And most years it's rather rough. The fast certainly cleanses our bodies, but that is not really the point. Even more, it cleanses our spirits and realigns us with God. It is a reorientation that makes way for this deep and lifesaving truth: *God, I love you more than all these things. You are my food, my drink. You are the fountain of life welling up within me, and with you I am fully satisfied. I choose union with you. I will not sell my body or my soul to less wild lovers.*

Come mid-January, Cherie will typically find me, at some point, standing in front of the refrigerator, looking with desperation at my false comforters that are once again exposed and off-limits. She's so empathetic; she looks at me and says, "Honey, I'm so sorry." But always with a wink, as she knows the voluntary deprivation is holy, a course correction for my soul.

Cultivating practices of abstinence, particularly in a culture programmed to expect instant gratification, has a way of uniquely disrupting the false self and the self-saving at work within us. As Willard suggested, in order for us to become the kind of king God can entrust with his kingdom, the starting point is often this: if you have an itch, don't scratch it.

The practices of abstaining are perhaps the most effective over time to recover the soul-saving way of Saint Francis of Assisi, who suggested we must "wear the world as a loose garment, which touches us in a few places and there lightly." To become a king is to cultivate a benevolent detachment from the world. It is only in detaching from the world and attaching more deeply to God that we can become the kind of man who brings the great goodness this world most desperately needs.

There is nothing like the practical, so let me name three examples of practices of abstinence I lean into to strengthen my no muscle and practice feeding directly on God's immaterial sustenance.

The Practice of Sabbath

For many years, we were like just about everybody else: unconsciously forsaking honest soul rest, always going, with overfilled calendars and little to show in the category of true rest and simple delight. Sundays were much like other days, packed with activity and low on rest, restoration, or sacred space. Out of immense pain and burnout, we began our recovery and eventually chose to cultivate a lifestyle fueled by weekly and annual sabbath.

Sundays are now no-fly zones in our house. We don't do things that aren't somehow connected to Eden and the restoration of all things. These days are set aside for conversation, space, and any sorts of activities that allow us to hit pause on all the "not yet" and "not done," choosing to delight in the goodness of the life we have experienced in God.

In general when we sabbath, the cell phones are off, we don't schedule things, we wake up and linger, and we play and take our time. It annoys friends and frustrates people who can't find us (but I believe it's my ministry to them now). It takes immense courage to stop and settle in, because you're never done. One buddy lamented this afternoon, "I will die with emails in my in-box." How do you feel about that? They'll be there, and they'll keep coming. It's never done. What was once nonexistent has become a weekly and annual rhythm.

In this modern culture, there are few things as important as sacrificially fighting for an extended annual sabbatical. As a family, we chose to make increasing two-degree shifts, unplugging more regularly, living below our means. In time, I was ready to take the next step. I approached my boss and told him I was ready to exchange income for time. "I'd like to consider taking a few weeks of unpaid leave this summer—in addition to vacation time—in order to fight for sabbath for our family." The impossible became possible, and in time we went off the grid. We were *gone* gone. No-find-us kind of gone—no cell phones, no computers, no social media. Less of everything: fewer people, fewer decisions, fewer choices. Just an abundance of time together, in nature, resting, playing, doing honest work with our hands, and immersing ourselves in shared adventure.

It took me, a driven overachiever, years to even begin to be comfortable with choosing real rest and restoration. Now I can hardly remember life without it. Sabbath becomes the fruit of a regular practice of abstaining from the many demands, requirements, and needs of our world and choosing instead the deeper reality of simply being and allowing our souls to know that all is well.

The Practice of Doing Nothing

Our souls are shaped in powerful ways when we practice sending our roots deeper and coming to a place where we can agree with Psalm 46:10: "Be still, and know that I am God." While others might name this a practice of stillness, I find it important to emphasize that this particular practice, at least in part, must have intentional time that does not include journaling, reading, writing, or any sort of activity. Rather it is a practice in the discipline of rhythm, the sacred pause among the frenzy of activity.

I had returned from a demanding overseas mission, honored to have partnered with some of the kingdom's most anointed leaders in Australia. And I paid the price. Returning home, the glow of the trip was quickly erased by the cost and implications of hitting pause on the rest of my world. Many real and practical demands clamored for my attention. I've learned, through pain and failure, that what was needed most in that moment was nothing. And I knew just where to find it.

I headed out in my truck and tucked into one of the many pockets of wild I've discovered right in the midst of the suburban sprawl of my hometown. I took the hundred-yard walk from my truck, equipped with nothing more than my camp chair (which lives in my truck for these moments), a cigar, and a cup of coffee. No Bible, no journal, no cell phone or any other tether to my world behind. It could all wait. And I sat, in stillness with God, for about an hour. It took quite a while, as immediately in the stillness the agitation and frenzy from within surfaced. But eventually I settled in. I began to watch the hawk riding the thermals in the early spring chinooks coming down Colorado's front range. I noticed tiny, robust green shoots of new life beginning to wrestle their way free of winter's dreary brown landscape. A blue jay lit upon a branch not more than two yards from my secret perch. I was rescued by stillness. It was a rescue that not only bore immediate fruit but also permeated every area of the life that waited for me back in the truck, in my home, in my office, and beyond. I was centered yet again in God's kingdom. Through stillness, intimacy was being restored.

Sometimes a practice is not two weeks, two days, or even two hours; it might be only two minutes. Even a "micro-practice" can become deeply transformative over time—a micro-rest, a micro-stillness, a micro-sabbath. Make it accessible. Do what you can. Everyone can find a few minutes. For me, whatever else I do, I stop at the end of my road when I drive home, before I turn onto my street; I have to physically stop to bless my work, releasing to God everyone and everything I have engaged—all the battles, all the stories—and turn my heart to my family. I breathe and center and receive the fresh life of God for my role as father and husband. *What has my wife's day been like? What are my kids contending with?* So often the Spirit will both refresh and reorient me in a lifesaving way.

The Practice of Limiting Our Technology

Our culture is in the midst of a titanic human experiment, the outcome of which will be uncertain for decades or perhaps even centuries. The technology revolution has enabled us to be instantaneously connected and falsely available to a limitless world of information, people, and experiences. It is more than the soul can bear. With all the undeniable benefits and blessings of technology, the data already supports that being plugged into digital devices without a fierce intentionality toward rhythm and times of unplugging has a negative impact on brain development and on one's soul.[12] Our great task is to learn how to live and love well in the times in which we find ourselves. And it is my passionate conviction that the most powerful kings and queens in God's kingdom leading the next generation into wholeheartedness will be men and women who've cultivated a lifestyle through practice and perseverance that is not ruled by technology and the plugged-in life.

Applying the practice of abstinence regarding our many digital devices, in the form of limitations and rhythm, is one of the primary frontiers for kingdom living in our age. To care for our own heart and the hearts of those entrusted to our care, we must ask some hard questions. *Father, how do we set life-giving limitations regarding the context of technology, the quantity of technology, and the nature in which we engage technology?* These are dynamic rather than dogmatic questions, as the intention is to safeguard a soul-filled life for yourself and your domain. The application of these life-infused limitations will, of course, change over time, yet they are intended to keep first things first, allowing technology to be in the service of love and to be an arena in which we exercise fierce mastery rather than submit to slavery to an inevitable cultural revolution. But in the spirit of practice, here are a few questions for your consideration.

- What spaces and places are good for technology use?
- What spaces in your home and kingdom are protected from technology?
- What times and spaces are set aside for conversations and shared experience and protected from the interruption of technology?
- What life-giving guidelines can be established around technology?
- How do you regularly create an atmosphere that diminishes our culture's demand that we be perpetually accessible and plugged into digital devices?
- How do you offer a larger story that increases the appetite for the real and decreases the appeal of the negative ways of engaging digital devices?

In every practice of abstinence, God is working to increase—not decrease—our desire for the good. What if, through these practices, he intends to reach down deep and raise from within us unfinished places in our souls that will not rest until they find their home in him?

Practices of abstinence are some of the most restorative and redemptive forces in all of the kingdom. And in God's profound generosity, there is far more available to us here than we've given ourselves permission to believe and receive.

Practices of Being Weird

Jesus said you will know them by the fruit they produce. If we are to ever become wholehearted men, we must risk exploring the weird, the practices that don't make sense to some but whose fruit is more of *us*, in time, being given over to more of God.

I guess that's how I landed in a sea of stretchy pants. For years my wife had graciously extended an invitation to me (not unlike her loving suggestion to see a counselor, which took me three years to take) to attend a Christian yoga class she was teaching. My internal dialogue went something like this: *Yoga? Are you kidding! What a waste of time. Especially when I could get a real workout. Yoga is a world for women. Besides, all those women will think I'm a pervert.* I finally yielded my pride, cynicism, and unbelief and slipped into the back of a room full of rubber mats at the YMCA. The only other man to be found was an old guy in the front row with a headband and very short shorts, probably left over from when he coached basketball.

And yet something happened deep in my soul. After an hour of holding my breath and making feeble attempts to stretch fossilized muscles, I found myself in "final relaxation." As the hour built to a time of rest and surrender, lying in stillness on the floor, breathing and receiving, tears began to come. It was the first time in my life I remember fully allowing myself to receive love. With each breath in, I could feel the *ruach*—the very breath of God—bringing dead places back to life. Somehow the experience of integrating my body with my mind and spirit, the hard physical work, the attempts to breathe deeply, and then finally surrendering was the combination that opened the lock.

I've never been the same. One class turned to many. Months into the practice, I finally touched my toes. Months after that, I found my breath. And I found a doorway into receiving mercy, comfort, and the mothering heart of God. I had yet to find in any other spiritual practice. It would be years before I understood that stretching and strengthening my core was a secret weapon to increasing my ability in bowhunting and other adventurous pursuits. It would be years before I began to understand how to be kind to myself, how to "try easy" and embrace the wisdom of knowing there's a time to go full throttle and there's a time to back off. It would be a decade before I understood how God was using this spiritual discipline to mother me, to heal my self-hatred, to teach me to receive Divine nuture, nourishment, and to facilitate the integration of my soul.

I asked my good friend Aaron to share some of his own weirdness he's been cultivating as a kingdom apprentice. Here's what he had to say.

I didn't grow up an artist. My dad's not a painter. But I started dragging a big marker kit to executive meetings in my company. One high-power meeting, there are six people sitting in the conference room, and everybody is in shirt and tie. They pull out their computers, and I pull out a big sketchpad and a bag of markers. They're busy taking notes on their digital devices, but eyes turn my way as I engage the business of drawing pictures, words, and ideas with my big markers. One by one, they pause and give me seething looks, as if to say, "Who the hell's that guy with the Crayola kit?" So I take my notes, do my thing, and choose twenty more seconds of courage. "God, I'm going to hold fast to my weird, trusting this is you in me and this is good."

That night, we're having beers back at the hotel, and the president of the company approaches me. "When you pulled out your crayon kit, I wondered what elementary kid showed up to that meeting." He was giving me crap about it, but I just laughed and responded, "Yeah, it's weird. I get it."

As I've cultivated this practice, I've found I'm able to use pictures and words to communicate the flow of ideas that others present. So I capture these ideas with my kit, then turn to them and say, "Here's what I hear on your behalf." It's an exercise for me in weird, in risking bringing good for men in my world. If it doesn't work, that's okay. But what I'm discovering as I become more of my true self—without a requirement of what that means or what it yields—is this specialized craft that I have. I sat down and did one of these for my CEO at breakfast a couple months ago, and I got promoted and a raise.

So that's my weird.

Everyone has a weird. Just look at the animal kingdom. Hippos, clown fish, giraffes . . . God has set us in a world that reminds us there are parts of who we are that are unique. Snowflakes and fingerprints are intended to remind us of that. There are parts of God we can bring as his unique image bearers, but also parts of him that can be known and enjoyed by us in a way no one else can fully know. It is in the ownership and practicing of our unique weird that we can cultivate some of the most robust dimensions of our intimacy with him and our particular assignment in his kingdom. Practicing and cultivating your weird is simply a way to access and bless that unique friendship being offered to you from and with God.

One friend has an Eddie Vedder signature guitar stashed in a mechanical room in the Fortune 500 company where he's a senior manager. He regularly hides away among pipes and ventilation to play a few riffs of life on his guitar.

Another elder in my life has a secret passion for the harmonica. One of his favorite ways of being with God is sneaking into the landscaping business next door after hours, sitting among stones and fresh mulch, and jamming on his harmonica. I've got another elder in my life who finds great joy in not having *any* tan lines. One of his most fruitful practices in nourishing his life in God is to find a sunny spot to hide out, buck naked, and sit and be still, soaking in the sun and saturating himself with the experience of God's enjoyment of who he made him to be.

Do you recall the Bud Light commercial from a past Super Bowl that featured wild fans cheering their team on to victory? Scene after scene, we saw the weird rituals each employed to rally their team. There were beer cans arranged in the shape of team logos, lucky socks, guys rubbing their buddy's bald head at the moment of the winning field goal kick. And after victory, one line was left on the screen: "It's only weird if it doesn't work."

The kingdom is—among its many qualities—a very weird place. For heaven's sake, demons are kicked out of a man, they are sent into pigs, and the pigs race to their own death. Jesus spits in the dirt, makes a mud pie, and shoves it into a guy's eyes to heal his sight. Manna, which sustained the Israelites for forty years, could not be grown, hunted, or manufactured. As Dallas said regarding the wildness of the Israelites being sustained on this food from God himself, "We're going to be living on weird stuff if we draw near to God."[13]

It's only weird if it doesn't work.[90] There is method to kingdom madness. God has much to dismantle, deliver, and restore in us in the process of making us kings. So choose your weird. As long as it works, it's worth it. Jesus was the first to admit that weird works. He had to reassure us we would know good things by their good fruit (Matt. 7:16), because it is often in the nonreligious and unexpected places where the soul can be most transformed. Cultivating a practice of being weird is unique to each man. You must risk exploring your own nature, the reality of the unique expression of the image of God you bear, and the unique relationship you alone occupy with him.

It's only weird if it doesn't work.

Risk being weird. It's okay. You'll never be as weird as the One who fashioned you. And your weird might be the very thing that gives the rest of us permission to push off from the shore and head toward deeper seas.

What Will You Practice?

Keep in mind that as soon as we talk practical examples, the risk is to become dogmatic or to focus on external activity. Becoming a king is always a matter of the heart. The lists go on. Practicing not having the last word. Practicing courageous vulnerability. Practicing taking responsibility for 100 percent of your impact on others. The spirit of becoming deep roots is to begin taking seriously whatever it is you intend to practice, so that in time and over time, these practices will establish your soul so deeply in the soil of God's life, even the most violent storm cannot harm the man you are becoming.

I've always been drawn to monastic communities. In my longing, years ago I found myself researching the lifestyle of a monastic community led by Father Thomas Keating. Here's the big idea that caught me: while the world tries hard to fit prayer into already full lives, this monastic community lives a life of prayer and finds a way to fit all the necessities of life into their lifestyle as apprentices of Jesus.

I quickly dismissed this lifestyle, thinking, *Sure, that's easy to say when these guys live without the pressures of society or the demands of family, conveniently tucked away in a mountain outpost where the primary work of their hands is brewing great Belgians.* Then the Holy Spirit disrupted my bitter interpretation and reminded me that a lifestyle organized around union with God is meant for us all. We are all human. We are all invited to immerse ourselves in the realities of the kingdom. Jesus tore the veil, forever separating secular from sacred. Through Jesus, all of life is declared holy, and we all "have equal access to the Father" (Eph. 2:18 MSG). Perhaps in spirit, my life can resemble a monk's far more than I have been led to believe.

The Father brought me this phrase: "the liturgy of life." He invited me into an adventure that has only expanded with every passing year, and now, with every passing decade. It's a daring kingdom experiment whereby my whole life can become liturgy.

I am being led in the process of a paradoxical shift, no longer finding ways to fit the spiritual life into the demands of modern living but rather living, breathing, existing in a life with God, finding ways to fit in the necessities of day-to-day life.

Dallas Willard was once asked by a young, eager man, "How should I use my fifteen-minute quiet time?" After Dallas's characteristic long pause, he responded, "I believe God is rather unconcerned with your fifteen-minute quiet time. He is far more concerned with how you choose to spend the other twenty-three hours and forty-five minutes of your day." He went on to offer this wildly winsome invitation: "You must arrange your days so that you are experiencing deep contentment, joy, and confidence in your everyday life with God."[14] This is the counsel that sits on my computer, the first thing I must contend with as I plug in each day. It entices and disrupts me along the ancient path of becoming a king.

Resolving to become the kind of man who arranges his days to experience deep contentment, joy, and confidence in his everyday life with God is the essence of our life becoming liturgy. Over time, as we grow in both our practice of and our consent to a lifestyle forged around our practices of engagement, abstinence, and being weird, we can trust that we will experience God and the manifestation of his power in a way that exceeds all we could have asked for or imagined (Eph. 3:20). We will mature in fierce mastery—in both the mandate and the invitation given to humanity at our creation—and become ready to rule and reign with integrity and wholehearted strength over all that God entrusts to our care. The liturgy of life, then, becomes our greatest asset to experience the present-tense reality of the gospel. While salvation is the door, the invitation deeper into the good news of the accessible kingdom is to venture along a narrow path toward divine *union*. Our everyday life, pursued and seen as liturgy, becomes the primary context for our transformation and the primary fuel for our joy. And through arranging our days around the narrow path of transformation and union, we become God's most effective weapon to bring the kingdom on earth as it is in heaven.

Jesus, Holy Spirit, Father, how are these practices, these big ideas, these ancient stones along the narrow path, intended by you to inform me by day and by decade? Holy Spirit, I am asking you to shine your light. What are you saying? Where are you inviting me to risk love? To risk receiving more of you? To risk giving more of me over to you and your relentless kindness in leading me along the path of becoming a king? Jesus, I am asking for your supernatural power, your resurrection life to infuse me with capacity to arrange my days around this reality. Father, I am asking for your full provision, protection, and pleasure to be my fuel as I choose to engage in the risks you are asking me to take.

YOU MUST ARRANGE YOUR DAYS — SO THAT YOU ARE — EXPERIENCING DEEP CONTENTMENT, JOY & CONFIDENCE — IN YOUR EVERYDAY — LIFE WITH GOD

— DALLAS WILLARD

BecomeGoodSoil.com

9

BECOMING LIKE-HEARTED

Things which matter most must never be at
the mercy of things which matter least.
—Johann Wolfgang von Goethe

Surrounded by ponderosa pines and tucked into the foothills of Colorado's front range, Craig's back porch was always a place of rest for my soul. Years ago I found myself there again, with a deep, unnamed wrestling in my soul. He met me with a confident smile, poured a few Manhattans, and offered a father's presence. After I explained the difficulties I was having with a few people I care about deeply, he quietly offered this observation: "You know, Morgan, one of the greatest indicators of spiritual maturity is the quality of our closest relationships."

I was exposed. "What do you mean? I have been heroically coming through for these people in more ways than I can remember. Doesn't that count for something?" He laughed and paused. He knows my story and how long I've attached my sense of being loved to coming through for people. He was gently creating space for my pain to teach me a deeper truth: Wisdom is proved right by her actions.

Since then, I've watched this truth find its way into my soul. Few other indicators in this world—specifically, in *our* world—provide a better litmus test of how we're maturing and being made whole and holy than the quality of our relationships. We must pause and soberly ask how well we are loving. Put simply, who and what gets the most and the best of us? If I asked the people closest to you what you're *really* like, what would they say?

Relationships are messy and vulnerable. They're the place in our lives where we have the least control of outcomes. And, as with all work of great meaning, true relationships require sacrifice and are disruptively inefficient by design. As I've journeyed further down the narrow path in pursuit of true and deep relationships, I see that vulnerability in this arena is one of God's strategies to expose and dismantle the false self and to recover the true self and its core desire to love, be loved, and move ever closer to the Source of love.[1] What's more, the untamed nature of relationships provides the frontier in which each of us must face the one thing we *can* control: the plank in our own eye.

Let's look at a visual symbol to provide a framework for closely examining both the problems and the possibilities of increasing health in relationship through this decade. I'm hoping that this symbol will serve as an invitation to take an honest inventory of your time, your money, and your emotional energy, that it will cause you to consider where you spend yourself and to whom you're giving your strength.

For our masculine soul to thrive, the foundation and priority of our lives must be intentional union with God. There is no substitute, shortcut, or alternative. The true self does not exist apart from union with God. As C. S. Lewis suggested, "Until you have given up yourself to him, you will not have a real self."[2] Union with God cannot happen apart from cultivating the care of your soul. As we covered in chapters 7 and 8, intimacy and union with God flow from arranging our lives around the habitat and habits of becoming a king. Though we're united with a limitless God, our personal reality does have limits. In the diagram, this is represented in the narrowing of each ascending tier of relationship: we simply have finite time, money, and soul capacity to give. And where and how we spend ourselves tells us much about what we believe and what kind of man we're committed to becoming.

Our Hidden Life with God

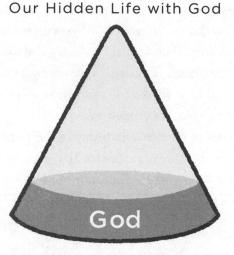

The foundation of the relational model for this decade is choosing to consistently and relentlessly cultivate the with-God life.

Years ago I sat across the table from a kingdom warrior who had become a father of the faith. At the age of seventy-five, he was making a pilgrimage from Australia to the United States to spend time with two of his mentors, Thomas Keating and Richard Rohr. I was a hard-charging and overachieving young man nearing thirty. I contacted him to ask if I could lean into his counsel. I showed up with an extensive list of questions, most of which we never got to. What I remember so vividly about the encounter was how my body immediately began to rest in his fatherly presence. In the atmosphere of his heart, I felt peace, I felt acceptance. I felt a deep sense of "all is well." And I remember these sacred words he shared: "In time, I am learning that my inward life must become greater than my outward life."[3]

His words and his presence were both disorienting and merciful. Disorienting because I was overwhelmed by the battles and demands on every side, and to primarily grow my inner life, at the time, seemed about as possible as walking on water. But deeper still, I could feel my Father's mercy. I knew this was bedrock truth for young men destined to become kings in our Father's kingdom.

Our hidden life with God is the central concern of our Father in heaven (Matt. 6:6); giving priority to an interactive relationship with God and his kingdom above everyone and everything else is the foundation of the narrow way (Matt. 6:33). As Schaeffer suggested, "Always there will be a battle, always we will be less than perfect, but if a place is too big and too active for our present spiritual condition, then it is too big."[4] Put simply, the process of becoming a king is a path by which our secret life can be steadily transformed from a place of shame into our place of greatest treasure.

We were born out of the heroic intimacy of the Trinity, a community of relational integrity that serves as a constant flowing river of life. As we considered in chapter 2, "Becoming a Son," our brother Jesus oriented his days around the superior reality of his oneness with the Father (John 10:30; 16:28). It is from this seat of intimacy that the heart of a true king is fueled.

Soul Care

Prioritizing soul care and arranging our days as apprentices are the primary means to receiving wholeheartedness and union with God. It was Oswald Chambers who said that "the lasting value of our public service for God is measured by the depth of our intimacy with him."[5] In other words, soul care is foundational to loving God and others effectively. In the wise words of Parker Palmer, soul care "is never a selfish act—it is simply good stewardship of the only gift I have, the gift I was put on earth to offer others. Any time we can listen to our true self and give the care it requires, we do it not only for ourselves, but for the many others whose lives we touch."[6] The habitat of good soil and the deepening roots of cultivated practices are intended to be an engine that makes it possible for our spiritual life to become first and foremost in our life.

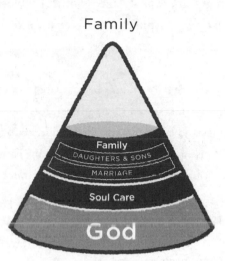

Family

Marriage

God assured us in Psalm 68:6 that both the lonely person and the lonely places within each soul are offered an invitation back into a loving family. Family is the first expression of the church. While for a single man this may not be a spouse, it is here where each of us must walk with God and ask him to reveal what he means by family in our story.

For the men among us who are husbands or intend to be, I think it's critical to take a moment and explore how, when we prioritize our inner life with God, we are able to give our hearts to loving our wives. Over time, we cannot become the man God intends us to be in other arenas outside of loving first and loving well in this covenant. Yet when I consider my marriage, what do I do with the failures I have accumulated and the confusion I have around what it actually looks like to give and receive love well? Here's the good news: this path we're on as men leads our masculine soul through the pain of brokenness in our marriages into the possibility of deep healing that we can substantially shift from self-protection to a sustained posture of mutual advocacy.

Marriage is intended to be the headwaters of the redemptive community of family in which all members can flourish and become who we are meant to be. But let's face it, there's nothing like marriage to both allure us and at the same time make us spontaneously combust with fear or anger at a moment's notice. In the middle years of marriage, youthful fantasies can give way to painful realities. Mike Mason spoke some of my favorite words on the disruptive power of marriage.

> A marriage, or a marriage partner, may be compared to a great tree growing right up through the center of one's living room. It is something that is just there, and it is huge, and everything has been built around it, and wherever one happens to be going—to the fridge, to bed, to the bathroom, or out the front door—the tree has to be taken into account. It cannot be gone through; it must respectfully be gone around. It is somehow bigger and stronger than oneself. True, it could be chopped down, but not without tearing the house apart. And certainly it is beautiful, unique, exotic; but also, let's face it, it is at times an enormous inconvenience.[7]

A decorated U.S. Special Forces warrior recently confessed to me, "I can handle any firefight and a three-hundred-man ambush, no problem. My role and objectives in war are clear. It is my life at home I can't handle—my marriage, my kids, my mortgage. I'm failing. I feel like I live in Afghanistan, and I'm deployed to my home in Texas."

Nothing will expose more of the unfinished places in us than our marriage. Marriage is the most difficult relationship in which to love well, because it is the one in which it is least possible to hide. Work and church typically provide buffers that enable us to pose for years without exposing our deep brokenness, but the day in, day out proximity of marriage eliminates all buffers. She's always there. You can't blow the whistle, throw a flag, stop the clock. It's real-time, live-ammo training for the masculine soul. She sees it all—or at least the results of it all.

It's not just us. Statistics tell us that counselors see more women in their midthirties than any other demographic. As experienced counselors point out, one reason for this is that often when a woman's children become the ages when she experienced her own childhood trauma, deep places in her soul are triggered. Much of the trauma that was shut off, managed, or dismissed out of self-protection and a need for survival begins to surface. Add to that the struggles of marriage and a woman's ache for intimate companionship, and the result is often a perfect storm in which the courageous women seek help.

As I've sat with dozens of sages who have given their lives to walking with God, I've unearthed a startling pattern. All these men—mature and heroic in their own right—fit, over time, into one of two groups. The first lands in the posture of "good enough" as far as what they have grown to expect in their marriages. While they deeply desire to rule as God's kings in his kingdom, they draw unseen lines in their marriages around relational minefields, choosing to engage only in the safe zone but not disrupt deeper layers of the false self in either their spouses or themselves. As a result, their marriages function more as static trade agreements than as unions growing and maturing in oneness. Whether this manifests in managing the finances or raising children, these no-fly zones point to underlying fissures of disunity. At the core of these marriages seems to be some deep agreement of formidable limits placed on what is available between husband and wife.

And then there is union. Oh, it is the rarest treasure I've witnessed on the earth, truly the pinnacle of human relationship. I have had the privilege of sitting with sages who have chosen unity over disunity. They have relinquished self-protection, self-salvation, and every external title, measurement, and outcome they were once committed to, in order to lay hold of the full portion of what is available between a man and a woman in relationship under heaven. The men and women in these marriages have fought for, invested in, and cultivated a lifestyle of increasing unity. And through coming again and again to the center of each other's heart and story, they have chosen to become increasingly aware of the impact they have on one another, particularly in their sin and brokenness but also in their joy and strength. Each husband has made a fierce commitment to contend with the plank in his own eye so he can become the kind of man who is able to tend with great care and patience to the speck in the eye of his bride. He has learned to lead with, "I'm sorry. I was wrong. Will you forgive me?" These couples have chosen to reflect the quality of relationship found in the Trinity alone; each spouse is so full of love that they are unwilling to merely be served by the other's submission. Instead each is intent on outloving, outgiving, outserving, outcherishing the other.

Cherie and I have witnessed that quality of union in the lives of a few, and we want it. Several years ago we were challenged by wise marriage mentors to begin our theology about marriage with God's design *before* the fall. These mentors invited us to meditate on Genesis 1 and 2 every day for three months in order to let God's design, God's desire, and God's intentions, expressed in the magnificent creation of Adam and Eve in relationship, find deep roots in us.

"Let *us* make mankind in *our* image, in *our* likeness, so that they may rule" (Gen. 1:26, emphasis added). Humanity was lovingly formed in the likeness of a heroic fellowship—Father, Son, and Holy Spirit. A mystery of one God who is also a holy community of persons, a unity of three being One. In Genesis 2, we are whisked directly into God's creative studio to witness his rendering of this holy mystery. God forms man from the dust of the earth, from organic compost. Then, in the most intimate and extraordinary act in all creative history, God "breathed into [Adam's] nostrils the breath of life, and the man became a living being" (Gen. 2:7). God's Spirit fills our mortal bodies with an inextinguishable life from his very own breath. He brings us to life with the intimacy of a kiss.[8]

Then he goes into this wildly mysterious and nearly preposterous story: Adam alone is not enough. Humanity is not yet complete and whole. Adam is the image of God, as a man, but not yet as a fellowship. So Adam falls asleep, a rib is drawn from his side, and woman is created, the "crown of creation."[9]

The very next sentence contains the secret Cherie and I missed for years: "Therefore," the text reads. In other words, "All that I have just shared was prologue for this next idea." *Okay, wild and creative Trinity, you have my attention.* "Therefore a man shall leave his father and his mother and hold fast [cleave] to his wife, and they shall become one flesh" (Gen. 2:24 ESV). A man and a woman become one. They are united.

The gospel of Matthew records Jesus' affirmation of this mystery of oneness in marriage. In an effort to test Jesus' fidelity to the teachings of Moses, a Pharisee asks Jesus to explain the grounds for divorce. Jesus subverts the trap entirely by rooting his response in God's original plan for marriage; he cuts to the heart by going back to God's design and intention.

> "Haven't you read," he replied, "that at the beginning the Creator 'made them male and female,' and said, 'For this reason a man will leave his father and mother and be united to his wife, and the two will become one flesh'? So they are no longer two, but one flesh. Therefore what God has joined together, let no one separate. . . . Moses permitted you to divorce your wives because your hearts were hard. But it was not this way from the beginning."
>
> —Matthew 19:4–8

For many years, Cherie and I had lost the plot of Love's original intention in marriage. We lived out a tag-team model, taking turns being on point, shuttling kids, making decisions out of efficiency, and yes, seeking God, but separately. We were missing the biggest point. Unity is the goal, not productivity. Not doing good things for God. Not making good decisions on behalf of our spouse.

Unity is the point.

Unity cultivates intimacy. And intimacy—in marriage with our partner and in union with our God—is the goal and the prize of this story. More intimacy is available than we had a vision for. Much, much more.

Now we are embracing a dream that our marriage could reflect more of the delighting, enduring union of the Trinity.

Prioritizing unity is deeply inconvenient. We've had to put the brakes on at many crossroads along this narrow path. We are punting on many decisions, off-loading commitments, slowing down. We are listening to each other's heart and pain like never before. We are coming to the center of how the other is feeling, seeing, and hoping, in order to be with each other in that place. We are seeking God together and on behalf of "we"—this holy union.

And the fruit is already ripening. Joy. Trust. Hope. Kindness. Unity. Strength. Cherie is becoming my sunrise, and the radiance of our healing relationship is casting a glow on every other relationship in my life. God willing, slowly, one day at a time, this "we," this union, will bring about something new in this world, something dreamed up by our God since before creation, some piece of his promise to a hurting world that "all shall be well and all manner of things shall be well."[10]

Outcomes are in God's hands. But we have a lifetime, and the mission never changes. No relationship holds more pain or possibility. Our time and our money and our calendar must speak of this. To become the kind of man over time whose life consistently communicates the message that his wife was cherished beyond all other relationships in his world, that she felt deeply known, deeply loved, and deeply fought for. This single conscious decision by day and by decade will unleash a power to bring all other aspects of becoming a king into deeper maturity and ultimately deeper joy.

> *Father, I want to choose the narrow path that leads to life. I stand in need with deep challenges in my marriage of which I simply don't know what to think or what to do. Jesus, I am asking for your life to infuse our marriage. I'm asking for you to give us your heart for each other. Holy Spirit, would you teach me how to love my wife? God, I'm asking for your grace to infuse me with a capacity to risk radically cherishing my wife and coming to the center of her heart and story, getting to know her more than I do, and choosing to be known by her more than I am. Would you shepherd me in this process as I take bigger risks? Would you help me increase my vulnerability with her? I agree with the full portion available for a man and a woman, two made one, under heaven. Expose my unbelief and shine light on where you are inviting us to go next in recovering everything you intend in our marriage.*

Parenting

A wise mentor told us once that if we ever are to consider evaluating how we are doing as parents, perhaps it is only safe—if safe at all—to even begin asking that question when our children are in their forties. With his words came such relief. There are land mines of disorientation in parenting because we long so deeply to love well, to make an impact for good, and to leave a valuable legacy. And yet Scripture is disruptively clear that to hitch our horses to the wagon of outcomes can have devastating implications. Nature is clear on the matter too; there are some dimensions of the human experience we cannot control. Every child has his or her own will. In a kingdom model of parenting, we are invited to relinquish the choices our children make as our report card and instead embrace something altogether contrary: *becoming the person we would like our children to be*. As Dan Allender has pointed out, the crux is that we become the parent we would like to be only through parenting.[11] It is process and not arrival, and always with live-ammo training.

Yet here we can take heart; we have a Father who will shepherd the process, promising to supply what we need in order to love and nourish our children so they can grow in wisdom and stature. Much of the time I blow it. Over this decade Cherie and I have diligently cultivated the practice of being present in our parenting.

Perhaps there is no season of parenting in which it's more challenging to be present and truly engaged than when the kids are young. And in general, there is no season that has more demands on the heart of a man and more temptations to miss the gold. I sit here today with pages and pages of counsel from old men regarding parenting. So many of them resound with the same plea: *"Be there."* The children are young only once. Work will always be there, but the kids grow up. And the deep bonds of love are formed in the early years.

- "I wish I'd fought for more vacations for my family."
- "I wish I'd been less distracted by work."
- "I wish I'd been present in the dailies."

The collective counsel of so many fathers can be summarized in two statements:

Quality time does not substitute for *quantity* of time.
and
Quantity of time does not substitute for *quality* time.

All parents live in this tension. I confess that sometimes my kids lose the battle for my time to things that in the end are far less important. I confess that sometimes I find myself there with my kids but distracted and not truly *there*. Loving our children well requires both quality time and quantity of time. How rare it is to find men who will consent to the process of becoming the kind of person who is no longer willing or interested in surrendering either quality time or quantity of time in the formative years.

The wake-up call for me came when Joshua was eight. He experienced some consistent spiritual warfare in the form of recurring night terrors. Through prayer, we uncovered the root of the problem: a strained relationship he had with a troubled friend. It took time and being present—in the middle of the night—to talk, hear his heart, engage, pray, walk him through the hard and holy long miles of a boy becoming a man. I lay in bed after that with tears, thanking God in this moment that *I was there*, not on yet another trip, not on sleep meds, not taken out by alcohol or exhaustion or passivity. Sadly, it is not something I could always say. But in this moment I was there, and it shaped me for the years to follow. It was a wake-up call and an affirmation. No matter how much time we give them, how much we are around, if our hearts are not healed and free, if we are not doing the work to become the kind of person we want them to become, we won't really be *there*. We will be limp and distracted, or overbearing and driven by the need for our kids to answer our own soul's question. And simply put, our kids won't receive what they need from God in us. Choosing again and again to say no to other things so we can consistently be there with our kids—physically, emotionally, and soulfully— disrupts the self-life and surfaces the many entanglements and unfinished places in our masculine soul. As wise sages have shown and as experience has proven true, the most sacred moments of parenting—God moving for us and for the formation of our children—take place far more often in these simple, "ordinary" moments. To be there, in quantity, is to unhinge the pressure and expectation from the special moments and milestones and give God an infinite canvas on which to form both ourselves and our children.

I recently sat with a man as he shared the story of his father's funeral. His dad was a well-known and esteemed man of great influence. Story after story was shared of how his father had impacted lives. After the recounting of the stories, he said with profound sincerity, "I sure would have liked to know that man. That was not my father. My father was never home."

Oh, brothers, let it not be our story. The window is so very short, and it will form the foundation, God willing, of decades of maturing connection ahead. One mentor said it with wisdom and precision: "The days are long, but the years are short." Even in the time I've invested in writing this book, I have watched as my kids have transformed from children to teenagers. The years are short.

And yet, while the years are short, they are also very impressionable. Belief is contagious. That's why, to steward our responsibility as parents, we must become conscious of our true beliefs, the ones exposed by our actions, habits, and body language more than by our creeds. We must turn inward and do some honest inventory. What do you really believe about God? About the nature of life and reality? What is the gospel you are modeling for your kids? If it's a religious appendage to a rather secular life, it will not capture their hearts.

Our hearts were born out of a story and are made to find meaning in a story larger than our own. Because of this, the human heart gravitates toward the biggest, best story we can find. If the gospel we are offering our children isn't all that big, bold, and beautiful, teeming with life and joy, their hearts will stay on pilgrimage to find a better story or, worse, settle for whichever small story provides them the most life at the time. This is essential for us to give honest consideration.

We can offer only who we have become; we do not provide what we do not possess. To choose the ancient path of becoming a king and to consent to God's process of restoration within us is the most sure path toward seeing our children become who they were meant to be.

The covenant relationships entrusted to our care under heaven are first and forever our wives and our children. I believe it's these relationships that will form the most central and heroic stories of our lives at the campfires of the kingdom. And it is through these few relationships, like none other, that our souls are intended to be restored and strengthened and made whole and holy on our quest to become the kings of God's kingdom.

God, what is in the way of this? What will it cost me that I am not willing to pay? What's beneath the places or patterns in my lack of either quantity of time or quality time in regard to my wholehearted attentiveness to my children? I want to become wholehearted and united with you more and more in the hopes that the children and young ones around me will be attracted to your life growing within me and fueling my life with courage, love, and vulnerability that surpasses understanding. Guide me in what is next for us here.

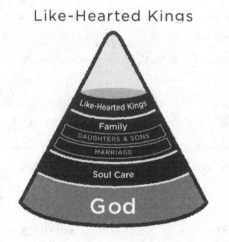

I didn't have time. The work on my desk wasn't done. The kids needed help with homework, and I had hours of moving furniture ahead because we were midstream in getting that new carpet. We'd negotiated a great price, but it cost me moving all the furniture in my house—twice. Still, I wouldn't give up the peace pipe. Bestowed on me by my hunting partner, Brian, who knows my heart and what I love, the pipe is fashioned from hand-cut pipe stone he chiseled himself, with a tiger maple stem he turned on his lathe. We pass the peace pipe in the great tradition of the first native warriors of our land. We smoke great tobacco, and as the smoke rises, we pore over maps and stories of campfires gone by, and we dream of our next adventure. We're practicing dreaming—everything from an Alaskan bowhunt for Yukon moose to our anticipation of introducing my son into our adventure this year for his very first big-game hunt. It was an hour I didn't have for beers and smoke and laughter, but an hour I couldn't live without. We both have young kids and amazing wives who had given more than their share today, who could have deeply benefited from more of us. Add to that a list of not-yet-done on the desk at work. But we fought for that hour as if it were the most important thing on earth. And it changed something. My soul was fed. It gave me hope and longing. It gave me a place to gripe and dream and not be alone in it all. It strengthened my soul. And it took years—*years*—to cultivate a few allies (it will ever only be a few) who want the very same things my soul longs for.

It took over a decade for me. I remember the conversation as if it were yesterday. It was a summer Sunday morning. Joshua was a year old, and Cherie and I were sitting on our green couch during his morning nap, reflecting on some of the pain I was feeling in the crucible of life. Very gently, Cherie said, "Morgan, you don't seem to have any peers. You have older men from whom you seek out advice and relationship, and younger men you offer to, but you really don't seem to spend time with other men your age. And can I make an observation? You've lost your smile. And I think those two things are connected."

Cherie was right. It was a profoundly painful admission. Yet at the same time, it was another risky and orchestrated invitation back along the narrow road and the ancient path that leads to life. I had gotten very serious in this battle for the hearts of others. Life's pressures were mounting, and I felt the pull of my false self to secure love by coming through for people. It was killing me. That slow death began by pushing out peer relationships. The peer circle we did have at the time included mostly single men and women, and we found ourselves awkwardly out of place—the only ones holding a crying baby at the gathering or scrambling for childcare beforehand. But peer relationships are intended to be oxygen for our masculine soul. It was Dan Allender's advice to me that gave me a framework for what I was most deeply longing for: "Find like-hearted kings living in the same direction. Sign treaties. When they are at war, you are at war."

He named what I'd been searching for all my days. It whispered through the way I would rally boys for epic childhood adventures like capture the flag under a moonlit summer sky. It echoed through my joining a fraternity, hoping to lock arms with a few to share some heroic adventure. But what I realized I was searching for all along was brotherhood that is only available in and through God's kingdom. To live the adventure and fight a battle side by side with a small band of heroic brothers. I wanted a few who were sold out. I needed like-hearted kings living in the same direction. I needed to sign treaties. And with a few, for a few, go to war.

As many miles as I'd traveled in various friendships, this level of soul-to-soul brotherhood with like-hearted kings was all frontier. I've discovered over years that it is less about finding the right men to sign treaties with than it is about becoming the kind of person with whom someone would *want* to sign a treaty. Slowly, I've become and am becoming that kind of man. Though it has taken years and is still a daily task of heroic love, I have cultivated several brothers-in-arms who have invested the same heart-filled miles. And it has made all the difference.

Men who want what I want and have to fight through the same crap to get it. Men fiercely committed to God. Men sold out to becoming more than they find themselves to be today. Men committed to becoming kings to whom God can entrust his kingdom. Men who won't fold their cards on marriage or throw their kids under the bus by working overtime to build another man's kingdom or to feed the mortgage beast or to keep pace with a culture of things. Men who pray for me every day, who know me and are known by me. Men who have access to my soul. Men who want joy and a heroic adventure, together.

It's messy. We live in a world at war. And we go to war with what we have and who we find ourselves with. Let's face it, we all look a bit like members of Wallace's army at the Battle of Stirling Bridge—brandishing a pitchfork for a weapon, holding the side of a wooden crate for a shield, and sporting a side ponytail and brutal neckbeard. But the Father often sneaks into our lives with what we need, not what we want. And when a small band of brothers is willing to put God at the center of their hearts, their relationships, their families, and their kingdom mission, it works, and it'll change the world. Most important, it'll change *your* world.[12]

In the film *Gladiator*, Maximus has become a slave and finds himself leading a sordid band of underarmed, malnourished prisoners against seemingly insurmountable odds, as they are tasked with entertaining onlookers in the Colosseum. As they ready for what should be an inevitable slaughter, he gathers his men in a tight formation. He instructs them to stand together as one man, and then he says to his men, "Whatever comes out of these gates, we have a better chance of surviving if we stick together." The fury is unleashed. Yet it appears heaven is on their side, and through cunning and courage Maximus rallies a tired and beaten-down group of slaves to draw in tight formation and unite together against evil. Heavily armed soldiers on horse-drawn chariots cascade fury, but Maximus refuses to relent. "As one!" Maximus calls out in the next volley hurled against them, and the men lock shields as one man. Together they advance, taking out evil. Through trial, fire, and some very real casualties, they come out more united and achieve victory against incalculable odds.

This decade, this path toward becoming a king, is a crucible intended to integrate our masculine soul and deepen our union with the Father on every level. God is training us for our increasing role, not only in this world but also in the coming kingdom. It was his design, desire, and intention that we forsake the safety of independence and self-sufficiency and risk giving our lives over to a shared life with a company of men. God is more invested than you are in cultivating that kind of brotherhood with like-hearted kings, kings who will sign treaties with you, and when they are at war, you are at war. One way to access a vision for the importance of peers is to ask yourself this question: *Who will carry my casket?*

I've had the honor of being a groomsman in quite a few weddings, offering an outward expression of the unspoken promise to walk alongside that man and that marriage into the unknown landscape ahead. Being a groomsman says, "I will." Carrying a casket is different. Carrying a casket says, "I did."

Solomon said a man is worse off than a stillborn child if he does not receive a proper burial (Eccl. 6:3). I can imagine few things more central to a proper burial than who will carry my casket. It will only be a few. Ask God. Speak their names. Offer your sword and your strength, with great discretion and sincere devotion, whatever the cost. (In the midst of writing this, I received a Mayday call from one of these men. Had to drop everything and go on a rescue mission. Treaties aren't cheap or convenient. But it's some of the best currency I spend.) The reward will last forever. Recovering the ancient path to becoming a king requires cultivating real and life-giving relationship with the few. And the first step is to become the kind of friend you long to have.

Mentors

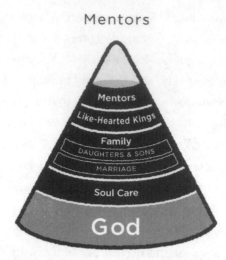

In every great story, the hero or heroine must turn to someone older or wiser for the answer to some riddle. Dorothy seeks the Wizard, Frodo turns to Gandalf, Neo has Morpheus, Timothy leans into Paul, and Luke Skywalker must find his way through the swamp to sit at the feet of Master Yoda. The mind is not sufficient for what the Bible means by knowing the truth. It's only when truth reaches down deep into the heart that it begins to set us free, just as a key must fully penetrate a lock to open it, or rainfall must saturate the earth down to the roots in order for your garden to grow. We were born into a culture that celebrates self-expression over Wisdom's long view of self-restraint.[13] To listen, to observe, to lean into the counsel of mentors is to train the masculine soul in recovering the ancient path. It is to repent of self-sufficiency.

> Counseling doesn't just flow to us directly from Christ, *only* from him; it flows through his people as well. We need others—and need them deeply. Yes, the Spirit was sent to be our Counselor. Yes, Jesus speaks to us personally. But often he works through another human being. The fact is, we are usually too close to our lives to see what's going on. Because it's *our* story we're trying to understand, we sometimes don't know what's true or false, what's real or imagined. We can't see the forest for the trees. It often takes the eyes of someone to whom we can tell our story, bare our soul. The more dire our straits, the more difficult it can be to hear directly from God.[14]

It was September 1998. I'll never forget the first time I experienced John Eldredge leading our fellowship of eager young hearts into the depth of God's larger story. It revolutionized my heart as a man. Next thing I knew, I was in his office. "I'm in. Where do I sign up? What do I do next to live in this gospel?" I couldn't have put it into words at the time, but what I was asking for was discipleship, real life-on-life kingdom apprenticeship as a young warrior in God's kingdom.

In reply, he offered this: "Real discipleship doesn't happen with programs or formulas. It is shaped by the questions. What are your questions?" I had no response. I had yet to do the soul work to identify and allow God to draw out the questions deep within my masculine soul. What began that day was the start of more than two decades of excavating the questions of the masculine soul and bringing them to the sages in my life, so they could walk with me deeper and deeper into my initiation. Henri Nouwen said, "Answers before questions do harm to the soul." In this age of gross overload of content, answers are abundant. But questions are rare.

Have you noticed how often Jesus teaches his apprentices with questions? He must be onto something. What are your questions, and who are you asking? We are invited to follow the ancient path—the tried and true path. One of the central places God has marked out for us to recover the ancient path that leads us back to life is by leaning into the few in the generation before us who have recovered the path afresh themselves. When the student is ready, the teacher appears. When the son is ready, the father appears. To become student and son, to consent to the ancient path, will surely shift your orientation, and you will begin to recognize the kind of people with whom your questions are safe. But it starts with your questions. And soulful questions are birthed only in a person who has consented to a growth mind-set over a fixed mind-set and has consented to this essential work in recovering the ancient path of becoming a king.

Everything Else in Life

If we are to live out the reality of our God-given design, with relational integrity at the center of our lifestyle, it will become evident that very little is left at the end of our finite (natural) resources. This is a hard, holy, and lifesaving pill to swallow if we so choose. Many a good man has been led like a lamb to the slaughter by a gross misinterpretation of Paul's statement about becoming all things to all people (1 Cor. 9:22). It is these natural soul constraints that align our eternal life increasingly with God's intention for our lives, by day and decade. As a gifted and unfinished man, you too will quickly and likely find that your kingdom has come to exceed your capacity to rule over it with wholehearted integrity. Like a transplanted tree that survives (if at all) by being propped up until the root base can grow and carry the weight of the canopy, so go too many men's kingdoms. In the context of a loving Father who leads us as students and sons, there will never be a better opportunity to consent to him for the "soul sizing" of your kingdom. Slowly, over time, doing the hard and holy work of pruning—beginning with motives—so that your external kingdom can align with the internal realities. What can you handle with wholeheartedness and integrity? I've found in my own life that it often takes a courageous set of shears—better yet, a chainsaw—to do the holy work of pruning and soul sizing so your kingdom can reflect with integrity where you truly are in your masculine journey, from the inside out. The invitation of the Father as he is cultivating kings is to prune and prune and prune. God is profoundly investing in the expansion of his kingdom. It is his intention, and it is his work. Our task is the holy pursuit of pruning and becoming.

In Summary

Let's circle back to the image of the Becoming a King relational triangle. Notice that the finite resources available and appointed become fewer and fewer as we engage further beyond the core foundation of our masculine soul in its growing union with God. There are many important, even critical, relationships not represented in this diagram. It's meant to be more portrait than photograph, more metaphor than prescription. A set of values and guidelines, not rules and dogmatism. Above all else, we must walk with God and partner with his uniquely wild path for the restoration of our masculine soul on our journey to becoming a king. The Father invites us to be responsive rather than live lives that are primarily reactive, shaped and driven by external demands. He wants us to respond to his leadership, his initiative, his way as it weaves a redemptive and restorative tapestry through every relationship in our lives. It's revolutionary. And it will save your soul.

Being shaped from the outside in rather than the inside out, our lives can quickly take on the inversion of this relational model. How often most of our energy is spent in our work and in trying to satisfy everything demanded of us. Armed with a masculine heart that has not received validation from God and is seeking to have its question answered through other people and things. Our God-intended desire and capacity to build continue to be motivated by the self life rather than be united with God and employed in the service of love on behalf of those entrusted to our care. Instead God is inviting us to create a paradigm that is ordered according to not only that which is good for God in our lives but toward the very initiatives that are intended to bring us deep and lasting life, over time. A well-ordered soul, in time and over time, will lead to a well-ordered kingdom.

The process of consenting to becoming a king could be more appropriately named the hidden years. When I'm honest with myself about my own soul and when I have invested most of me into who and what matters most to God, the sober truth becomes apparent. There's not much of the true *me* left to give to other people and things. *And that's okay.* Friends, I give you *permission.* Your Father extends his *permission* and his blessing over you. Remember Cherie's words at the beginning of this chapter: nothing more is required of us than that which we can do in union with God. Our limitations are not to be resented. In the process of becoming a king, they become a faithful friend sent by God himself. God is perfectly capable of saving the world he created. He is far more invested in and intent on your becoming than you may have been led to believe.

The Inconvenient Truth

Before we can get to cultivating our yes to our primary relationships, we have to tackle an inconvenient and offensive prerequisite: cultivating our no. We have to be able to say no to the pull to make these the building years, in order to have the energy and resources to consent instead to the season of the hidden years.

Only our *no* to many temptations and pulls will enable us to say yes to what matters most. It is within this decade the world calls the building years that most men wreak havoc in their own lives. They are filled with desires, many from God himself. Yet out of youthful enthusiasm and an unanswered question, men make the fatal mistake of setting out to fulfill those desires, never asking the second question: *Father, when would you have me fulfill that?* We fight bravely and die quickly, because we have not yet become the wholehearted and integrated man who can handle the weight of the call. And we come to painful conclusions about ourselves, even questioning our desires. Pastors walk away from the calling to lead God's people and end up in some obscure role far from their dreams. Entrepreneurs walk away from their dreams and settle for the safety of a cubicle and a paycheck. The desire was from God, but it was meant to be first and foremost our fuel. Fuel to become, to take a journey through wilderness of soul, through our own story, and to come to know God and our own heart and learn how to live the interactive life with God in his kingdom. And then from *that* place of a heart restored and initiated we become the kind of man, the kind of king, who can fulfill that God-given desire.

The narrow way is filled with story after story of God unearthing a man's desire—and then hiding him. David was told he'd be king, then spent the next fourteen years hiding out in caves with a bunch of misfits. Joseph was told he'd be elevated to a place above all his brothers, then was thrown into a pit by those brothers and sold into slavery. It was many years and much suffering before he was ready, in his soul as a man, to lead all those God had entrusted to his care.

Again, the ascent of the masculine soul is powered by this radical idea: our inward life is intended to become greater than our outward life. In God's humor and wildness, he seems to often use this decade that puts more external demands on our lives to invite us deeper into this internal process. Rather than taking the bait to build the kingdoms of uninitiated kings or follow my own drive to build, I must pause, take inventory, and ask, *Who do I want to become?*

One sage put it this way: "Look at most men in their forties, fifties, and sixties. Ask yourself this question: What took them out?"

What a painful exercise it was. I looked around and saw many men—good men—who started out at the same juncture I was at. They wanted great things. Yet so many were taken out. And they'd have given anything to get back what had been lost, stolen, or surrendered.

How are we to avoid that story line and recover and restore the places where it has already become a reality? The sages had my attention. "These years, you should have very little available beyond your family." They were such hard words to hear at the time. So many opportunities were coming to me; older men were pulling me into leadership roles that felt affirming—"Lead this group," "Lead this initiative," "Come on this rescue mission with us." But the voice of the few brave souls along the narrow path were offering something very different.

Jesus' warning on this is clear. It is so important for our souls to know, he addressed it explicitly: "You will always have the poor among you" (John 12:8). This doesn't mean "Don't help the poor." The point is that it's an unwinnable strategy to be ruled by the needs of others. There will always be another need asking for your time, your money, your energy. To live in reaction to those needs because of an unanswered question in your soul will lead to exhaustion. It is in the vulnerability of weariness that the Enemy wears us down and makes us a target. He prowls like a lion. I've had the privilege to watch lions hunt. They are slow and methodical, watching for the weak and vulnerable, patiently waiting for the perfect opportunity. And their strikes are effective and deadly.

It doesn't have to be your story. In this painful place of too much, we are forced to start making tough choices. It is here where we are invited by a loving Father to begin to cultivate our yes to the right things and the core things, out of true motives, so that we can, with courage and increasing confidence, say no to the many other good things not meant to be ours. If you want to be apprenticed in kingdom living, if you want to become what God meant when he meant you, if you want to become a wholehearted king, the only way you can do it is to say no, in love, to most people and most possibilities.

No, I can't lead that project, that mission.
No, I won't take that promotion, because it costs me too much of what
matters most.

No, I won't rush.

No, I won't upgrade my house, my car.

No, I won't take on that debt.

No, I won't work late tonight.

No, I won't let your fifteen years of bad choices be my crisis today.

I'm choosing some soul care so that I have something worth offering. More important, I'm choosing the union with God that can provide me discernment about how to love well and love deeply.

I'm choosing to be present to those entrusted to my care.

I'm choosing to invest my time in becoming the most wholehearted and true version of me to bring to the world.

I would love to be able to, but I can't.[15]

Some of the earliest sages in the Christian faith called it benevolent detachment.[16] It's the heroic work of loving well and deeply, fully engaged in the present moment, and then, with just as much courage, simply letting it go and entrusting it to God's care. It is holy defiance against the self-sufficient life. Humility can have its way and be formed in us, and we can grow in our ability to trust God to do all he has said he will do. No one models it better than Jesus. His capacity to disappoint people was profound and pervasive. A simple study of the Gospels gives ample illustrations. In the words of Dallas Willard, if you follow Jesus long enough, he will surely disappoint you.[17]

One of the great tragedies of the spirit of the age is this gospel of infinite possibility. Hear the paradox: yes, God is infinite in his capacity to bring forth his kingdom on earth as it is in heaven, yet he has created a world with a great number of limitations. We have limitations as well. They are meant for our good, to inform, guide, teach. This season in the masculine journey, more than any other, confronts us with the painful reality of our limitations. Limitations are scoffed at by a culture steeped in the idea that you can be anything and anyone you want to be. But our limitations help us live honest, wholehearted lives. They validate that unique expression of God in us that is constantly assaulted by false comparison. We crash into what feels like invisible walls and are brought face-to-face with our limitations. They're actually God's gift to help narrow the focus of our lives. Embracing what they are telling us helps us zero in on the unique glory of God we are intended to bring. They will teach us if we let them.

I am intense. I am deeply introverted. I love engaging people and diving into their stories and watching and working with God to see their restoration and freedom realized. But in order to do that, I require much solitude. Nothing fills my heart and soul like wilderness; being alone with God in wilderness is a regular requirement, not just to thrive but to function. I'm woefully limited. But I'm learning to see it as one of God's greatest and kindest teachers. Begin with your emotional energy. Move to your budget, then your calendar. In the little that is left, this precious sacred trust, it would do you well to ask the Father how it should be spent.

In time, you'll find what Frederick Buechner discovered of vocation: it's the place where your deep gladness and the world's deep hunger meet.[18] You will find that place only by becoming the person who can inhabit it, wholehearted, daring, strong, and true. And in time, you will find such an intimacy with God and an integrity in the relationships closest to you that the nagging of *What do I do with my life?* will ease, and you'll find satisfaction in a day well lived. You will find that the heartbeat of your life will move from scarcity to overflow. The abundance from which Jesus led and served will be yours (John 1:16).

Father, I receive your blessing of permission.

Men, you have his permission.

Men, *you* have his *permission.*

Permission to let it be okay that time, energy, and resources are finite.

Permission to embrace the hidden years.

Permission to embrace limitations as kind and instructive guides.

Permission to know God is up to deep, transforming work well below the waterline that, in time, will reap huge rewards.

Permission to be young in the places that have yet to be initiated and the places being trained to rule.

Permission to put first things first.

Permission to disappoint those who are not God's mission or intention for you in this day or in this decade.

I bless your masculine soul with permission. You are on time. This is on time.

Guide me, Father, so the things that matter most to you are never at the mercy of the things that matter least.

10

BECOMING A KING

It is not what a man does that is of final
importance, but what he is in what he does. The
atmosphere produced by a man, much more
than his activities, has the lasting influence.
—Oswald Chambers

Travel with me for a moment back to the narrow dirt roads of a first-century Roman military outpost. Imagine hand-sewn animal hide military tents, their interiors illuminated by the flickering glow of oil lamps, the fur-covered tent flaps barely holding at bay the chill of the evening wind. Inside this tent is the captain of a division of about eighty Roman soldiers, a centurion. Laying his sword and shield aside, the centurion is quietly kneeling next to one of his men, who is clearly in deep distress. Let's pick up here with Matthew's account of the story.

> When Jesus had entered Capernaum, a centurion came to him, asking for
> help. "Lord," he said, "my servant lies at home paralyzed, suffering terribly."
> Jesus said to him, "Shall I come and heal him?"
> The centurion replied, "Lord, I do not deserve to have you come under

my roof. But just say the word, and my servant will be healed. For I myself am a man under authority, with soldiers under me. I tell this one, 'Go,' and he goes; and that one, 'Come,' and he comes. I say to my servant, 'Do this,' and he does it."

When Jesus heard this, he was amazed and said to those following him, "Truly I tell you, I have not found anyone in Israel with such great faith. I say to you that many will come from the east and the west, and will take their places at the feast with Abraham, Isaac and Jacob in the kingdom of heaven. But the subjects of the kingdom will be thrown outside, into the darkness, where there will be weeping and gnashing of teeth."

Then Jesus said to the centurion, "Go! Let it be done just as you believed it would." And his servant was healed at that moment.

—Matthew 8:5–13

Though a Gentile, this Roman centurion knew of one who had the power to heal his servant. Jesus' reputation as a powerful healer had continued to spread in the region of Galilee and Syria (Matt. 8:4). In fact, the centurion had heard Jesus teach on several occasions, and he recalled that Jesus had recently gathered with a multitude of his disciples on a hillside above Capernaum. Gazing upon the rigid body of his servant, the centurion determined to find Jesus; he would risk seeking out the Jewish rabbi and asking him to heal this man under his care.

After Jesus entered Capernaum, the centurion found him. "My servant lies at home paralyzed, suffering terribly."

Instead of responding with cultural spite, Jesus gazed into the eyes of this Gentile Roman soldier. The external identities of Jewish man and Gentile soldier were eclipsed by the superior reality of their identities in God's kingdom. It was the King of kings gazing into the eyes of another king, in unity of soul and purpose under heaven. Jesus listened with absolute focus. Maintaining eye contact, he asked, "Shall I come and heal him?"

Notice the steadfastness of the centurion. He was neither confused nor unsteady, nor did he frantically provide Jesus with directions to the tent where his servant lay suffering. No. He had become the kind of man who was well acquainted in his soul with Jesus' authority and the way in which his kingdom worked. With strength and conviction, the Roman captain matched Jesus' gaze. Soul to soul. Brother to brother. King to king. In intimate heart knowledge, these two men united over the restoration of another. The centurion responded, "Master, just say the word, and my servant will be healed. For I myself am a man under authority, with soldiers under me. I tell this one, 'Go,' and he goes; and that one, 'Come,' and he comes. I say to my servant, 'Do this,' and he does it."

"When Jesus heard this, he was amazed" (Matt. 8:10).

That's it. Period. In this very text is hidden some treasure that causes the heart of God to be astonished.

The Greek word conveying Jesus' response is *thaumazo*, meaning "to marvel, have in admiration, to wonder." This is the only instance recorded in Scripture when Jesus marveled at the faith of a man—and it is a Gentile, no less. What was it that caused Jesus to be amazed, astonished, to marvel at this man? What was it that Jesus saw inside the soul of this man that evoked such an unprecedented response from the King of kings?

Jesus, a Man Under Authority

As we contemplate the substance of the centurion's faith (Heb. 11:1), what stands out is his recognition of and active reliance upon the reality of *authority*. This Roman soldier grasped what those in Israel, who were "supposed to know all about God and how he works" (Matt. 8:10 MSG), had missed: Jesus had supreme authority over all of reality, seen and unseen (Col. 1:16–20). The Gentile captain had become the kind of man who understood and walked in accordance with the nature of authority. He knew what it was like to have servants under him who followed his commands. He knew as well what it was like to have authority over him and to submit to leadership over his life. The centurion was familiar with the nature of authority, and he recognized Jesus as the One who has supreme authority over all things.

This faith-filled Roman centurion embodies this central treasure of the restored masculine soul: heroic strength in conscious submission to a greater authority. This submission is the Rosetta Stone of the masculine journey. The treasure of the kingdom is a man who is fully yielded to Jesus' authority. A man who has given full consent for his King to lead him. A man who has crucified self-sufficiency in exchange for a reliance upon Trinitarian fellowship that empowers him to act in a manner that conforms to the will of God and makes a way for the impossible to become possible.

The Western worldview has done great harm to our understanding of authority. We live in a culture that deeply values self-sufficiency and is steeped in self-determination. Our culture cherishes the icon of the self-made man, and we spend most of our energy building, protecting, and preserving our personal kingdoms. Most of us have come to resent being under authority, because our experiences have confirmed the message that being under authority causes harm and constricts our liberty. Yet the kingdom of God is fundamentally different from the fallen kingdoms of this world. The kingdom of God prizes our willful consent to make the goodness, truth, and beauty of the true authority for which we were made under the care of God to be our ultimate refuge and seat of inextinguishable strength.

The thought that Jesus was not an independent man might be a new one. But the Scriptures are clear that the power and provision of his life flowed from union with his Father. He was dependent, not self-sufficient. Take Jesus' words as recorded in the gospel of John: "I'm telling you this straight. The Son can't independently do a thing, only what he sees the Father doing. What the Father does, the Son does. The Father loves the Son and includes him in everything he is doing" (John 5:19 MSG). The Father and his Son are inseparable in action. Jesus wholeheartedly consents to his Father's leadership over his life. And *from that place*, the reign of his Father flows into the lives of ordinary humans, allowing for the impossible to be made possible under Jesus' leadership and care. Consent to and dependence upon his Father's authority over all things is what Jesus knew. Intimate knowing is what he operated from. He knew he was a *son*; his identity was rooted in sonship.

Jesus knew he was an *apprentice* and had grown over decades in wisdom and stature and in favor with God and man; he knew he was a *warrior*, bearing the image of his Father, who would prevail against evil. He knew he came from heaven and was returning to heaven, and so he could serve from the lowest seat with a kingly heart. It is from this consent to authority that Jesus' power as a king flowed in strength, courage, and love. Jesus' earthly life came to its apex on the cross, where he voluntarily endured the weight of fallen humanity. When faced with the imminence of suffering and death, Jesus said, "Father, if you are willing, take this cup from me; yet not my will, but yours be done" (Luke 22:42).

The Stories We Love

It is amazing how often this theme of a hero voluntarily sacrificing his life for the sake of others is brought forth in the stories we love.

Let's revisit the story of Maximus in *Gladiator.* The general who became a slave. A slave who became a gladiator. And a gladiator who unseated an evil leader from the throne. Remember the words of Maximus as he owns his true identity and stands face-to-face with evil.

My name is Maximus Decimus Meridius,
commander of the armies of the North,
general of the Felix Legions,
loyal servant to the true emperor, Marcus Aurelius.[1]

Here's the piece of the story critical for us to grasp: Maximus was not an autonomous man. When, at the climax of the story, he proclaims to his enemy his true identity, he describes himself as the loyal servant to the true emperor. Maximus, like Jesus, was a man with great authority. But he was also a man *under* authority. Maximus was a man who understood authority and how it works. Like the centurion, he had faith that would astonish the heart of God. It was the secret weapon to his powerful life.

The story of Maximus shows evidence of the kingdom thread woven through the great narratives given to us to help orient our hearts. Think with me for a moment about heroes in the stories that you love. Luke Skywalker was a Jedi Knight being trained by Master Yoda. Sergeant Mitchel served under the command of General Eisenhower. Frodo was under the guidance and faithful care of Gandalf. The legendary figures change, yet all of their stories carry the power of one common narrative: they all find themselves filling heroic roles by consenting to bring their strength under care and connection to one who is greater still.

This crux in the masculine journey surfaces these central questions: Who is truly at the helm of your ship, and who is in command of your kingdom? What parts of you have been consecrated and given fully over to the care and connection of the King of kings?

The ability for us to live a powerful life and to become a wholehearted king in God's kingdom is directly proportional to the consent we give God to have active and supreme authority over our lives. This is the crux of the heart of a king. Understanding and living in alignment with kingdom authority is the secret place where the soul of man thrives and the world is made right. And it is the secret weapon in recovering the path to becoming a king.

The degree to which we live in consent to God—literally where he has been given say over the moment-by-moment reality of our lives, where we have consented to God's authority to have the final say over what is good and beautiful and true—is the degree to which we will become the kind of man to whom he can entrust his kingdom. Our willing alignment with kingdom authority gives Jesus permission and access to break the limits we have placed on who he can be, what he can do, and how he can do it in our lives. Consent to Jesus' authority enables us to not just survive the unknown but flourish in it. In submission, we receive the fortitude to endure the risk and peril of living by the day and measuring by the decade on the frontier of the masculine journey. Jesus is inviting us to be intimate allies and step into our inheritance as kings in his kingdom. A consecrated life is the one and only place that allows the culture and atmosphere of the world to be eclipsed by the culture and atmosphere of the kingdom of God. We must allow our soul to be sustained by the blessing of living under and from the authority of the King of kings.

Harnessed Strength

Where have you come from, and where are you going?

These are two fundamental questions of the human experience, two questions the Son of God also answered in his fully human life. And his answers were the foundation from which he lived out his vocation as the true King. In the company of his closest companions, on the night before he was crucified, Jesus demonstrated holy kingship. He had traveled countless miles over the previous three years with this wild crew. They had experienced triumph and tragedy together and had ignited a revolution in the human heart and in the power structure of the cosmos. I can only imagine the laughter, banter, intimacy, and joy they experienced together—the camaraderie that, throughout human experience, is the treasure of men who have fought and bled together for a purpose greater than themselves. It was in this intimate context that Jesus did the unthinkable. He stooped down, lowering himself, and took into his hands the dirty feet of his friends.

> Jesus knew that the Father had put all things under his power, and that he had come from God and was returning to God; so he got up from the meal, took off his outer clothing, and wrapped a towel around his waist. After that, he poured water into a basin and began to wash his disciples' feet, drying them with the towel that was wrapped around him.
>
> —John 13:3–5

It's difficult, from our cultural perspective, to grasp how humiliating it would have been for any Jew to assume the position of a servant in this way. In fact, as we can see from the strength of Peter's response, to see Jesus humiliate himself in this way was unacceptably offensive. Aghast, Peter said, "No, . . . you shall never wash my feet" (John 13:8). But Jesus was relentless in modeling love in action; he was showing what it looks like to be a king in God's kingdom. Jesus lived out of a deep knowing that he had *come from the Father and was returning to the Father.*

You see, if we are to model our lives after the King of kings, it is critical to understand the heart of Jesus in this story.

He knew *who* he was.
He knew *whose* he was.
He knew where he had *come from*.
And he knew where he *was going*.

"I came from the Father and entered the world; now I am leaving the world and going back to the Father" (John 16:28). Jesus' masculine need for validation and identity was securely met in the heart of his Father. His selfless offering flowed from a rootedness in ultimate reality. From this place, Jesus lived heroically with a harnessed strength beyond anything this world has ever seen. From this security, he could love freely, boldly, without any concern over outcomes. He was utterly yielded to the Father. His strength was harnessed under the rule and reign of God. This humility allowed him to thrive as a king and embody a gospel that liberated him from the limitations of his own will and from the tyranny of unmet desire. It is from this place that Jesus could rule with the heart of a servant and serve with the heart of a king.[2]

Jesus' humility makes a way for us to become good and true kings in his image. But it's important for us to understand this, especially in light of how our religion and culture have often identified humility with passivity or acquiescence: *kingdom humility is harnessed strength, not passivity or absence of strength*.

The Hebrew word often translated into the English word *humility* is *anah*. As scholars have explained, it is a term used to communicate the reality of a wild stallion being brought under reign. It is completely different from passivity. A horse is a powerful being, but until it is harnessed and brought under reign by the love and care of a master, its strength is of little use. Such is true of the masculine soul.

God has set within us an indescribable power, yet that power can be harnessed for good only when it is brought ever-increasingly under his rule and care. With that strength, under the rule of our King, we can become trustworthy kings under whose strength people and portions of creation entrusted to our care will indeed flourish.

What's Right with the World?

In the mid-twentieth century, the *Times* in London ran an essay contest, inviting highly respected thinkers and leaders to respond to the question, "What's wrong with the world?"

G. K. Chesterton offered this as his full response:

> Dear Sirs,
>   I am.
>
>   Sincerely yours,
>   G. K. Chesterton

Chesterton was in contact with the reality of the masculine soul. In apprenticeship to Christ, he had taken personal responsibility for his part in what is wrong in the world. Chesterton consented to a process of masculine initiation, a putting to death of the false self, this ancient path epitomized in the life and death of Jesus and described concisely by Joseph Campbell in these words: "Where we had thought to slay another, we shall slay ourselves."[3] Through apprenticeship to Jesus, Chesterton had become the kind of king who could be entrusted with more and more of God's kingdom. We are invited to join him at the side of our elder Brother, so that one day the inverse of the question offered by the *Times* might be answered positively by us all:

What's right with the world?
I am.

Never Give Up

Along this ancient path of relentless pursuing—becoming part of what is right in the world as an apprentice of Jesus—we would do well to glean one more lesson from another good man who has gone before us. Major Richard Winters is one whose story can continually orient and fortify our own. A simple farmer from rural Pennsylvania, Major Winters became the heroic leader of the 2nd Battalion, 506th Parachute Infantry Regiment, 101st Airborne Division in World War II, playing a critical role in the victory of the Allied forces against the Nazi regime. Though his deep goodness was ever present to the lives of the soldiers with whom he shared a foxhole in the appalling conditions of Bastogne, it was not until Stephen Ambrose's book *Band of Brothers* was published that the heart of this man caught the public's attention.

One rainy spring day several years ago, I found myself feasting again on Winters's memoir, *Beyond Band of Brothers*. In this very personal offering, Winters takes us into his internal world as a young man. Of all the wisdom he shares about being a soldier, being a leader of men, and enduring violence, trauma, and loss, one virtue and mandate stands out above all else:

Keep going. Or, in the words of his era, hang tough.

This mandate embodies all I've gleaned from the ethos of all the noble warriors who have gone before us. It is the virtue that characterizes whole-hearted kings:

They never quit.

A lot of days I want to quit. I want to give up. I want to quit risking, quit loving people, quit fighting the good fight, quit running the race and keeping the faith. I want to quit believing that God's goodness prevails even in the dark hour in which we live. I want to settle for a happy little life off the grid. I want to desire less and make life work on my own terms.

But then the sun pierces the darkness yet again, and I'm reminded of a God who is filled with vibrant life and limitless joy. A God who is pursuing me. A God who really cares. A Father who is at work today to orchestrate invitations for my heart and soul to believe in the more that he has promised and planned. A Father who is willing, given our consent and participation, to fill us, this very day and this very decade, with abundance. To partner with us to become the kind of men in whom there is no lack.

I see the sparkle of life and hope in my daughter's brilliant ocean-blue eyes as she descends our outdated and tired staircase dressed and ready for a new school day. Her hair is drawn in a bun with a delightful floral headband, and her ring of her daddy's delight proudly adorns her finger. She is radiant, alive, filled with promise and love. And she is looking again today, as she does every day, for a dad.

I look at my little bear-cub-turned-young-man-overnight. He's tall, lean, and chiseled. He's filled with more words and jokes and dreams and hopes than my groggy soul can process. He is heroic, strong, and more true than I. My son grabs me and lifts me off the ground. We wrestle, and I barely prevail, but I remind him, for now, I'm still the herd bull. My reminder is playful and inviting, as he and I both know that his challenges are mounting and—to my utter joy—I will soon be dethroned. He will stand on my shoulders. I want to become the kind of man and the kind of king I hope he, too, will one day become.

I catch a glimpse of my wife in the kitchen. It is the most normal of days, midweek in our suburban life: making lunches, getting ready for reading group, preparing to shuttle kids to school, and then teaching a movement and meditation class at a transition shelter for single mothers. And she is radiant; she takes my breath away. I'm so deeply in love. A love hard fought and hard won over nearly two decades. I know in my soul, deeper than words, something of what Solomon knew when he voiced, "I am enthralled with your beauty" (Ps. 45:11, my paraphrase). I feel yet again both the sobriety and the dignity of being entrusted with the heart of this daughter of my King.

As they depart and I descend into my half-finished basement to soak in stillness and meditate on Psalm 23, I find my footing in the richness of God yet again, and I'm lifted up and out of my circumstances. I am led in prayer for a handful of faithful allies out there going after the hearts of men and influencing distinct realms upon the earth with the love of God. One by one I see their faces. And then I see even more in my heart. An army of warriors. Row upon row of a fellowship of men who have consented to becoming kings in God's kingdom. I stand in agreement with God's Spirit on their behalf. The worship once again sets my tired heart ablaze. I'm on their sidelines, armed—a bow in one hand and a tambourine in the other. I'm wild-eyed, celebrating their triumph and the strength of who they have become and who they are becoming. Love wins. Love prevails.

Doubt gives way to faith.

Despair gives way to hope.

I see the faces of those I love. I remember that we are all unfinished. We have all been given an invitation to receive the fresh life of God. Each of us is being invited to be an apprentice, to be shaped by him. Formed to become like Jesus so that our lives might look more and more as they would if he were us, living our lives in our day. We are each given everything we need for our lives to take on more and more the quality of eternity that marked his.

We can each become more relaxed, more unhurried, more true, more trusting, and more consecrated. One choice at a time. I'm reminded that it begins by receiving this lavish love reaching out to us right now, beckoning us upon the narrow path. I am reminded that this moment will give shape to this day. This day will become my decade. This decade will become my eternity. And eternity is what I have set my heart-strength upon.

I am a pilgrim in this world. I don't belong. And neither do you. Yet God is making a way where there is no way. Our sorrow does not eclipse his joy. His assignments never eclipse his resources, generously poured out to make it so. He is readying us for an expanding kingdom he is entrusting to our care. Our task is to consent to his leadership and receive his provision so that we might become the kind of man, the kind of king, who can be entrusted with his kingdom.

I call to mind the words of Psalm 27:

> I'm sure now I'll see God's goodness
> > in the exuberant earth.
> Stay with GOD!
> > Take heart. Don't quit.
> I'll say it again:
> > Stay with GOD.
>
> —Psalm 27:13–14 MSG

In these words, in the strength of the Spirit, and in the company of these other men, I will not quit.

Brothers, this book is my gift to you. Shaped by forge, hammer, and axe.

Hewn by blood, sweat, and the tears of two decades. From a broken soul who became first a student, then a son, and even more, an apprentice of a good, good Father. And who in small and steady ways is becoming the man and the king God meant when he meant me.

Jesus knew there would be enough of his called-out ones who would consent to carry his purposes through to the end of the age. He knew there would be the few in every generation who would choose apprenticeship and live beyond their own gifting and self-sufficiency. The few who would risk everything to learn to rely on the unlimited resources of the kingdom of heaven being made available today. The few who would come to know a love so deep, so wide, and so vast that even the most ruined soul could be restored to the likeness of God himself. A love that is utterly personal and ever pursuing. A love that is wild, unfettered, and free.

God knew that there would be a few who might risk a wholehearted yes on this day and in this decade.

Yes to a decade of letting God build our character rather than building our own kingdoms.

Yes to taking the lowest seat at the table.

Yes to excavation before building.

Yes to no shortcuts.

Yes to becoming good soil.

Yes to becoming deep roots.

Becoming students.

Becoming sons.

Becoming warriors.

Becoming, over time, the kind of men, the kind of kings, God can confidently and joyfully entrust with his kingdom. And this few would be enough to carry his purposes through from one generation to the next, so that the whole of the human race and creation would be blessed unto the restoration of all things.

You can have your integrity back. Your masculine soul can be restored and set free. This is the wildly preposterous invitation of the gospel. Here. Today. No matter who and what you have become. God, your Father, knows who you are. Even more, he knows who you can become. You can become the king you were meant to be if you choose to start today. To give your consent. To live in the day and measure in the decade. If the message of this book can be summarized in two words, it is this:

Invitation and Process

Becoming a king is an invitation to a process of becoming the kind of man to whom God can entrust his kingdom. The greatest revolution in human history began through twelve men saying yes to a personal invitation from the King of kings to recover the ancient path. It's not easy, it's not cheap, and it's not quick. The path is made available to all, but few choose it. It has always been so.

Your Father is pursuing you. He is at work. Next comes your response. Writing this book was my response to his ongoing apprenticeship. Engaging this book was part of your response to his pursuit. If you've made it this far, you are well on your way along the ancient path to becoming a king. There are more than enough resources portioned out from the kingdom of God for your becoming. He knows your heart. He knows your story. He will lead you deeper into wholeheartedness and full integration of your masculine soul if you will let him. If you are willing to give God your yes—a yes from the deepest places of your being, from your deepest fears and from your growing courage—he will open the floodgates. And you will, over time, find yourself among the few.

With tears, I conclude, filled with this deep hope:

That one day I shall see you.

We shall be together, side by side around a campfire in the kingdom.

We will feel together the warmth of the fire and look at each other, soul to soul, standing amidst a small, heroic fellowship.

We will raise a glass and drink the finest drink.

We will roll up our sleeves, bare our scars.

And we will share the stories of the days we were given.

Stories of walking through the narrow gate.

Stories of choosing the narrow path.

Stories of becoming.

Stories of partnering with God and a few brave souls to recover the gospel for this generation and the next.

Our laughter will echo off the canyon walls. Consenting to a revolution seated in the restoration of human hearts and loosely and deeply organized into small and growing tribes of like-hearted kings. We will stand among the few who are choosing to participate in the life of God, to will what is good for God, in the portion of his kingdom entrusted to our care. The choice is yours. This day and this decade. And there is no more sacred space in all of creation than the space the Father has reserved for you, his son, in which to consider this choice.

This is my personal invitation to you to join me in a decade of becoming. If you say yes, your life will never be the same. Momentary choices will give way to days. Days will give way to decades. And decades will become our eternity. What would it look like today to say yes to God's initiative and respond with relentless pursuit of becoming the kind of man and the kind of king to whom God can entrust his kingdom?

To my God and my King, to my Father and my Friend, I say this:

You have my strength and my sword.

You have my yes.

You have me.

I look forward with hope and eager anticipation to being with you at that campfire in the kingdom.

Strength and honor,

Morgan

A FELLOWSHIP OF KINGS

God shapes people through people. We shape people by becoming the kind of people God intended us to be and bringing the person we've become to our world. Who needs this message in your world? Which ten people in your world could most benefit from this message? Pause right here for a few moments. Ask God to show you their faces. Write their names here. And gift a copy of this book to them, in love. Go ahead, change the world. In this generation, the revolution begins with you.

_____   _____

_____   _____

_____   _____

_____   _____

BECOME GOOD
SOIL PRAYER

The Become Good Soil Prayer embodies the heart of *Becoming a King*. As a next step and also as a regular way of reestablishing your heart in God, I invite you to join me and many others in praying through this prayer. As Eugene Petersen (author of *The Message* translation of the Bible) suggests, prayer is about being and becoming before it is about getting and doing. May this prayer be a path for you to rest in your Father's initiative, to respond to him with confidence and curiosity, and to become the good soil in which he can deeply establish his kingdom.

Father, I confess that what I want is for my heart to be made whole and my life to be integrated. I confess that I want the freedom and the restoration of my strength through the integration of the whole person. And I invite you to do it. I invite you to partner with me to become a man who astonishes you because we are united in love, and I've learned to do nothing apart from you.

Father, I agree with your relentless love, your relentless pursuit—that you will stop at nothing to continue to open the doorway to invite me home, for me to give access to you to the whole man, to be made whole and holy.

Father, I confess the parts of me that have yet to yield to you, that are resistant, and I give you the shame and the fear and the disappointment and the hurt. I give you my belief in life being found in self-determination and self-reliance, and I say your love is greater still—your love is stronger than death. I ask that you would shine your light, that you would expose every place in me that has yet to come home to you as my good Father.

Jesus, Holy Spirit, Father, I receive you afresh today, and your inextinguishable life. I receive your kingdom come and your will be done on earth as it is in the kingdom of heaven. I arise once again to trust you in your mighty strength, uniting my heart with your heart.

Jesus, I ask that you would break every limit I've placed on who you can be, what you can do, and how you can do it. I ask for your forgiveness for those limits, and I say break them in your power and in your name. I say in that place that I am rooted and established in your love. It is infinite, ever-present, and always flowing.

Father, I name that you care about me, that I matter to you, that you are the one who sees me. I say it out loud: You are the One who sees me, and I have seen the One who sees me. I name you as the One Who Sees Me.

I receive you afresh in this place. I ask that you would make me good soil. I say I want more. I ask that you would dismantle the self-promotion, self-protection, self-reliance; that you would dismantle the self and restore the true man, making me whole and holy by your love. I give you permission to my body, my soul, and my spirit.

I receive your inheritance. You have given me unlimited resources. That is my inheritance, and I claim it, I receive it. I ask that you would help me to access it more: your favor, your life—to accept it and receive it.

Through your death, your resurrection, and your ascension, I choose union with you. Forgive me for trying to arrange so many things to feel good. You alone are contentment, and so I choose you to be my place of contentment. And I choose to receive that smile of the Holy Spirit that says you alone bring true joy.

I receive you, Holy Spirit, afresh today—your breath. You are the wild one. You want to partner with me. You know what I need. You are my counselor, my comforter, my strength, and my guide. So I choose you, Holy Spirit. I ask that you would increase my awareness to sense your moving, your leadership. Show me how to move. Give me the shoes of the readiness of the gospel of peace so that I can move in step with you—your pace, your rhythm, your way.

Holy Spirit, I believe that you usher in this mothering that I so deeply need, that you alone can nourish me to fullness—robust well-being. You alone, through mothering me, can make me feel safe and loved, make me feel ten feet tall and bursting with joy. I want that, Holy Spirit, so would you mother me in new ways? I confess you're good at mothering. I want to know and believe that I am loved because I am yours. I am worthy of love and belonging.

Father, I confess that I still resist you, hiding as an orphan and a slave. I want to come home to you. Today afresh, Father, I ask that I could come home to you—home to your love, home to your generosity, home to your abundance, home to your provision, home to your protection. Father, all that I am, in union with all that you are. I do it through the life of Jesus Christ.

Jesus, I receive you as my brother, as my Savior, as the Doorway, the Pathway—your life spent so that I could have life. Through you, my old man is given to death, and death rises to new life. I rise with you, Jesus—your unstoppable life and strength and force. Jesus, you have my yes. Validate me. I receive my name from you, my place in the kingdom, my inheritance through you, Jesus.

God, in that place I confess all the sophisticated ways I have created a life to protect me from engaging in true relationship, all the ways I've arranged to disengage from relationship—the ways that I move against people, the ways that I move away from people and move toward people, all searching for validation, searching for love. I ask that you would dismantle all of it in me, God, that you would restore my style of relating and restore my relating with you, that I would see you move and walk, that you would cultivate a love language with me more deeply than ever before, that I would find myself laughing because you know me! This is our moment, just us. I hold a part of your heart no one else does, God, and you hold a part of mine. Can we cultivate an acquaintance? I confess that I need to *live more deeply in a habitat that allows my soul to thrive. To cultivate that acquaintance, I know there's unfinished business here, and so I give you the habitat of my life, and I ask that you would bring it into alignment with the habitat that's right for my soul. Unforced rhythms of grace, learning to live freely and lightly, putting down everything that is heavy-laden, and everything that is ill-fitting, that doesn't fit me. And help me to be comfortable in my own skin. Help me to like me as you like me.*

Restore my soul. Integrate the whole man. God, I give you permission. I pray that you would cultivate the habits that are necessary so that I can be available to receive that which I can't arrange for. What do I need to abstain from? And what do I need to engage in? Teach me; I'm your student. Let's try it on, try it out—let's practice; let's blunder around. Allow me not to go to shame or self-reproach.

I want to be a student, and I want to be a son. And so I name that over my life, God: student and son. As you restore my true self from the inside out, I consecrate my motives to you, I consecrate my beliefs to you, and I choose to adopt a worldview that is steeped in and seated on wisdom and not simply gifting or the spirit of the age. I choose to partner with Wisdom that you set as the Craftsman at your right hand, that is in the fabric of all of creation. You say that he who finds wisdom finds life, and I ask for wisdom, because I need life.

God, I stand with you against my enemies; against every scheme that has been set against me as a man, against my masculinity, and against my masculine line. I say, "It stops with me." In the authority of Jesus Christ, I say no. I take my stand with you, and I say, "It stops with me, in the authority of Jesus Christ." And I ask for you to begin a new work in me, to establish a new legacy, a new generation; to restore what you originally intended since before creation. Show me the warfare set against me; and in your authority, I stand against it. I choose against it by your power and through your life.

And, Jesus, in the spirit of the age, I confess how much I've agreed with a distracted life, with this "temporary atheism" where I so often find myself living apart from you. Lord, you never give any man too much to do. And so I ask for your forgiveness for every place I find myself feeling overwhelmed and alone. I break every agreement I've made with drivenness and hurriedness and busyness; and I ask in its place that you would give me intimacy, that you would cultivate acquaintance. Give me intimacy with you.

Father, I give you every way that I have elevated myself in a kingly realm in a way that was beyond what you entrusted to my care. I ask for your forgiveness, and I give you access to sort it all out. Jesus, I ask that you would heal my heart in the traumatized places where I have been set as a king by uninitiated men, where I have been maimed and harmed and used and abused. I forgive them, for they know not what they do. I release them and bless them, and I say to have your way with them, God. I ask that you would heal my heart in those places and help restore the false conclusions I've come to about my life and calling because of the pain and the hurt and the violation.

Father, I ask that you would dismantle every shortcut that I've willfully chosen. I pray that you would reveal again the shortcuts I've taken, that you would dismantle them; and I choose the long, holy, and narrow road you have for me that is truly life. I want to be your apprentice, God. You are accepting master students, and I say yes! I want to work with you; I want to watch how you do it. I'm signing up. Show me how to grow in fierce mastery over all of it, the fullness of my domain. I pray that you would right-size it; shrink it where it needs to shrink. And help me with my body, with my soul and spirit, with my imagination, with my mind.

I give all of my kingdom to all of you. I bring it back under the rule and reign of Jesus—every piece of it. I ask for your blood to wash it and for your anointing to come. And I'm asking for your favor over my kingdom. I set it apart for your life.

Father, I ask for forgiveness: I've played it safe in a lot of ways. I haven't risked because I've been fearful. Help me exercise risking—risking love, risking courage, risking generosity. Meet me in this frontier. I want to trust you more. I believe that you want to increase the stakes, and this is my practice.

I ask for your forgiveness for every way I've agreed with the spirit of false comparison with other men and had jealousy and envy and want of their lives. I confess that the only life worth living is my life in you. Father, forgive me for comparing part of my life with part of his life. I release him. I bless him. And I cut off every judgment, every value I have made, every way I've cursed inadvertently. I ask for your forgiveness, and I bring blessing in the place of cursing. I choose in the heavenlies with my will to cause good on behalf of those men.

And I own my life, my story—you as Author, me as participant and partner and friend. Father, I invite you into all of my suffering. You're the only person who can handle it. And you can handle it. So I invite you into it. I ask that you would make something beautiful come out of it. I ask that you would show me what to do with it, that you would make it worth it, Jesus, that you would tell me that it matters to you. All of it. And that you're not far off, that you're moving toward me.

Jesus, would you show me how to rest? And play? Would you show me how to receive love? There are places in me that just avoid it and fear it. Show me how to receive. Show me how to play. Show me how to become the kind of person of whom my kids (or future kids) would one day be able to say, "He was playful. He was so fun to be with." Take off the burden. Lift the burden.

Father, I give you all of my relationships: my marriage (or future marriage), my kids (or future kids), my friendships—I give them all to you. In the area of marriage, I give you my dreams and my dilemmas. And I am asking that you would simply breathe life into the here and now, that you would show me what needs to be done, that you would help me come to the center, and that you would give me your heart for my wife. Father, at every one of those junctures where it's going sideways, I pray that you would help me be mindful to simply turn again to you and say, "Give me your heart for her." I pray that you would help me believe that you are my defender; I have no need to defend myself. I ask that you would heal my marriage, restore my marriage; and I pray that you would bring my wife onto the same parallel journey as a woman and as a bride. Only you can do that, and only you can orchestrate it. I give you my marriage, I trust you with the pain, and I ask for a miracle. Today. A miracle. I agree that she's the one you chose for me, and you don't make mistakes. So I break every agreement I've made around an alternative path, and I receive her again in love. I renew my heart for her because of you.

Father, I give you my children. I give you what I've missed of their hearts. I give you the hours and the days I've missed; and I stay in your love, where you say, "Love covers a multitude of sins." I'm banking on it, Jesus. And I believe that the only way to become the kind of parent I want to be is through parenting. So I receive grace for myself as a parent.

I pray that you would teach me how to be present; that you would work my schedule supernaturally, flowing out of my beliefs, to give my family more of my time—and also out of my beliefs, more of my heart; that you would help me be present to the regular, day-to-day moments when you are asking me to bring them into deeper realities and wonder of the kingdom of God; that I would model a larger Story, bigger than anything they find; that I would give them access to you, Father; that I would turn and that they would see my model of turning to you, the One with unlimited resources. I don't have to have it figured out, God. I confess all the pressure I put on myself to have it figured out. And I pray, God, that you would help me bring them deeper into the kingdom of God, to know your heart.

I confess that these are the hidden years. I give you permission to hide me in the ways you want to hide me. Only you can figure that out, and only you can resolve that. But I ask that you would clarify and consecrate my yes. Help me understand what it is that I am to say yes to and who it is that I am to say yes to. Help me establish my yes and amen as it is in the kingdom of heaven, so that I can have confidence to say no to everything and everyone that's a no from you. Help me discern; help me walk in that.

Father, I pray for pure relationships. I ask, God, that you would give me one, that you would give me two, that you would help me see like-hearted kings who want what I want and have to fight through the same stuff to get it. Help me fight for those. Show me where I need to sacrifice *more. Pour your robust life into those relationships. Give us shared mission so that we can lock arms and move toward something larger, as a context to dive deeper into the restoration of our hearts together. Give me a few. I believe that it's your idea, it's your design, it's your desire, and it's my destiny. So would you bring me those men? Father, bring me the peers, bring me the mentors, bring me the men; order my expression of the body of Christ, my community, my story, that I would own my life and I would cast off every other story. I release it. I own my life.*

Father, the love that you have for your Son, Jesus, is the same love that you give to me, the love that you offer me. I receive it today. I receive it with confidence. I receive it with joy, with expectation. I receive your love afresh today.

And I put on the armor afresh today as your son, the armor of God: shoes of the gospel of peace, whereby I can move in step with your Spirit; a belt of truth, whereby I love the things you love and I hate the things you hate; a breastplate of righteousness, whereby I choose what you choose and I refuse what you refuse. I put on the helmet of salvation, whereby my hope is seated and established in the kingdom to come and the place that you have carved out for me. My hope is in the intervention of heaven today. I take up the sword of the Spirit, that you would arm me with the Word of God; and the shield of faith, whereby I am sure of what I hope for and certain of all that I do not see. I put it on.

I am your son, and I say, "Your kingdom come, your will be done on earth as it is in heaven." I choose you today; I invite you into this decade. I invite you to shape it, to lead it and guide it. Father me. Apprentice me in your kingdom. I am an unfinished man, but I choose today to give all of me to all of you. I accept your acceptance of me. I choose to live in the present moment. I ask for a wise and discerning heart. I unite my heart with your heart. I choose to listen to your voice. I receive your peace that passes understanding. I receive your courage, I receive your strength, I receive your joy. I love you. I trust you. I choose to become good soil. You have my yes.

ACKNOWLEDGMENTS

It was a story shared by a mentor twenty-four years ago, and yet I find myself carrying it in my heart like it was yesterday. A boy and his uncle were exploring the wildness of the Mississippi River Delta together. They ventured out, only to realize they were surrounded by quicksand, sinking and incapable of self-rescue. The following day a search-and-rescue team came upon the boy, almost entirely submerged and barely conscious. After removing the boy from the quicksand and reviving him, they asked him if he knew the whereabouts of his uncle. The boy's eyes grew wide as moments from the previous day flashed before him. He looked up at them and said, "I am standing on his shoulders."

For over two decades this image has been stored as treasure within me. As I look to express my inexpressible gratitude for the heroic women and men who have prayed for, fought for, and championed this book in me, this story is my soul's picture: I have stood on the shoulders of those who have gone before me.

An inexpressible thank you to:

Cherie, for becoming the champion of my heart and a lifesaver when the heavy seas have threatened to take my strength and my breath. For twenty years you have been the light in my life that pushes out darkness more than any other. All I have is yours.

Joshua and Abigail, for your constancy of joy and lavish forgiveness. You are role models beyond telling. When I grow up, I want to be more like you. You stand on my shoulders, and nothing has brought me more joy than being entrusted with the gift of being your father.

Mom and Dad. You have given us the very best of what you have been given. We stand on your shoulders. You have deposited in us—your kids and your grandkids—your faith, your hope, and your love. It's an inheritance that can never be taken. Thank you for choosing love in the face of unspeakable adversity. I love you.

John, for opening the door to masculine initiation and sharing with your very life a gospel that was finally big enough to carry hope for every sorrow and possibility for every dream. For inviting me to wrestle with questions my heart didn't even know to ask. For the Monday mountain bike rides in Ute Park; for being with me at Lance's funeral. For sharing Moab campfires and encounters with bugling bull elk. For a thousand unseen times you have said yes to God.

Bart, Mark, Jim, Craig, Sam, Brad and the facilitators of a decade of Become Good Soil Intensives. You are the Rosetta Stone of this generation. You are the few among us who have become the kind of men who are restoring the father heart of God in the land. You all make me want to grow old.

Jan, for taking my call and welcoming me to share a seat on your porch swing on a summer's evening when I was on the precipice of losing everything that mattered most in my life. You were the face of God. Your truth-telling and feminine presence helped me find an unknown courage to keep heart and travel the impossible road ahead back to life. The beauty born of your suffering will one day be realized. You are my hero.

Parker, Brian, Jon, Alex, and Aaron, daily life with you men has been my hidden fuel for becoming. I'm indebted to your willingness to offer me the benefit of the doubt and to teach me to fight for joy.

Laurence, Pablo, Jay, Tim, and the heroic fellowship of graduates of the Become Good Soil Intensives. Your lives are the stuff of holy headlines on the day when all stories are told rightly. Your yes to God and to the ancient path of becoming is the great treasure of our age. Let's keep going.

Linsey, Jessica, Jim, John, Chuck, Jeff, Simon, Jon, Rob, and the many prayer warriors who have fought by my side to see this work come to pass over these many years. Prayer is the greatest work of the kingdom. I'm grateful for you and the others who have prayed with such stamina and devotion.

Karen and Cherie, for the incalculable investment you made with hammer and chisel in the many early drafts of this manuscript. This effort would have stalled out a dozen times were it not for your vision, patience, and brilliant editing.

Chris, your strength, winsome leadership, and advocacy made it possible for this message to reach outposts of the kingdom around the globe. Your steadiness and honest counsel have been the faithful guide for me to navigate wild terrain.

Megan, Daisy, Dawn, Kristi, Mark, and the entire team at W Publishing and HarperCollins Christian Publishing. Your heart-centered and passionate partnership has made it possible to open this newly recovered doorway to hope for so many.

Darren, your contribution carried us through the fourth quarter and across the goal line.

Stasi, John, and the Wild at Heart and Ransomed Heart team. Thank you for your love and patience with me as we've grown up together for two decades, seeking as a fellowship to consent to the slow and steady process of becoming. Your lives are proof that the transforming power of the gospel is being realized on earth. You are men and women after God's own heart.

Father—this is all yours. May my gratitude for all of these hearts, named and unnamed, be a hidden fuel to keep going, to keep risking, and above all else, for putting on love.

And may all of us, by day and by decade, recover the greatest gift of all: more portions of us coming home to more of you, God.

My deepest thanks, Father, I give to you.

We stand on your shoulders.

NOTES

Uncovering the Ancient Path to Becoming

1. Louis L'Amour, *Lonely on the Mountain* (New York: Bantam, 1984), 1.

Chapter 1: Becoming Powerful

1. John Eldredge, *Waking the Dead* (Nashville: Thomas Nelson, 2006), 166.
2. John Eldredge, *Fathered by God* (Nashville: Thomas Nelson, 2008), 160.
3. Oprah Winfrey, "Lance Armstrong's Confession," Oprah Winfrey Network video, January 17, 2013, http://www.oprah.com/own/lance-armstrong-confesses -to-oprah-video.
4. Mackenzie Carpenter, "Family. JoePa did not die of broken heart," *Pittsburgh Post-Gazette*, January 25, 2012, https://www.post-gazette.com/sports/psu/2012 /01/26/Family-JoePa-did-not-die-of-broken-heart/stories/201201260357.
5. If you need more data, a quick search gives us this piece by the *New York Times*: Sarah Almukhtar, Michael Gold, and Larry Buchanan, "After Weinstein: 71 Men Accused of Sexual Misconduct and Their Fall From Power," updated February 8, 2018, https://www.nytimes.com/interactive/2017/11/10/us/men -accused-sexual-misconduct-weinstein.html.

Chapter 2: Becoming a Son

1. For additional scriptures pointing to the mystery of Trinitarian Reality, see John 1, John 14–17, 1 John 1, and Colossians 1–2.
2. Jane Willard, John Ortberg, and the Dallas Willard Center, *Living in Christ's Presence* (Downer's Grove, IL: InterVarsity Press, 2014), 101.
3. For behold and contemplate the lavishness of love and affection that the Father

has given to us, that we should be called children of God—and that is who we are! 1 John 3:1, my paraphrase

4. Christine Winquist Nord and Jerry West, "Fathers' and Mothers' Involvement in their Children's Schools by Family Type and Resident Status. Table 1," NCES 2001–032 (Washington, DC: US Department of Education, National Center of Education Statistics, 2001).

5. National Center for Fathering, Fathering in America Poll, January 1999; these statistics as reported by National Center for Fathering, http://fathers.com /statistics-and-research/the-extent-of-fatherlessness/.

6. John 17:3 (my paraphrase).

7. John Ortberg, *Soul Keeping* (Grand Rapids: Zondervan, 2014), 50.

8. George MacDonald, *Unspoken Sermons* (Somerville, TN: Bottom of the Hill Publishing, 2012), 162.

9. MacDonald, *Unspoken Sermons*, 162.

10. MacDonald, *Unspoken Sermons*, 192.

11. MacDonald, *Unspoken Sermons*, 242.

Chapter 3: Becoming True

1. Photo by Jeremy Bishop.

2. Mike Mason, *The Mystery of Marriage* (Colorado Springs: Multnomah Books, 2005), 21.

3. Gerald May, *Addiction and Grace* (New York: HarperCollins, 1988), 1.

4. Thomas Keating, *Centering Prayer in Daily Life and Ministry* (New York: Bloomsbury, 1997), 29.

5. Mason, *Mystery of Marriage*, 39.

6. John Eldredge, *The Journey of Desire* (Nashville: Thomas Nelson, 2016), 67.

7. There are many references like this in the Gospels, such as Matthew 3:2, Matthew 4:17, and Mark 1:15, my paraphrases.

8. Ortberg, Willard, and the Dallas Willard Center, *Living in Christ's Presence* (Downers Grove, IL: IVP Books), 15.

9. Over two decades, I've spent time regularly with men who have created an external world filled with success and accolades, but who are living in fear, shame, and deep brokenness in their marriages. Reconciling the interior life of the soul with the exterior life is first and foremost done through engaging this ongoing process of motive, exposing the false self, so that it might be put to death and the true self might be resurrected.

Chapter 4: Becoming the Man You Were Born to Be

1. David Franzani, John Logan, and William Nicholson, *Gladiator*. Directed by Ridley Scott. DreamWorks, Universal Pictures, 2000.
2. Gerard Manley Hopkins, "As Kingfishers Catch Fire," *Poems and Prose* (Penguin Classics) (New York: Penguin Putnam Inc., 1985).
3. Dallas Willard, *The Divine Conspiracy* (New York: HarperCollins, 1998), 15.
4. Fran Walsh, Philippa Boyens, and Peter Jackson, *The Lord of the Rings: The Return of the King*. Directed by Peter Jackson. New Line Cinema, 2003.
5. Lilly Wachowski and Lana Wachowski, *The Matrix*. Directed by Lana Wachowski and Lilly Wachowski. Warner Bros., 1999.
6. George MacDonald, *Unspoken Sermons*, (Somerville, TN: Bottom of the Hill Publishing, 2012), 40.
7. William Nicholson, Alain Boublil, Claude-Michel Schönberg, and Herbert Kretzmer, *Les Misérables*. Directed by Tom Hooper. Universal Pictures, 2012.
8. Eph. 1:1, Phil. 1:1, Rom. 1:7, Col. 1:2, all my paraphrases.
9. Dallas Willard, *Renovation of the Heart* (Colorado Springs: NavPress, 2002), 248–9.
10. A. W. Tozer, *The Knowledge of the Holy* (New York: HarperOne, 2009), 2.
11. This idea was formed in me through a mentor who taught me from Francis Schaeffer's teaching on "The Lord's Work in the Lord's Way" in *No Little People* (Wheaton, IL: Crossway, 2003). He explains (p. 29), "We should consciously take the lowest place unless the Lord himself extrudes us into a greater one. The word *extrude* is important here. To be extruded is to be forced out under pressure into a desired shape. Picture a huge press jamming soft metal at high pressure through a die, so that the metal comes out in a certain shape. This is the way of the Christian: he should choose the lesser place until God extrudes him into a position of more responsibility and authority."
12. MacDonald, *Unspoken Sermons*, 41.
13. MacDonald, *Unspoken Sermons*, 115.

Chapter 5: Becoming a Generalist

1. Gerald Manley Hopkins, "As Kingfishers Catch Fire," *Poems and Prose* (New York: Penguin Putnam, Inc., 1985).
2. "Remarks Concerning the Savages of North America" (1784) by Benjamin Franklin, https://founders.archives.gov/documents/Franklin/01-41-02-0280.
3. Wendell Berry, *The Unsettling of America* (Berkeley, CA: Counterpoint, 1977).
4. C. S. Lewis, *The Abolition of Man* (New York: HarperOne, 2015), 27.

5. "Strong's G4982," *Blue Letter Bible*, https://www.blueletterbible.org/lang
   /lexicon/lexicon.cfm?t=kjv&strongs=g4982.

6. Of course, this is not exhaustive or prescriptive, merely a few common examples
   of the kind of activities God allows to initiate the boy into a man. This process
   of initiation through the path of becoming a generalist is unique for every
   man. Yet for every man it involves choosing to engage in the activities that are
   uncomfortable, fearful, unknown, and risky.

7. Walt Harrington, *The Everlasting Stream* (New York: Grove Press, 2002), 146.

8. C. S. Lewis, *Mere Christianity* (New York: HarperOne, 2015), 192.

9. Garrison Keillor, *The Book of Guys* (New York: Penguin Books, 1993), 17–18.

10. Dorothy Sayers, *Letters to a Diminished Church* (Nashville: Thomas Nelson,
    2004).

11. Aldo Leopold, *A Sand County Almanac* (New York: Oxford University Press,
    1968), 6.

12. This is nothing more than the space created by a gracious wife who allows us to
    take over the kitchen with a couple hundred pounds of wild game meat still on
    the bone.

13. Watch *Alone in the Wilderness*, a documentary. It's fantastic.

14. You can begin your search at the Allies Network: RansomedHeart.com/allies
    /search.

Chapter 6: Becoming a Warrior

1. Jessica Buchanan, "The Rescue of Jessica Buchanan." *60 Minutes*. CBS, May
   12, 2013.

2. Dan Baker, *What Happy People Know* (New York: St. Martin's Griffin, 2004), 38.

3. Leif Enger, *Peace Like a River* (New York: Grove Press, 2001), 4.

4. Dallas Willard, *The Divine Conspiracy* (New York: HarperCollins, 1998), 72.

5. John Eldredge, *Waking the Dead* (Nashville: Thomas Nelson, 2006), 17.

6. John and Stasi Eldredge, *Love and War* (Colorado Springs: WaterBrook,
   2009), 39.

7. Cade Courtley, *SEAL Survival Guide* (New York: Gallery Books, 2012), xvii.

8. In *SEAL Survival Guide*, Courtley generously offers to teach much about
   survival to all who have ears to hear and a heart to understand. While most of
   the book is dedicated to surviving specific life-threatening situations, the first
   twenty-nine pages read like a training manual for The Abundant Life 101. The
   basic principles aren't sexy or particularly heroic, but practiced and harnessed

by the Spirit of God, these strategies hold kingdom secrets for maintaining our footing in a world at war.

9. Courtley, *SEAL Survival Guide*, 20.

10. "At the time GOD made Earth and Heaven, before any grasses or shrubs had sprouted from the ground—GOD hadn't yet sent rain on Earth, nor was there anyone around to work the ground—GOD formed Man out of dirt from the ground and blew into his nostrils the breath of life. The Man came alive" (Gen. 2:7 MSG).

11. John Ortberg, *Soul Keeping* (Grand Rapids: Zondervan, 2014), 39.

12. C. S. Lewis, *The Screwtape Letters* (New York: HarperOne, 2015), 75–76.

13. Ole Hallesby, *Prayer* (Minneapolis: Augsburg Books, 1994), 14.

14. Dallas Willard helped us understand that a kingdom is the range of our effective will; it is where what we want done is done. A great resource for more definitions from Dallas is http://www.soulshepherding.org/2013/05/dallas -willards-definitions/.

15. Francis Schaeffer, *No Little People* (Wheaton, IL: Crossway, 2003), 30.

16. Willard, *Divine Conspiracy*, 291.

Chapter 7: Becoming Good Soil

1. Yvon Chouinard, in *180° South*. DVD. Directed by Chris Malloy. New York: Magnolia Pictures, 2010.

2. A. W. Tozer, *The Pursuit of Man* (Chicago: Moody Publishers, 2015), 20, emphasis added.

3. Brené Brown, "Listening to Shame." TED Talk at TED 2012, Houston, TX, March 2012. Accessed December 7, 2017, https://www.ted.com/talks/brene _brown_listening_to_shame/transcript?quote=1652.

4. Theodore Roosevelt, "Citizenship in a Republic" (speech). Paris, France, April 23, 1910, https://www.theodorerooseveltcenter.org/Blog/Item/The%20Man %20in%20the%20Arena.

5. Cade Courtley, *SEAL Survival Guide* (New York: Gallery Books, 2012), 12.

6. Find out more at www.WildAtHeartBASIC.com.

7. Francis Schaeffer, *No Little People* (Wheaton, IL: Crossway, 2003), 28.

8. C. S. Lewis, *The Screwtape Letters* (New York: HarperOne, 2015), 75, 77.

9. Tozer, *Pursuit of Man*, 20.

10. John Ortberg, *The Life You've Always Wanted* (Grand Rapids: Zondervan, 1997), 77.

11. Richard Swenson, *Margin* (Colorado Springs: NavPress, 2004).

12. John Ortberg, *Soul Keeping* (Grand Rapids: Zondervan, 2014), 20.

13. Richard Foster, *Celebration of Discipline* (San Francisco: HarperSanFrancisco, 1998), 1.

14. Eugene H. Peterson, *A Long Obedience in the Same Direction* (Downers Grove, IL: IVP Books, 2000).

Chapter 8: Becoming Deep Roots

1. Dallas Willard, *The Spirit of the Disciplines* (New York: HarperCollins, 1988), 3–5.

2. Dallas Willard et al., *The Kingdom Life* (Colorado Springs: NavPress, 2010), 25.

3. George MacDonald, *Unspoken Sermons* (Somerville, TN: Bottom of the Hill Publishing, 2012), 146, 142.

4. Now there's a paradox—kind of sounds like the vice president of candy bars at Weight Watchers. Oh, the irony in kingdom living.

5. Brené Brown, *The Gifts of Imperfection* (Center City, MN: Hazelden Publishing, 2010), x.

6. Brown, *Gifts of Imperfection*, x.

7. Charles Spurgeon, *Lectures to My Students* (Charleston, SC: CreateSpace Independent Publishers, 2014), 151.

8. John and Stasi Eldredge, *Captivating* (Nashville: Thomas Nelson, 2001), 125.

9. John Eldredge, *Wild at Heart* (Nashville: Thomas Nelson, 2001), 5.

10. John Muir, *The Yosemite* (Charleston, SC: CreateSpace Independent Publishing, 2014), 125.

11. Theodore Roosevelt to Senator Albert Fall, 1904.

12. "A 2016 survey of 17,000 kids found that about 13 % had a major depressive episode, compared to 8 % of the kids surveyed in 2010. Suicide deaths among people age ten to nineteen have also risen sharply, according to the latest data from the Centers for Disease Control and Prevention. Young women are suffering most; a CDC report released earlier this year showed suicide among teen girls has reached forty-year highs. This follows a period during the late 1990s and early 2000s when rates of adolescent depression and suicide mostly held steady or declined.

    "These increases are huge—possibly unprecedented," said Jean Twenge, a professor of psychology at San Diego State University and author of *iGen*, which examines how today's super-connected teens may be less happy and less prepared for adulthood than past generations. In a peer-reviewed study that will appear later this year in the journal *Clinical Psychological Science*, Twenge showed that, after 2010, teens who spent more time on new media were more likely to report mental health issues than those who spent time on non-screen activities.

"Using data collected between 2010 and 2015 from more than 500,000 adolescents nationwide, Twenge's study found kids who spent three hours or more a day on smartphones or other electronic devices were 34 % more likely to suffer at least one suicide-related outcome—including feeling hopeless or seriously considering suicide—than kids who used devices two hours a day or less. Among kids who used electronic devices five or more hours a day, 48 % had at least one suicide-related outcome.

"Twenge also found that kids who used social media daily were 13 % more likely to report high levels of depressive symptoms than those who used social media less frequently. Overall, kids in the study who spent low amounts of time engaged in in-person social interaction, but high amounts of time on social media, were the most likely to be depressed."

Taken from Markham Heid, "We Need to Talk About Kids and Smartphones," *Time*, updated October 10, 2017, http://time.com/4974863/kids-smartphones-depression/.

13. The original power of this playful reality is borrowed straight out of Jesus' teaching in Matt. 7:16–19.

14. John Ortberg, *Soul Keeping* (Grand Rapids: Zondervan, 2014), 89.

Chapter 9: Becoming Like-Hearted

1. Gerald May, *Addiction and Grace* (New York: HarperCollins, 1988), 1.

2. C. S. Lewis, *Mere Christianity* (New York: HarperOne, 2015), 227.

3. Rob Jones, Centre for Men, Australia.

4. Francis Schaeffer, *No Little People* (Wheaton, IL: Crossway, 2003), 30.

5. Oswald Chambers, *My Utmost for His Highest* (Grand Rapids: Discovery House, 1992), January 5.

6. Parker Palmer, *Let Your Life Speak* (Hoboken, NJ: Jossey-Bass, 1999), 30–31.

7. Mike Mason, *The Mystery of Marriage* (Colorado Springs: Multnomah Books, 2005), 39.

8. Interview with Jonathan David Helser, *Become Good Soil* Podcast.

9. John Eldredge and Stasi Eldredge, *Captivating* (Nashville: Thomas Nelson, 2010), 26.

10. "Article #31," *Christian History Institute*, https://christianhistoryinstitute.org/incontext/article/julian.

11. Dan Allender, *How Children Raise Parents* (Colorado Springs: WaterBrook, 2005).

12. Keep in mind that it will only ever be a few. How many fronts can you fight on before the ranks are simply spread too thin? It's a sobering and helpful guideline that can give you permission to prune relationships and give your very best to fewer so that they might truly flourish.

13. This is brilliantly explored by David Brooks in *The Road to Character* (New York: Random House, 2015).

14. John Eldredge, *Waking the Dead* (Nashville: Thomas Nelson, 2006), 130–31.

15. Some of this proclamation was formed from an idea originally offered by Seth Godin on *Seth's Blog*, "No Is Essential," May 13, 2014, http://sethgodin.typepad.com.

16. These sages were known as the desert fathers. If you want to go deeper on this, Anthony the Great and Athanasius of Alexandria would be good ones to look into.

17. Quote came from the first audio file by Dallas Willard, "Teaching Series," http://www.dwillard.org/resources/section/teaching-series.

18. Frederick Buechner, *Wishful Thinking* (San Francisco: HarperOne, 1993).

Chapter 10: Becoming a King

1. David Franzani, John Logan, and William Nicholson, *Gladiator*. Directed by Ridley Scott. DreamWorks, Universal Pictures, 2000.

2. Bill Johnson, Bethel podcast on Sonship, April 12, 2015, http://podcasts.ibethel.org/en/podcasts/sons-and-servants.

3. Joseph Campbell, *The Power of Myth* (New York: Anchor Books, 1991), 151.

ABOUT THE AUTHOR

Morgan Snyder is a grateful husband of twenty years and a proud father of a wildly creative and witty daughter and a joyful and passionate son. He serves as a strategist, entrepreneur, teacher, writer, and speaker. His passion is to both be shaped by and shape the men and women who are shaping the kingdom of God. In 2010, he established BecomeGoodSoil.com, a fellowship of leaders whose global reach offers guidance for the narrow road of becoming the kind of person to whom God can confidently entrust the care of his kingdom. Morgan serves on the executive leadership team at Wild at Heart and Ransomed Heart Ministries and has contended for the wholeheartedness of men and women alongside John and Stasi Eldredge for more than two decades. He has led a decade of Become Good Soil Intensives and sold-out Wild at Heart men's events across the United States, United Kingdom, South Africa, and Australia. Morgan goes off the grid every chance he gets, whether bowhunting in the Colorado wilderness or choosing the adventurous life with his greatest treasures: his wife, Cherie; his son, Joshua; and his daughter, Abigail.

BECOME
GOOD
SOIL

Ready for more? Join us.
www.becomegoodsoil.com

New Video Study for Your Church or Small Group

If you've enjoyed this book, now you can go deeper with the companion video Bible study!

In this six-session study, Morgan Snyder helps you apply the principles in *Becoming A King* to your life. The study guide includes video notes, group discussion questions, and personal study and reflection materials for in-between sessions.

Study Guide
9780310115243

DVD
9780310115267

Available now at your favorite bookstore,
or streaming video on StudyGateway.com.